Neoliberal Frontiers

CHICAGO STUDIES IN PRACTICES OF MEANING

Edited by Jean Comaroff, Andreas Glaeser, William Sewell, and Lisa Wedeen

Neoliberal Frontiers

An Ethnography of Sovereignty in West Africa

BRENDA CHALFIN

The University of Chicago Press   Chicago and London

BRENDA CHALFIN is associate professor of anthropology at the
University of Florida and the author of *Shea Butter Republic: State Power,
Global Markets, and the Making of an Indigenous Community*.

The University of Chicago Press, Chicago 60637
The University of Chicago Press, Ltd., London
© 2010 by The University of Chicago
All rights reserved. Published 2010
Printed in the United States of America

18 17 16 15 14 13 12 11 10   1 2 3 4 5

ISBN-13: 978-0-226-10059-3 (cloth)
ISBN-13: 978-0-226-10061-6 (paper)
ISBN-10: 0-226-10059-6 (cloth)
ISBN-10: 0-226-10061-8 (paper)

Library of Congress Cataloging-in-Publication Data

Chalfin, Brenda.
   Neoliberal frontiers : an ethnography of sovereignty in West Africa /
Brenda Chalfin.
       p. cm.
   Includes bibliographical references and index.
   ISBN-13: 978-0-226-10059-3 (cloth : alk. paper)
   ISBN-13: 978-0-226-10061-6 (pbk. : alk. paper)
   ISBN-10: 0-226-10059-6 (cloth : alk. paper)
   ISBN-10: 0-226-10061-8 (pbk. : alk. paper)
   1. Ghana. Customs, Excise, and Preventive Service. 2. Neoliberalism—
Ghana. 3. Neoliberalism—Africa, West. 4. Customs administration—
Ghana. 5. Customs Administration—Africa, West. 6. Sovereignty.
I. Title.
HB127.5.G6C53 2010
382'.709667—dc22

                                                   2010005834

⊚ The paper used in this publication meets the minimum requirements of the American National Standard for Information Sciences—
Permanence of Paper for Printed Library Materials, ANSI Z39.48-1992.

For Safi and Eliot

Contents

Illustrations

TABLES

Acknowledgments

It is nearly twenty-five years since I first visited Ghana. Hence, the list of those to whom I am indebted is understandably long. The project from which this book derives was initiated on the heels of my dissertation, sparked by the lingering preoccupations of research in a highly dynamic African border zone. When I interviewed for my position at the University of Florida, I recounted my fascination with cross-border flows and the complex ways state authority is constituted at the national frontiers. A few months later I wrote a series of research proposals composed in a carrel at the University of Denver library where I was teaching part-time while caring for my infant son, Eliot. I initially sought to study an array of border authorities, highlighting the operations of Ghana's Customs Service as well as the Ghana Immigration Service, two bodies whose personnel I became familiar with during my Ph.D. research stint in Ghana's Upper East Region. A conversation on a Colorado hiking trail with friends turned my focus to a single state agency and the contrasts among operations at different types of border zones.

Although I was tentative about returning to Ghana with a toddler in tow, the prospect was becoming ever more likely. My husband, Daniel A. Smith, had just received tenure at University of Denver and was awarded a Fulbright fellowship in Political Science at the University of Ghana–Legon. In turn, my application for a Small Grant for Exploratory Research focusing on Customs personnel and sovereignty in the context of Ghana's neoliberal turn was approved by the Cultural Anthropology section of the National Science

Foundation. Soon after the UF administration and Anthropology chair, Allan Burns, agreed to postpone my start date at UF by a year, I received a postdoctoral grant from the Wenner-Gren Foundation. In the summer of 2000 Dan and I packed up our house in Denver and said good-bye to our many friends and neighbors who supported our early efforts to balance parenting and professional aspirations and had grown used to our incessant talk of Africa: Barb and Earl Walker, Robin Calland and Imelda Mulholland, John and Cherry Grove, Chris Keating and Sarah Landeryou, Kamala Parell, Jennifer Pap and Robert Urquhart, and Dean and Martha Saitta.

Rather than being based in the northern savanna zone (the region I knew best from my dissertation work in the 1990s), we made our home in Accra, Ghana's coastal capital. In addition to accommodating my husband's teaching and research obligations and my concerns about child care, this arrangement allowed me easy access to my proposed research sites at Ghana's airport and Tema Harbor on the outskirts of the capital, along with the Aflao border post on the Ghana/Togo frontier a few hours east. The Bawku border zone, my old stomping grounds in Upper East, was initially part of the research but after a couple of exhausting forays north and a round of post-election violence in December 2000, I realized that pursuing this case study too was untenable.

I made initial contact with the principals at Ghana's Customs Service through my graduate school colleague Kathryn Geurts, who had also conducted her Ph.D. research in Ghana. I soon gained an introduction to the Customs commissioner to plead for permission to conduct my study. The commissioner's consent, along with the requisite letter of introduction, was readily granted. Despite the efforts of some Customs officers to deflect my queries, I found Ghana's Customs officials, like their countrymen more generally, to be both affable and surprisingly at ease with my presence. Not only did they tolerate my efforts to conduct interviews and observe their work sites and activities, many reflected with great insight on the culture and structure of the Customs bureaucracy and appeared to relish the opportunity to analyze their profession and its politics. As my follow-up visits became more frequent, so did the relationships and discussions become more relaxed.

The names of the many Customs officials with whom I worked deliberately go unmentioned in these acknowledgments and the text that follows despite my desire to personally recognize their generosity. This is to protect their privacy and prevent my interpretations and representations from in any way jeopardizing my sources. My debt to the personnel of Ghana Customs Excise and Preventive Service, however, is vast. I thank all the Customs officers with whom I interacted for their tolerance of a stranger in their midst, especially in light of the startling license to prod and probe their work-world provided to me by their commanding officer, the Customs commissioner. Indeed, I did not at first recognize my position as an emissary of executive authority. I apologize for my unwitting participation in this world of injunction, armed with little guarantee that I could be trusted except my own word. I hope that the initial command to participate in my research was eventually secondary to the relationships and rapport forged in the course of conversation and consecutive visits. I am grateful to each officer who contributed to my knowledge and understanding of Customs and Ghana's political and economic landscape more generally. The Customs corps is now part and parcel of my universe of past and present associates in Ghana. Whether borne out of memories of my incessant probing, or the common experience of political upheaval shared far from the security and comforts of home (Customs officers are posted around the country on a temporary and rotating basis), even today the relationships are amazingly fresh, easily renewed in phone, email, or subsequent visits to Ghana.

Given the many challenges of conducting fieldwork with state officials across a range of venues, my support network in Ghana was absolutely critical to my research endeavor. Besides the unflagging support of my husband, ever ready to care for our son Eliot, I am foremost indebted to my research assistant, Raymond Kwaku Afawubo. I was introduced to Raymond by Leigh Stallings, a recent University of Denver graduate who had returned to Ghana with us. Leigh spent her junior year at the University of Ghana and had remained in touch with her Ghanaian classmates. She knew a few students harking from my intended research site of Aflao, Raymond included. Fresh from university, with degrees in political science and French in hand, Raymond visited me at our borrowed house in Adenta, a far-off suburb of Accra. A few days later we made our first foray to the port of Tema to feel out Customs operations there. Although Raymond had no formal training in anthropology, he was a natural. An exceptional writer and recordkeeper, Raymond was a thoughtful observer and careful raconteur with a keen ability to navigate the diverse personalities, ranks, and relationships we encountered in our work with Customs. Tireless and ever available to engage in and reflect upon our work, Raymond was equally patient with the unanticipated twists and turns of ethnographic research. As we traipsed up and down the quays and warehouses of Tema Harbor, he sometimes doubled as a bodyguard. In Aflao he was the consummate guide, leading me through the deep sandy lanes of the town in daylight and the darkness of dawn and dusk to greet friends and family members or search for provisions before or after a day at the border post.

My debt goes beyond Raymond to his family, especially his mother, Victoria Abla Agbemeza, for generously allowing me to reside at her home in Aflao; his father, Raphael Afawubo, and his uncle, Simon Afawubo, for introducing me to the business of Customs Clearance; and his cousin Bebe, for her masterful food preparation. In Accra, Clara Sewor, Raymond's wife, was a source of moral and logistical support for our research endeavors as well as an occasional assistant with data entry. I derive great pleasure that the completion of this book coincides with a number of important events in the lives of Raymond and Clara. Raymond received his law degree from the University of Ghana and was called to the bar in 2005. He is now a barrister and solicitor of the Supreme Court of Ghana. Clara gave birth to their daughter, Malike Sika Afawubo, in Sacramento, California, in 2008.

Equally crucial to the success of my field research, on the academic front, I was able to secure an affiliation with the Institute of African Studies at the University of Ghana–Legon. IAS director Takyiwaah Manuh, lawyer, activist, and anthropologist, was readily available for discussion despite the many demands of her post. Her interest and encouragement enabled me to better reflect on and carry out my project. Paul Gifford, professor of religion at London's School of Oriental and African Studies, in Ghana at the same time to research charismatic Christianity, egged me on with his challenges and questions, requiring me to both recognize and defend the boundaries of my study. Paul Nugent, professor of history at the University of Edinburgh, and a student of Ghanaian politics and frontiers, also proved a reliable source of information and advice over the course of fieldwork and write-up.

Baffour Agyeman-Duah, co-founder of Ghana's Center for Democratic Development, longstanding friend, political scientist, development professional, and a co-coordinator with my husband and me of the study abroad program we ran through the University of Denver, provided valuable intellectual support and commentary throughout my research. However puzzled, he was always accepting of my attempt as an anthropologist to comprehend the workings of the Ghanaian state. The same is true to Professor Emanuel Gymah-Boadi, co-founder and executive director of CDD, and a foremost analyst of the Ghanaian political scene. Baffour and his wife Dang were extraordinarily generous in helping us settle for a year in Ghana. Our weekend visits to their home in Akosambo were an especially welcome respite from our busy lives in Accra.

The friendships my family and I forged in our Adenta neighborhood remain a fixture of my experience in Ghana despite our eventual move to the Fulbright House on the University of Ghana campus. The warm welcome we received from the Wuarko family, especially Ma and Pa Wuarko, and both "Big" and "Little" Ama can scarcely be repaid. At Legon, Sammy Danso always provided humor and aid. Afi Sulaiman tirelessly managed the many demands of our household. Evelyn Asamoah was a wonderful teacher and companion to Eliot. Student Fulbrighters Susan Gagliardi and Jon Temin were great friends to our whole family and were always ready to explore the nuances of Ghanaian culture and politics as well as the far-off corners of the country. Each continues to prove their commitment to Africa in different ways. On break from graduate school at Johns Hopkins, Kwaku Nuamah was also a fixture of our life during the first few months of our stay in Ghana, at once a source of critique, companionship, and trademark ironic insight.

As this book project has been a constant companion for nearly a decade, following me on a trail of academic appointments and fellowship opportunities, my debts extend far beyond Ghana. Upon our return from Africa in 2001, we relocated to Gainesville, Florida, where I assumed the position of assistant professor of anthropology at the University of Florida. I put the borders and sovereignty project on the back burner in order to focus on the publication of my first book, *Shea Butter Republic* (Routledge, 2004). With the shea manuscript still in the works, unable to resist a call for proposals on the comparative study of corruption, I nevertheless applied for, and received, a fellowship at the School of Social Science at the Institute of Advanced Study in Princeton. At the Institute Jennifer Hasty and I found ourselves the two anthropologists among a sea of political scientists and economists. Buoyed by the presence of Clifford Geertz, professor emeritus and the defining voice of American anthropology, I sought to pose the perceived corruption of public officials such as Customs officers, not as a "problem to be solved" (as favored by our economics and political science colleagues) but, first and foremost, as a problem to be understood, with complex political, economic, and cultural underpinnings and effects.

IAS is truly an academic paradise, with spacious offices and apartments, tranquil surrounds, engaged scholars, an excellent library, and the world's very best day nursery, all on a single campus. My second child, Safi, was born just a few months before my appointment at the Institute. I faced the difficult choice of taking parental leave from UF or relocating to New Jersey with the children while my husband commuted to Denver, where he still held his academic post. Fully dependent on the wisdom and support of the dedicated teachers and caretakers at the Institute's Crossroads Nursery School, I chose the latter.

I am sincerely grateful to the IAS/SSS faculty, the late Clifford Geertz, Michael Walzer, Joan Scott, Albert O. Hirschman, and Eric Maskin, for the invitation to join the Institute in 2002–3. It was a privilege to be part of the School of Social Science cohort and partake in an intense year of conversation of debate. Alerting to me to both the disjunctures and points of resonance among the social sciences, the comments I received on my early efforts to analyze my research on Customs and neoliberal sovereignty in Ghana have gone a long way to shape the content and interdisciplinary aspirations of this text. Geertz's work has been a source of inspiration since I discovered anthropology as an undergraduate at Amherst College. His attention to my perspective and progress and his willingness to engage in casual conversations as well as more pointed critiques speaks to his lasting intellect and immense generosity. Moving the conversation across disciplines, Michael Walzer was especially supportive of my efforts to tie the investigation of the official and unofficial operations of African bureaucracy to the issue of sovereignty. Jennifer Hasty, Joao Biehl, Neil Englehart, Michael Johnston, Madeline Kochen, Rachel Neis, Charlie Kurzman, Adam Ashforth, and Bill Sewell were all incredible partners in discussion, whether at lunch, in our living rooms, or around the conference table. At the close of 2003 Bill graciously urged me to share my Customs manuscript with the editorial board of the University of Chicago Press Practices of Meaning series, a suggestion I kept at the fore in the long interim between the manuscript's conception and completion.

My year-long residency at the Institute also afforded the luxury of branching out into new research areas, ultimately leading me to redefine the scope of my inquiry into Customs reform and the transformation of state authority in the context of globalization. Specifically, the opportunity to investigate the historical underpinnings of Customs policy in West Africa alerted me to the strongly international context in which national rubrics are forged. Most of all I became aware of the heavy hand not only of nineteenth-century imperial templates, but perhaps more important in the twenty-first century, the abiding weight of a handful of international organizations. So informed, my study's analytical scope shifted from a consideration of the trickle-down effect of abstract global imperatives on the specifics of border management and state sovereignty in Ghana, to a consideration of the actual crafting of so-called global agendas, how and why they become attached to specific national institutions, and the ways in which on-the-ground operations contribute to the valorization of specific global projects all the while fulfilling national imperatives. Rather than seeking to identify local variations of the global, I sought to treat the local, national, and global with equal specification— a perspective central to the arguments presented in this book.

This point of view became evident to me as I tracked the production of a global customs template through the activities of the World Customs Organization (WCO). In the spring of 2003 I attended my first WCO meeting. My inquiries were enthusiastically received by the organization's leadership. I am especially grateful for the encouragement for further research I received from Secretary General Michel Danet, Council Chairperson Pravin Gordhan (now South Africa's minister of finance) and the aid and advice proffered by their assistants, Patricia Revesz and Erich Kieck. I was welcomed to the WCO Brussels headquarters library and archive by Edmond Galle, who educated me on the history of global Customs policy. I would later learn more about the WCO mission from Chriticles Mwansa, Marc Declunder, and Bob Mall. Jouko Lempiainen kindly approved my request to attend the WCO Directors General and Policy Commission meetings in 2005. Michael Schmitz extended the organization's invitation again in 2006. Here I could witness the forging of a shared language of economic governance and along with the play of the U.S.-driven post-9/11 Customs security agenda. These visits equally afforded me the opportunity to meet with African delegates and observe their efforts to build cross-continental coalitions and respond to the pressures and incentives of more powerful states at the same time their countries experimented with a whole range of Customs innovations.

Though delaying the write-up of my field data from Ghana, my affiliation with the WCO and its members deepened my understanding of both the Customs profession and the overarching contours of Customs policy. John Malone of the Taxation Directorate of the European Commission tutored me on the language and genesis of various Customs conventions and, most of all, alerted me to the renewed alliance between the World Customs Organization and the World Trade Organization and the multiplex agenda of trade facilitation. With WCO assistance I also gained an introduction to Customs principals from around the world and visited Customs installations at the ports of Rotterdam and Antwerp, Europe's major trading centers. Here, much to my surprise, I found fascinating parallels with the Ghana case. Though my European research has spun off in a direction of its own, this book would be incomplete without a hearty thanks to Tanja Peterson, Rik Houben, and Vincent Huys in Belgium, and Rob van Kuik, Kees Visscher, and Ton van Hoorn in Holland.

ACKNOWLEDGMENTS

A spring 2006 fellowship at the Woodrow Wilson International Center for Scholars in Washington, D.C., allowed me to follow up on these leads as well as probe the formative influence of the World Bank as well as U.S. Customs and Border Protection on the design and enforcement of Customs protocols worldwide, as I worked toward the completion of this manuscript. Benefiting from my affiliation with the Africa Program led by Howard Wolpe, I was aided by the Wilson Center's terrific staff, including Lindsay Collins and librarian Janet Spikes. I was lucky to join two other Africanist fellows at the Wilson Center, Sara Berry and Karen Hansen, scholars I have held in high regard since my early days of graduate study. Not only was their companionship both stimulating and enjoyable, their on-going commitment to an African Studies thoroughly engaged with present dynamics and dilemmas remains an invaluable source of inspiration to me.

Whether on campus or further afield, throughout the process of research and write-up I continued to be sustained by my colleagues in Anthropology and African Studies at the University of Florida. At the UF Center for African Studies, I have benefited from the unsurpassed support of Leo Villalon, Todd Leedy, Renata Serra, Alioune Sow, Luise White, Sue O'Brien, James Essegbey, Fiona McLoughlin, Goran Hyden, Vicki Rovine, Corinna Green, and Ike Akinyemi. In Anthropology, I have gained much from my friendship and exchange with Ken Sassaman, Peter Schmidt, Stacey Langwick, Kesha Fikes, Anita Spring, Tony Oliver-Smith, Susan Defrance, Florence Babb, Mike Heckenberger, Maria Stoilkova, and Susan Gillespie, as well as the help of Karen Jones and Patricia King. All the while, my graduate-school mentors from the University of Pennsylvania, Sandra Barnes, Tom Callaghy, and Lee Cassenelli continued to provide encouragement, incisive commentary, and models of vibrant scholarly careers.

Graduate students at the University of Florida, especially those enrolled in my Anthropology of the State seminar, equally contributed to the development of the themes addressed in this book. From questions of sovereignty and citizenship, bureaucracy, territoriality, or the techniques of state ethnography, the ideas and approaches developed in student research and critiques benefited mine. Foremost, I thank Jean Dennison, Lauren Fordyce, Michelle Kiel, Jennifer Hale Gallardo, Noelle Sullivan, Sarah Page Chan, Becky Blanchard, Wynie Pankani, Rahmane Idrissa, and Michael Degani for their thoughtful input and enthusiasm for the ethnography of state processes. At UF I also benefited from the editorial assistance of Jill Pease, Rachel Harvey, Josh Toney, and Kate McHarry.

Larry Leshan provided excellent advice on graphics. The fine maps are the work of Edward Gonzalez-Tennant and Diana Gonzalez-Tennant.

Throughout the development of this book, the University of Chicago Press has been a paragon of professionalism. I have been impressed by care and attention to prospective authors and manuscripts expressed by Executive Editor David Brent from our first meeting in San Jose in November 2007. Over the course of manuscript review, revision, and publication, David keenly guided this project without letting his vast editorial experience overcome his respect for original research. It is an honor to work with an editor who has done so much to further scholarship in Anthropology and African Studies. Acting on Bill Sewell's initial recommendation, David encouraged me to share my manuscript with the Chicago Studies in Practices of Meaning editorial board: Jean Comaroff, Lisa Wedeen, Andreas Glaeser, and Bill Sewell. The opportunity to present my manuscript to the board at the University of Chicago Center for Contemporary Theory (3CT) in April 2008 proved incisive, helping me refine my arguments and bring my ethnography to bear on inter-disciplinary debates. I cannot thank the editorial group enough for the questions they raised or their enthusiasm. The timely comments of two anonymous reviewers enabled me to further hone my work. Once I was under contract, University of Chicago Press Editorial Associate Laura Avey deftly guided the production process, serving as a tireless liaison with the graphics, design and marketing divisions.

Along with the University of Chicago Press, I gratefully acknowledge the permission to reproduce and refer to my previously published work. Chapter 6 draws upon "Cars, the Customs Service and Sumptuary Rule in Contemporary Ghana," *Comparative Studies in Society and History* 50, no. 2 (April 2008): 424–53. Chapter 7 brings together "Border Scans: Sovereignty, Surveillance and the Customs Service in Ghana," *Identities: Global Studies in Culture and Power* 11, no. 3 (June–September 2004): 397–416 (reprinted by permission of the publisher, Taylor & Francis, Inc.), and sections of "Enlarging the Anthropology of the State: Global Customs Regimes and the Traffic in Sovereignty," *Current Anthropology* 47, no. 2 (April 2006): 243–76. Chapter 8 is based on "Sovereigns and Citizens in Close Encounter: Airport Anthropology and Customs Regimes in Neoliberal Ghana," *American Ethnologist* 35, no. 4 (November 2008): 519–38. I would also like to acknowledge the permission to publish illustrations graciously provided by Ghana Customs Excise and Preventive Service, Ghana Post Company, the *Accra Mail*, and Azhar Architecture. Unless otherwise indicated, all field photographs are my own.

My greatest debt is ultimately to my family. My mother, Leita Chalfin, made weekly visits to Princeton to care for Safi so I could pursue my fellowship and work on this manuscript at the Institute of Advanced Study. My father, Robert Chalfin, has always been a great listener, helping me sort through my thoughts. Over the years he has learned to resist the impulse to inquire "how is this anthropology?" and come to appreciate a broad-based effort to theorize the human condition across cultures. My in-laws, Ron and Sue Smith, have not only tolerated my travels and preoccupations but provided an ever-ready source of aid and support, whether in Ghana, Washington, D.C., New Jersey, or Florida. My sisters, Jayne Davies and Sonia Chalfin, have always brought me back into the fold of the familiar, insisting on family gatherings and races up the rock scrambles at Mohonk, even if I was just back from Africa or immersed in the myopia of research, writing, and teaching.

Most of all, I thank my husband, Dan, and our children, Eliot Chalfin-Smith and Safi Chalfin-Smith, for their unfailing affection and support throughout the life of this project. They have been an enduring source of love and ever open to making Africa, especially Ghana, part of their way of being in the world.

Toward an Anthropology of Neoliberal Sovereignty

Introduction:
An African Perspective on Neoliberal Sovereignty

Building on the insights of ethnographic inquiry conducted across an array of sites and tactics of governance within and outside of Africa, this book explores the implications of neoliberal restructuring and the allied dynamic of global economic integration for the sovereignty of postcolonial states. I specifically consider how transformations of state sovereignty are brought into being through the everyday spaces and agents of rule—bureaucrats and local functionaries, government offices, checkpoints, and registries—typically held to be the target, though not the authors, of reform. And I probe why, in an era of profound transition, the contours of state restructuring on the global periphery portend shifts occurring in all corners of the world.

I focus on the West African nation of Ghana. Strongly attuned to comparative implications, I address the question of neoliberal sovereignty through an ethnographic portrait of a single governing apparatus, Ghana's Customs Service. In Ghana, as in many postcolonial states, bureaucratic orders such as Customs have long served as the "effective sovereign" (cf. Weber 1995), providing the bulk of state revenue, guarding territorial boundaries, and covering the whole of the nation with a highly visible administrative web. I investigate the work of Customs officials at Ghana's land, air, and

Figure 1.1 Customs officers in Aflao take a break between drills.

maritime frontiers and the shifting array of fiscal, territorial, and social controls under their command brought about by the neoliberal milieu.

Neoliberalism reigns supreme as the preeminent political economic pathway of the late twentieth and early twenty-first centuries the world over and is marked by a systematic commitment to freeing financial flows and nearly every mode of social welfare from state control (Harvey 2005). African states' engagement of the neoliberal turn dates back to the debt and oil crises of the 1970s and the coincident retooling of Bretton Woods agreements and institutions that had earlier delimited the possibilities of post–World War II political economy. I argue that programs of neoliberal reform in both core and periphery thrive in the "far reaches" of the state such as Customs. Not only do Customs authorities' privileging of things over persons fit well the fundamental materialism of neoliberal ideology, their common technocratic orientation obscures the politicized motives and outcomes of neoliberal interventions, making Customs a particularly "efficient" site for wider projects of governmental reform.

This book, then, is at once a foray into *international political economy*—the macro shifts underwriting state restructuring on a global scale; *politics*—the accompanying re/distribution of alliances and authority, and contestations thereof within, across, and upon national boundaries; and fore-most, *political anthropology*—the way these formulations are endowed with meaning and sentiment and subsequently shape and reflect social relations and the experience and exercise of power.

Homing in on the work and private lives of Customs officers in Ghana and their interactions with the citizen-civilians who travel and trade across national frontiers, I employ the lens of ethnography to track the concrete ways the authority of Customs officials—and in turn, state sovereignty—is asserted, understood, challenged, and transformed in the context of political economic change driven by the worldwide neoliberal turn.

Sovereignty, in conventional terms, denotes the manner and extent to which the state reigns supreme in its realm. This is not so much a *maachtstat* wielding a monopoly of power, but the state's capacity to claim, curb, and distribute power—to ultimately call the shots (or be perceived to) in the face of competing interests, whether by means *de jure* or *de facto* (Biersteker and Weber 1996; Bodin 1992; Philpott 1995). Such authority is typically realized on several fronts: the state's control of domestic affairs (domestic sovereignty), the oversight of movement across its territorial and other boundaries (interdependence/territorial sovereignty), the opportunity to set the terms of participation in the in-ternational community (international legal sovereignty), and the state's right to resist the incursions of other states or organizations in internal affairs (Westphalian sovereignty) (Krasner 1999, 11).

An ethnographic approach to the state, however, relying on exten-sive fieldwork across the higher and lower echelons of the apparati of governance, makes it possible to view the many faces of sovereignty as intersubjective and historically derived rather than abstract or wholly formalized figurations of power. "Sovereignty," from this perspective, in the words of international relations scholar Richard Ashley (1984, 272 n.101), "is a practical category whose empirical contents are not fixed but evolve." Unpacking the production of sovereignty in neoliberal times via an ethnographic optic focused on meaning, experience, and the neces-sary disconnect between the professed intent and actual outcomes of rule, likewise provides a critical means to move outside neoliberalism's own analytic and programmatic constructs to consider the practical and ideological work they do (cf. Comaroff and Comaroff 2001, 45).

In this project, I do not take Customs for granted as an arena of re-search, national authority, or international intervention, but probe the circumstances in the present and over the *longue duree* through which Customs regimes in Ghana and elsewhere are constituted as such. With a focus on Customs authorities over time and within and across space, the strongly bureaucratic *cum* technocratic turn of my analysis is driven by an effort to conduct ethnography wherever power in late-modernity is concentrated and renewed yet works to hide itself (cf. Ferguson 1994; Marcus 1998). As John Gledhill (2004, 338) puts it: "Not only is neoliberalism highly "politicized," but the most important part of the politics may lie backstage."[1] Though the discipline of anthropology has gravitated toward the examination of extra-state institutions in neoliberal times, whether multinational corporations, nongovernmental and multilateral organizations, or transnational networks (Ferguson 2006; Ferguson and Gupta 2002; Ong 1999, 2006; Malkki 1995; Nordstrom 2004; Sawyer 2004; Tsing 2005), this book returns state bodies to the center of an anthropology of the political without losing sight of the substantial macroeconomic and macropolitical shifts which anchor the contemporary moment.

Anthropology in the twenty-first century is prone to point to the neoliberalization of nearly everything (cf. Gledhill 2004, 340): from bodies and family life (Ellison 2009; Greenhalgh and Winkler 2005), to urban space and experience (Babb 1999; Dávila 2004), aesthetics (Edmonds 2007), nature and the environment (Tsing 2005), and even spirituality (Newell 2007; Rudnyckyj 2009). In contrast, I take a more orthodox approach to the matter, homing in on specific macroeconomic and macropolitical interventions geared to the promotion of private enterprise and the market logics strongly associated with economic globalization and the spread of multinational capital. Led by scholars such as Aihwa Ong (1999, 2006), anthropologists have made important steps to capture both regional variants of these modalities of social and material regulation (pace Ong's treatment of "neoliberalism with Asian characteristics") and recognize the overall tendency of neoliberalization toward exception and aberration. Further probing the relation between case and norm, my findings from Ghana demonstrate how specific national paths of neoliberal reform actually inflect global models, to shape their replication and ongoing dissemination.

Neoliberal Riddles and Fieldwork Forays

Long before I sought to theorize neoliberal state formation from an African vantage point, I became acquainted with its paradoxes when I first traveled to Ghana as a college student in 1985 to participate in an international work camp. Though Ghana was touted as a middle-income

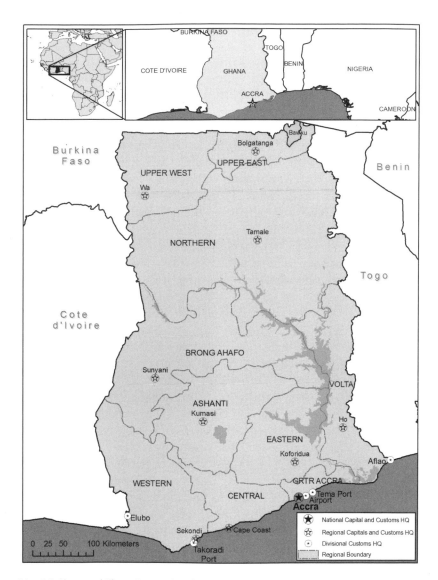

Map 1.1 Ghana and Ghana Customs jurisdictions.

country at independence in 1957 due to its high earnings from cocoa and gold exports, when I arrived in the 1980s the country was climbing out of a long decade of political instability and economic decline marked by a succession of military coups, agricultural downturns, and balance of payment crises.[2] Despite the rise of J. J. Rawlings's populist regime and the promise of economic recovery, imported goods and manufactured of nearly any sort were in short supply and infrastructure was in grave disrepair. This was so notwithstanding the Rawlings' government's assent to the strict conditionalities of the International Monetary Fund and World Bank structural adjustment program in return for massive infusion of financial aid. Establishing Ghana as a neoliberal pacesetter (and supposed success story), this was an arrangement that was virtually unprecedented on the continent at the time (Herbst 1993; Rothchild 1991; World Bank 1984). Here, as later tried elsewhere in the developing world, market logics lay at the crux of reform with the Government of Ghana disavowing industrialization, subsistence provisioning, state enterprise, and other tenets of the developmental state in exchange for the supposed allocative guarantees of competition, comparative advantage and the market's invisible hand (World Bank 1994a).[3]

In this economic climate, on my first day in Accra the leader of our volunteer group insisted we exchange our dollars through legitimate channels, not wanting to further undermine the still-decrepit formal economy (or take the responsibility of introducing college students to any new transgressions). The only outlet available was the head office of the Bank of Ghana, its massive gilded doors and ornate entrance sharply contrasting with the tattered *cedi* bank notes we received. Petrol and operable vehicles were scarce, forcing us to travel via whatever means we could find, from worn-out mammy wagons to, on one occasion, a secondhand ambulance. My friends and I hitched north, finding a ride on an unroofed maintenance vehicle after several hours of waiting. When we returned south via a rare intercity bus, I vividly recall a middle-aged woman being ordered off at a road block when army officers uncovered a cache of imported Maggi bouillons (a highly desired soup ingredient) smuggled from neighboring Togo, with which the border was closed. In hidden spaces, the black market nevertheless thrived. One evening a Ghanaian friend led us through the forest adjoining the campus of the University of Science and Technology in Kumasi to attend a clandestine night market. In addition to tinned food, imported soap, and clothes, gold nuggets could be had at the market's edge.

I returned to Ghana five years later in 1990 as a graduate student to conduct research on markets in northern Ghana and was astounded by the changed economic climate. In the Northern Region capital of Tamale, though far from the bustle of Accra and Kumasi, imported goods could now be had with ease. By the roadside, nearly every household boasted a wood-and-wire kiosk filled with Nestle condensed milk, Lipton tea bags, and Lever Brothers detergent—now staples—for sale. Much larger market stalls flanked the town square. Brightly painted and overflowing with goods stacked in elaborate pyramids rivaling American supermarket displays, they invoked the pleasures of consumption and newfound economic possibility. Buskers set up games of "commodity ring toss," laying plastic mats on the ground topped by a grid of kerosene lanterns, boxes of sugar, batteries, and so on, which could be had for a chance. The foreign exchange market, too, had been liberalized and even in this sleepy regional center it was possible to change money not only at the bank but at privately owned "For-Ex" shops requiring little more than a storefront and a money-counting machine.

At my main research site of Bawku, a border town located in the Upper East Region in Ghana's far northeast corner, the cast of political economic transition was somewhat less certain. Here the socialist-styled Committees in Defense of the Revolution and People's Militias founded in Rawlings's early days still thrived. Amidst groundnut and millet farming, the mainstays of the local economy, there was nevertheless a brisk trade with Cinkasse market in Togo just ten miles away. On market days, streams of people crossed the border by lorry, bike, and foot. I accompanied a neighbor on shopping trips where she purchased thousands of dollars of Togolese and Nigeria-made cloth and hired couriers to smuggle it into Ghana in head-loads and vehicle panels using clandestine bush paths. Unencumbered at the border-crossings, we would casually greet officials (usually residents of the area) as the old friends and relatives they were.

In 1994 I traveled again to northern Ghana for dissertation research on rural women's livelihoods and nontraditional export promotion. I could not help but notice that the changes in Ghanaian economic and political life, in both their scope and inconsistency, continued apace. By this time, the economy had turned the tide nationwide, with import and export the fastest growing arena of activity throughout. [4] In Bawku both legal and illicit commerce skyrocketed. It seemed as though nearly everyone in town was involved with cross-border trade. Otherwise sticking to the traditional millet-based diet, my pious rural host family's garbage pile routinely included imported plastic bottles of Fanta soda, and a trip to Cinkasse market had become a typical Sunday excursion conveniently scheduled at the close of church.

Cinkasse market itself, not just the border, was full of Bawku-people, both merchants and customers. I recall receiving a ride back to Bawku from a high-ranking Ghanaian civil servant whom I met as he filled the boot of his car with imported beer and soft drinks—banned for sale in Ghana—for a family celebration. At the canteen at the Border Post near my house, the same items, though still officially controlled in an effort to protect the few remaining Ghanaian industries, were in steady supply through an informal concessionary agreement. In Bawku, supplementing the few beat-up taxis and pickups that had long served as the primary means of local transport, well-off merchants had started to purchase private cars. There were now Mobil and Goil gas stations and mini-marts even in this town at the margins of Ghana's economic mainstream.

Though the Defense Committees and militias were officially disbanded, the border posts, checkpoints, roadways, and bush paths of a once-again prospering and democratically endowed Ghana teemed with a host of public officials—police, Customs, immigration officers, and occasionally soldiers. Typically harking from different corners of the country, they were largely unfamiliar with the local language and culture. All of us far from home, I often shared conversation and drink with them at day's end, catching the rare evening breeze at the Border Post, or watching CNN on the generator-powered TV at the canteen.

It was hard to discern to what extent these state agents had any bearing on the lives—economic or otherwise—of the citizens and sojourners in this far-off area of the country. Were these individuals simply complicit, partaking of the luxuries of liberalization, like the rest? Were they using the proliferation of cross-border commerce to reinstate older modalities of extraction and intimidation? Did they simply lack the knowledge and social ties required to have any impact on trade at all? With Ghana a celebrated partner to the neoliberal agenda of "rolling back the state," was I to assume they were enacting a new orientation as market facilitators without reverting to personal enrichment or abuse?

Replaying the arguments of the day regarding the diminution of state power in the context of global integration, I wondered to what extent the international border surrounding Bawku could be considered to serve as a marker of state sovereignty. Was I witnessing the last throes of a bureaucratic authority soon to be trumped by the force of society against those of the state and the exigencies of a global capitalist vision promoted by the international financial institutions controlling Ghana's purse strings?

As an anthropologist, I was ultimately curious about the human dimension of Ghana's economic and political reforms in Bawku's borderlands, especially how they were understood and negotiated by the state actors who were their direct and indirect target. With my focus on shea (*karite*), my main research program at the time had come to center on the privatization of state agricultural enterprise and the promotion of non-traditional exports from northern Ghana (Chalfin 2004). Further drawing me to the outlooks of state actors, I was astounded to discover how neoliberalism's ostensible project of political streamlining provided surprising opportunities for the survival of state institutions and expanded mandate for some state employees. Yet the day-to-day experiences of state officials continued to be a crucial missing piece in the growing number of scholarly discussions of either border-zone processes or neoliberal reform emerging at the time. When I returned to the United States, I continued to wonder about the state agents involved in these arenas. I wanted to know more about the terms of their consent, resistance, and reworking of both the older and newer norms defining their work, along with the attendant shifts in their political, social, and economic standing.

After I completed my PhD, I made my way back to Ghana to make these questions of neoliberalism, sovereignty, and state agency the central focus of my research, not just in the northern part of the country I knew best, but in the context of the nation's biggest and most active frontiers. Funded by grants from the Wenner-Gren and National Science Foundation and with a year of concerted research time at my disposal, it was at this juncture that I turned to Ghana's Customs Service, officially known as the Customs, Excise and Preventive Service and popularly referred to by the acronym CEPS. With a mission devoted to the oversight of all goods entering or leaving national territory and the persons (real and corporate) in any way involved with their conveyance, Customs, among all state agencies, appeared to be directly mired in the processes of trade promotion and economic integration at the heart of the neoliberal agenda deeply affecting contemporary Ghana. A powerful proxy for state power in neoliberal times, Customs officers were the prime dependent variable of my study as I sought to capture if and how their enforcement practices and attendant self-understandings varied with the context and conditions of free trade across national frontiers. As I began to systematically explore the workings of Customs administration in Ghana, I realized that Customs presented a far more complex and revealing case than I had ever anticipated. I soon learned that Customs was the state agency most deeply embedded in the history of Ghanaian state formation, a position affirming its status as a bellwether, not only of political economic change, but of Ghanaian statehood and hence, state sovereignty, more generally.

Thematics and Loci of Inquiry

The story I tell in this book takes place within airports and shipping harbors, frontier stations, government ministries, corporate offices, multilateral meetings, and the unbounded space of popular imagination, public life, and international regulatory rubrics. My account draws on a year of fieldwork among Customs officers in Ghana along with extensive archival and policy research. Moving from West Africa to Brussels and Geneva, Washington, D.C., and Singapore, the research also encompasses the array of international bodies involved in Customs regulation and reform on a global scale. It is further grounded in comparative analysis of the place of Customs authorities within the modern state apparatus.

In part 1 of the book, chapter 1 recounts the extraordinary history of Ghana's Customs authority, which was established in the mid-nineteenth century as a precursor to the founding of the Gold Coast Colony and later, the modern nation-state of Ghana. These developments are placed within a wider comparative frame exposing the enduring significance of revenue authorities such as Customs to early state-making in the European core and subsequent processes of European imperial expansion in Africa, Asia, or the Americas. Moving from the imperial age to the late-modern moment and uncovering a common logic of governance running across of the two eras, the chapter further reveals the centrality of Customs to a broad range of neoliberal organizations and initiatives at the dawn of the twenty-first century.

Chapter 2, continuing in a comparative vein, relates the terms of Customs' late-modern revival to other predominant modalities of neoliberal state restructuring, which challenge state claims to exclusivity. Occurring in finance, law, and industry, these are typically portrayed as largely legalistic and technocratic developments. Asking how the case of Ghana Customs partakes of and stands apart from these trends, the chapter argues that their implications for state sovereignty cannot be well understood without a fully anthropological theorization of the state attuned to how the prescribed modalities of neoliberal governance are constituted and struggled over in practice and the forms of knowing and being on which they depend. While sustaining the close reading of political economic circumstances suggested by established approaches, the methods of inquiry advocated here address the state's embeddedness in complex social relations that may well transcend the structural imperatives of governance. Prevailing depictions of the neoliberalism's instrumental logics are similarly complicated by the chapter's consideration of the state's strongly ideological and affective rendering. Finally, claims of epochal transformation under neoliberalism are supplanted by a concern with the ongoing interplay of diverse state projects.

These theoretical and methodological insights and attendant comparative arguments lay the ground for ethnographic inquiry in part 2 of the book. Each chapter in part 2 focuses on a particular research venue and with it a specific dimension of state sovereignty in the face of neoliberal restructuring. In addition to substantiating the comparative significance of the case of bureaucratic *cum* fiscal reform in Ghana across time and place, four themes prevail: (1) the historical patchwork of governing logics within the postcolonial state; (2) the rise of indirect and evidence based modes of governance; (3) the political contradictions of transparency; and (4) the affective and embodied dimensions of state authority.

Chapter 3, the first ethnographic chapter, situates neoliberal interventions in the context of the historical development of the Ghana Customs Service and the Ghanaian state more generally. Addressing the problematic of territorial sovereignty, the chapter focuses on Customs operations at Ghana's land frontier at Aflao on the Ghana-Togo border from the beginning of the twentieth century to the dawn of the twenty-first. This opening portrait of Customs traces the operations and physical layout of the Aflao border post over time and space to expose the diverse and not always compatible political strategies pursued by Customs at the frontier and the resulting dependence of Customs officials on the knowledge and services of border-zone residents.

Contrasting the embedding of frontier installations in the lives and livelihood of the border's residents and sojourners with the unsettled place of border controls in the life of Ghana's national state, evidence from Aflao brings to light the distinction between the functioning of territorial boundaries *in situ* and the tenuous coherence of broader claims to territorial sovereignty espoused by a shifting cast of national governing regimes. Ghana's Aflao borderlands expressly demonstrate that the tensions of territorialized sovereignty hinge not only on the inherent challenge of controlling mobile persons and things, but also, equally, on the uneasy layering of national political logics. An outcome of the ongoing process of governmental reform characteristic of the postcolonial polity and its strong infrastructural cast, this dynamic reveals the frontier to be a site for expression of excessive state power, however fragile or dependent its constitution or effects. Challenging assertions that the neoliberal era is characterized by the diminution of the state's territorial investments, the chapter moreover makes it clear that Customs operations at the Aflao borderlands are situated within a double axis of territorial authority at once shared between border-zone residents in place and the lingering bids of national administrations over time.

Also based at the Aflao frontier, chapter 4 trains its lens on neoliberally inspired good governance initiatives to provide a closer look at the changing tactical and spatial configuration of Ghanaian sovereignty at the millennium's turn. The chapter brings to light the recalibration of bureaucratic hierarchies occurring at the border zone, with the usual vertical rendering of sovereign authority cross-cut by more networked forms of power as Customs and the wider governing edifice respond to the pressures of neoliberal reform. Heightening the strain between Customs administrative headquarters and Customs officers and operations at the frontier, these contentions are evident in the rising number of disciplinary measures meted out by the Customs commissioner in the name of donor mandated anticorruption programs. Stemming from the same democratizing impulses, it can also be seen in the government's contradictory efforts to purge the state of older military tendencies and simultaneously build Customs military capacities through a generalized mandate of force and the assignment of paramilitary loyalists to Customs offices.

Exacerbating the perennial tensions between Customs administrative center and periphery, at Aflao the conventions of Customs bureaucratic authority are additionally compromised by the adoption of World Trade Organization (WTO) rules requiring the transfer of work off-site to private sector partners and the accompanying devaluation of Customs site-specific expertise. Rather than generating greater political transparency as promised, these moves undermine established modes of bureaucratic accountability and revitalize the authoritarian potentials of state executives. At the same time, they extend expressions of state authority away from the border to a range of alternative spaces, less public or permanent. The result is a reconfiguration of sovereignty, both top-heavy and dispersed, that confounds neat notions of hierarchical state authority whether based on territory, administrative capacity or the exclusive control of force (cf. Weber 1968).

Moving the lens away from particular border zones and Customs installations, to the persons and things Customs rules over, chapter 5 speaks to the struggles between the Ghanaian public and Customs authorities with regard to property rights in neoliberal times. A vital switch-point between state and society, questions of property (private as well as public) expose the conditions and contentions of popular sovereignty (pace Locke 1960). In chapter 5 the question of property and popular sovereignty is unpacked through the case of motor vehicles, a form of movable property whose handling by Customs has sparked heated and ongoing public controversy in Ghana.

Using evidence gleaned from newspapers, radio, and the archives of popular culture via film, literature, religious imagery, and advertising during Ghana's 2000–2001 electoral interregnum, the chapter investigates perspectives on vehicle access and ownership espoused by Ghana's highly mobile citizenry. Public conceptions of personal property are juxtaposed with the elaborate bureaucratic procedures required by Ghana Customs for car ownership and importation (surprisingly, supported anew by Customs international partners) to reveal competing notions of entitlement endorsed by a succession of ruling regimes. Once again betraying the grip of the past on contemporary politics, these divergences provoke the public's outrage over the lingering influence of socialist and military-era commercial controls on state-sanctioned property regimes despite the country's apparent commitment to democratization and free market principles. Yet, giving voice to a popular sovereignty deeply inflected by neoliberal values in which ideals of the market and individualized consumption are mobilized to collective ends, the ensuing debates about the proper modalities of car disposition extend the space of democratic politics and ultimately curb state authority.

Chapter 6 takes the operations of the Customs Service at Ghana's Tema Harbor, the country's primary port and most active and profitable commercial frontier, as its centerpiece. Since independence Tema has been transformed from a fishing harbor and industrial site to an international trade-hub accommodating global shipping lines, cargo carriers, and logistics firms in order to serve the West African coast and subregion. The case of Tema brings into focus the outsourcing of state operations, the increasing reliance on information technologies and other forms of virtual communication, and the growing breadth of multilateral directives—all critical dimensions of neoliberal intervention.

The chapter specifically examines the inauguration of two cutting-edge Customs technologies at Tema: a giant x-ray cargo-scanner and a countrywide and multistakeholder electronic data network. Funded and managed by multinational corporations involved in security and trade logistics, these developments put Ghana on the forefront of twenty-first-century Customs reforms. Notwithstanding the threat of denationalization these technical innovations bring, Customs' assertion of state sovereignty is augmented by them. The chapter analyzes the new governing tactics availed by Customs' high-tech enhancements and the ensuing adjustments for the public as well as Customs officials. In a rather stunning development, Customs mastery of these high-tech services give the consortia who govern them products to sell to other developing and transitioning states. Rendering Ghana a global model, here technological innovation and international standardization combine to create a form of profit-bearing "derivative sovereignty" functional to capital and the nation-state.

Chapter 7 maintains a focus on sovereignty's subjects, agents, and objects as it shifts the locus of analysis to yet another space of rule: Ghana's Kotoka International Airport (KIA). Examining a decade of foreign and domestic investment in airport expansion, the chapter argues that international airports in Ghana and elsewhere comprise a key yet largely overlooked frontier of neoliberalism and serve as a vital infrastructure of global mobility. Chapter 7's ethnographic content showcases the encounters between Customs personnel at KIA and Ghanaians by birth or citizenship whose livelihoods and lifestyles increasingly depend on transnational mobility due to the constraints and opportunities of the neoliberal era. These observations suggest that citizenship and sovereignty are forged in the same crucible. As the details of passenger clearance makes clear, in the setting of the airport Customs control of Ghanaian and other African nationals is much more important to the assertion of state power than the control of nonnationals.

The political implications of these adjustments are multiplex. While the authority of Customs officers at KIA is enlarged due to their involvement in international training programs and exposure to international protocols, Customs officers find themselves dependent on the knowledge, status, and material wealth of the rising ranks of Ghanaians who travel abroad. Travelers, in turn, draw upon their political experiences overseas to challenge the entreaties of Customs officials. But mired in political nostalgia, they remain invested in preserving Customs' bureaucratic excesses as an icon of a discrete and knowable state authority. The airport as a result operates as a centerpiece of a hybrid sovereignty, at once national and transnational, native and cosmopolitan, authoritarian and liberal, internally felt and externally endowed.

The conclusion, brings together the many reasons why Ghana, though construed as part of the global periphery, represents a paradigmatic case of neoliberal transformation. Hidden behind the shallow but much noted spectacle of democratization, demilitarization, and decentralization, the revitalization of Customs regimes consolidates state sovereignty within an ostensibly depoliticized fiscal-administrative nexus. Contributing to the renewal of an institutional realm at the heart of modern state-making (pace Tilly 1985), in the late-modern context, international coordination rather than domestic authority is at the fore of Customs mandate. The result, as evidenced in the chapters that follow, is the nearly unguarded expansion of highly bureaucratic and technocratic political arrangements. They are tempered only by an emerging set of nationalist and transnational loyalties, themselves informed by neoliberal logics in combination with pre-existing modalities of domination and affiliation.

I argue that Ghana stands as a prime laboratory of governmental reform due to the longstanding strength of the country's bureaucratic apparatus, the fragile nature of political accountability, and the increasing impossibility of economic autonomy. Facilitated by a combination of bureaucratic resilience, executive autonomy, and the necessity of economic extraversion, here neoliberal experiments can be pursued with ease, fostering a form of "sovereign availability" that sets the stage for their replication worldwide. Gaining force in the states of the global north as well as the global south, these trends I suggest warrant recognition as defining features of late-modern statehood.

The Possibilities and Limits of an Anthropology of the State

Because I carried out my research within an institution and a moment intensely politicized, my access to the operations and outlooks of Customs officials across Ghana's bureaucratic and border installations was at once exceptional and admittedly partial. These limitations reveal much about the internal power structures of Customs and the self-images of Customs officials. Hence, this book does not aim to turn Customs "inside-out"; it is not a "tell-all" of the administration's inner-workings and back-room deals. Rather, it probes the "public face" of the state (see Navaro-Yashin 2002) and how that face comes to be constituted over time by shifts in policies, practices, and individual interests and understandings. Here I stand by the epistemological and political contention that before we can understand how the state is subverted or undermined, we need to consider how state power is manufactured, institutionalized, and recursively inscribed.

Nevertheless, eliciting the informed consent of my research subjects and collaborators was riven with dilemmas and uncertainties. Although ambiguities of power and purpose between researcher and researched are inherent to ethnographic field research, I found this to be particularly true of this study. Not only was I seeking to conduct my investigation in a privileged and, I should add, strongly hierarchical realm of the state, I sought to do so at a moment of acute political transition. My 2000–2001 fieldwork experiment spanned a critical democratic turn. In addition to being Ghana's third consecutive national election, it was one in which the reigning head of state, J. J. Rawlings, with two decades of party and government leadership behind him, was constitutionally required to leave office. This laid the groundwork for a heated political contest, not just between the ruling party and a single opposition, but among a plethora of parties—old and new—vying for power, and within the ruling party itself. The old regime, in which Customs was firmly ensconced, was simultaneously under attack and subject to myriad counter-efforts to maintain the status quo.

Whether this was a prime or inopportune time to conduct field research is left for the reader to decide. What is clear is that in this climate my efforts to establish rapport—or even the most basic forms of access to the Customs bureaucracy—were unavoidably politically tinged. In turn, I found myself both a perpetrator and a victim of the sort of "ethnographic complicity" described by George Marcus (1998) in his discussion of the "changing mise-en-scene of anthropological fieldwork." Straddling a thorny ethical divide, I am at once indebted to my many interlocutors as well as in cahoots with them, sympathetic to their vulnerabilities and celebratory of their victories, even if exploitative or abusive.[5] In striking this epistemological *cum* moral compromise, my aim is not to suspend judgment in a hyperrelativist mode, but to reveal the workings of power on its own terms: to confront it fully with all its enticements and distortions.

In this regard, I owe my greatest debt to the commissioner of Customs, who granted me permission to pursue my study within his realm. In a manner typical of Ghanaian sociality and in conformity with the tried-and-true ethnographic strategy of "snow-ball sampling," I gained an introduction to the Customs commissioner through a friend of a friend. Upon our first meeting there was a quick, if not somewhat forced, camaraderie reflecting the sort of innocent complicity that comes from a common sense of being here and elsewhere, what Marcus calls "shared outsiderness" (1998, 118). American-educated and a long-time resident in the United States, the commissioner appeared to welcome me as a compatriot with full respect and recognition of my academic concerns.

Little did I know that his approval may also have been founded on a more problematic ethical partnership. Unbeknownst to me at the time, Customs' ranking officer was facing accusations of corruption and was on the cusp of official investigation. Thus his willingness to put his cadres under the ethnographic microscope was potentially self-serving, as it indicated to the press and federal investigators that he had nothing to hide. More troubling, perhaps, was the fact that in the steep hierarchy of Ghana's Customs administration, what I took to be a simple letter of permission to conduct research was as much a legal order from the commissioner to his underlings to cooperate with me. Evincing a full-fledged, even if unknowing, political complicity, in this arrangement my presence and inquiries were never mine alone but a by-product of the commissioner's authority. I was an agent and beneficiary, however unsuspecting, of his power. In this setting, as in many other contemporary ethnographic situations, given the inevitabilities of complicity, as Marcus (1998, 121–22) notes:

The inequality of power relations, weighted in favor of the anthropologist, can no longer be presumed. . . . The fieldworker . . . may deal with persons much stronger in power and class positions than his own, in which case both the terms and limits of ethnography are managed principally by them. Here, where the ethnographer occupies a marked subordinate relationship to informants, the issues of use and being used, of ingratiation, and of trading information about others elsewhere becomes a matter of normal ethical concern.

Thus aligned, I was subject to rote compliance from officials throughout the Customs Service. With little choice but to consent to my inquiries and interview requests and allow me to occupy their work site for the course of my observations, Customs officers at times put forth a ready resistance to my entreaties, shunning efforts to go beyond the most superficial exchanges. Between these two poles of command and evasion, individual officers and I nevertheless forged our own grounds for rapport separate from the commissioner's exactions to which we were both prey. In another effort to distance my research from the pressures of political affiliation, much more than I had initially planned, I also utilized the potentials of proxy research (Ellis and MacGaffey 1996), asking my research assistants to pursue a variety of independent assignments. In addition to carrying out the usual standardized interviews, they became experts in participant observation, making themselves present in venues and situations where I would be too conspicuous and forging relationships with those whose backgrounds they shared.

Variously driven by boredom, a personal tendency toward extraversion, the enticements of my own status as an American academic, or the skill of my research assistants in breaking the ice, a cross-section of officers let their stories be heard. In each venue—harbor, land frontier, airport, and private Customs service provider—there was a group of officers with whom we established a relaxed sort of parity (and in many cases, real friendships) and built our knowledge and extended our relationships. One close associate in Customs labeled this cohort Customs "intellectuals," singling them out for their curiosity and capacity for self-reflection. As the Customs Service carried out a major recruitment of university graduates (many in the social sciences) in the late 1980s and early 1990s, these were in many cases persons with whom I held something in common.

As my presence at various Customs offices became regularized, I experienced a reciprocal effort by Customs officials to bring me into the fold on their own terms. In their own bid for transparency, senior officers took to calling me into offices to share their version of events before I could formulate my own questions and observations. Neither was it unusual for them to share the spoils of a typical Customs shift—ostensibly categorized as "taxi fare" and "chop money."[6] Whether or not my newfound colleagues' largesse bought my silence or sympathy, it did at least initiate me into their point of view.

As Ghana's political tensions built both pre- and post-election (Smith 2002a), so too did the willingness (and indeed, desire) of Customs personnel from the very highest to the lowest ranks, to share their experiences and interpretation of events. The context of political uncertainty, like any other liminal phase, it turned out, provided a profound opportunity to observe the inner workings of an organization. Customs officers were eager to open up and share their secrets about Customs' past and speculations regarding Customs' future despite my status as an outsider. Whether an attempt to gain critical distance from their own circumstances or the expression of a self-consciousness that comes with the breaking-open of otherwise unspoken truths, this was a complicity that comes at the edge of crisis. But as much as I found this sort of bearing witness professionally expedient, it posed risks to my cooperants. The stakes were very real, with the potential to impact their own access to resources, employment and reputation and that of their coworkers, friends and families. For these reasons, I strenuously avoid mentioning Customs officials' actual names, or specific dates and places whenever possible. In this spirit, I pose my work as a meaningful account of events rather than a complete record. The insights and ellipses that come with this stance will become clear in the chapters to follow.

PART ONE

ONE

Customs as Effective Sovereign: State Logics across Time and Place

Introduction:
The Genealogy of the Ghana Customs Service

Ghana Customs, Excise and Preventive Service traces its roots to the very earliest days of British colonial rule in the Gold Coast. This began in 1828 when the responsibility for financial administration of British settlements and trading posts along this stretch of West Africa's Atlantic coast was ceded to a committee of London merchants. In 1839, half a decade before the official establishment of the Gold Coast Colony in 1844, the same merchant council was authorized to collect duties of one-half percent on all goods and merchandise coming into Gold Coast settlements for the British government, a directive involving the legal establishment of a designated "Collector of Customs."[1]

From the start, Customs cast a web of obligations to the emergent colonial state as it capacitated its very operation. According to historians, in the Gold Coast colonial financial administration lay at the foundation of governance overall, with Customs agents (both fledging and official) involved in peacekeeping, treaty-making, and hearing of court cases in addition to their core function of fundraising. Asserting British overrule even in the absence of its formal ratification, this strategy of governance paved the way for the legalization of colonial and, later, national territorial claims.

Far more successful than efforts to collect direct revenues from poll and household taxes, throughout the nineteenth century at the height of Europe's competitive "scramble for Africa" the tariff ordinances authorized by Customs underwrote imperial expansion in terms of the development of infrastructure, administrative accountability, and exclusive territorial control. Indeed, so strong was the relationship between fiscal administration and territorial authority that by 1885 the Customs and Treasury departments were one and the same. Customs stations were likewise established at the maritime ports of entry as well as inland frontiers of the Gold Coast (Anim-Asante 1988, 8–10, 22–23).

Completing the triumvirate of bureaucratic administration, bounded territorial rule, and monopoly of legitimate violence essential to a Weberian (1968) definition of the modern state, by the turn of the century Customs added the control of force to its official purview. This occurred with the establishment of a semimilitary Preventive wing in 1897. Operating within the Gold Coast as well as the boundaries of the colony's fledgling protectorates in Asante and the Northern Territories (Anim-Asante 1988, 26), Customs' Preventive department was clearly an instrument of imperial sovereignty charged with shoring up the reach of an expanding state. Moving beyond tax collection and Preventive Services, Customs status continued to grow through the colonial period. Customs eventually accrued the responsibilities of handling import licensing and controls and excise taxation, compiling trade and manufacturing statistics, running and policing harbors, and disseminating public information to traders and travelers. For the duration of the colonial era Customs remained accountable for the lion's share of revenue, consistently collecting over 50 percent of government receipts, rendering it the virtual lifeblood of the colonial state. At independence in 1957 Customs was among the largest and longest-lived bureaucratic orders within the new nation of Ghana.

Through the thick and thin of Ghana's alternating rounds of civilian and military rule post-independence, the might of the Customs Service persisted. Customs remained in play from the First Republic of Nkrumah established in the early years of nationhood, to the rise of the National Liberation Council, which captured the state via coup in 1966, and the return to civilian rule under Busia's Second Republic in 1970. It endured the reign of the militarist National Redemption Council and Supreme Military Council under Acheampong, the brief stand of Liman's Third Republic in 1980, and the first decade of Rawlings's military/populist statesmanship from 1981 to 1992. Facing the democratic dawning of the Fourth Republic in 1992 and the subsequent eras of electoral rule, Customs has continued to stand strong. Customs mandates shifted slightly in each period, reflecting the extent of political and economic austerity and the concomitant imposition or lifting of import and export controls. The division of labor between Customs and other security bodies, whether the army or specialized corps of border guards and paramilitary units, also waxed and waned depending on the leanings of the regime in power, but the organization's protective mandate never dissolved completely.

Customs remained a critical force in national governance with a strong hand in both revenue and security matters, with an administration spanning both the Ministry of Interior and Ministry of Finance for more than twenty-five years between 1960 and 1986. In the late 1980s, when other state agencies were being rationalized out of existence due to the pressures of neoliberal reform, Customs was promoted to a full-fledged government service located exclusively within the Ministry of Finance. Thomas Hansen and Finn Stepputat comment on the political significance of this sort of bureaucratic endurance, stating, "Certain sectors of the governmental apparatus, due to their origins in the colonial order or military or authoritarian legacy, have been allotted considerable autonomy and over time have developed extremely resilient forms of organization [. . .] that few political parties dare to confront" (2001, 29–30). Ghana Customs fits the bill.

Attested to by the many Customs officers I met who had maintained their positions for decades despite the rise and fall of various regimes, Customs has proven to be flexible enough to serve diverse governmental ends, yet strong (and important) enough to maintain its core functions of taxation and protection. With more than 500 employees in the early years of national independence (Anim-Asante 1988, 46), when I began my research forty years later Customs ranks had grown sevenfold, to over 3,500 employees. Customs, too, remained Ghana's most visible frontline agency generating the bulk of state revenue and maintaining an expansive and highly visible administrative web with multiple sanctions at its disposal.[2] Ghana is not at all alone in this regard as the fiscal might, and attendant political pull, of Customs is region wide.[3]

Clearly, Customs lies at the foundation of what Michael Mann (1986, 2008; see also Soifer 2008) has called the state's "infrastructural power," at once territorially expansive in its reach, centralized in authority and penetrating the social fabric of the nation overall. Although the two are not mutually exclusive in their ends and operations, in Mann's (2008) conception, "infrastructural power," deeply bureaucratic and invested in the ordering of daily life, is distinguishable from the purely "despotic power" of state elites cut off from the society at large.

On Modern State Formation: Customs in Comparative Perspective

Of supreme significance to this study, the association between the ascendance of Customs administration and modern state formation in Ghana is in no way unique. Scholars working from a wide range of theoretical vantage points note the importance of fiscal capacity to the rise of the modern state.[4] This is evident in Douglass North's (1981, 148) by now–classic assessment that "[t]he interplay between the government and its subjects with respect *to the expansion of the state's* right to tax was particularly important" (italics in original) to the dynamics of state formation in early modern Europe. Drawing on Mann's (1986) notion of infrastructural power, Mitchell Dean (1996, 147) likewise sees taxation as a political technology crucial to the production of the state effect, that is, a perception of an overarching governmental apparatus, external to and ruling over society. Saskia Sassen (2006) draws new attention to this point of view to assert: "The state bureaucracy for extracting revenue, particularly the capacity to implement increasingly standardized taxation, helped make the state the most significant economic actor at the time" (20).

Charles Tilly's groundbreaking historical synthesis put forth in his essay, "War Making and State Making as Organized Crime," offers a powerful explanation of this correlation. Alongside the examination of the development and legitimation of national states' coercive capacities, Tilly addresses the financial basis of modern statehood, succinctly capturing the prime interlocking facets of early modern states' military/fiscal nexus (1985, 181): "War making: eliminating or neutralizing rivals outside territory; State making: eliminating or neutralizing rivals inside territory; Protection: eliminating or neutralizing enemies of their clients; Extraction: acquiring the means to carry out the first three." Tilly, moreover, argues that a state's monopoly over the means of violence relies wholeheartedly on the monopolistic extraction of revenue from those who seek membership within that polity (172):

Power holders' pursuit of war involved them willy-nilly in the extraction of resources for war-making from the populations over which they had control [. . .]. In the long run, the quest inevitably involved them in establishing regular access to capitalists who could supply and arrange credit and in imposing one form of regular taxation or another on the people and activities within their spheres of control.

Particularly relevant to the arguments I seek to develop, embedded within Tilly's more general formulation is a reference to the significance of the extractive efforts of Customs authorities to state building.[5] Taking seventeenth-century Britain as the paradigmatic case, Tilly writes, "Britain has the advantage of drawing more of its tax revenues from Customs and Excise, taxes that were, despite evasion, significantly cheaper to collect than land taxes, property taxes, and poll taxes" (1985, 180).[6] Here, Tilly draws inspiration from economic historian Gabriel Ardant's encyclopedic *Histoire de l'impot* (1971, 1972). Arguing that "[t]he fiscal system was the transformer of the economic infrastructure into political structure" (1975, 220), Ardant documents the centrality of a range of modes of indirect taxation—nearly all of which are the purview of Customs authorities—to funding states as well as building state oversight and accountability across early modern Europe. At this time, agrarian populations' limited ties to markets and the small scale of most productive enterprise, in Ardant's view, made the extraction of revenue in the context of trade and transport and the close monitoring of commerce the only viable fiscal option for Europe's fledgling states. Proving his thesis that "political institutions do not change as rapidly as the circumstances from which they arise" to be especially "valid in the case of financial techniques" (Ardant 1975, 171), these same strategies were replicated over the course of European political development well into the eighteenth and nineteenth centuries.[7]

It is worth noting that a nearly identical logic of fiscal extraction via Customs, for many of the same reasons, emerged as a major mechanism of colonial conquest during the era of European high imperialism. Bringing to life Tilly's observation that "secondary states are typically characterized by the extensive bureaucracy of fiscal surveillance" (1985, 185), not only in Ghana but across Africa, Asia, and the Americas (including the Thirteen Colonies), this template was replicated in the designs of imperial state-making (Arasaratnam 1998; Dirks 2007; Prince and Keller 1989; Sen 2002).[8] These arrangements served the dual purpose of generating revenue and establishing the infrastructure of colonial governance at the very same time the taxing of tropical imports served to shore up states' administrative capacities in the metropole (Ardant 1975, 220).

In this historical context, as Benedict Anderson (1991) demonstrates more generally in his colony-centric explanation of the rapid spread of the nation-state, Customs presented a decidedly modular political form both highly functional and conveniently transposable.[9] Here Customs regimes stand as an early example of what has more recently been called an "immutable mobile" (Latour 1987, 234): "A technoscientific form that can be decontextualized and recontextualized, abstracted, transported and reterritorialized," in the words of Stephen Collier and Aihwa Ong "and is designed to produce functionally comparable results in disparate domains" (Ong and Collier 2005, 11). Customs transnational circulation, even at this time, stands out as a case of "technostructural" transposition with clear political origins and impacts.[10]

Indeed, in situations where claims to persons and landed property operate according to standards unfamiliar to the occupying power, as in most colonial locales, Customs authorities were a supremely efficient means of administrating wealth, society, and territory all at once. As evidenced in the Gold Coast, the bureaucratic and spatial reach of Customs authorities along with their fundamental commercial orientation also allowed for Customs assimilation of the other modalities of state violence described by Tilly, such as the neutralization of external and internal rivals or the protection of clients (in this era, typically drawn from the ranks of merchant capital). Attuned to the enduring significance of this logic of rule in the African case, Frederick Cooper (2002, 5) has gone so far as to define African states as "gatekeeper polities": "Colonial States had been gatekeeper states. They had weak instruments for entering the social and cultural realm over which they presided, but they stood astride the intersection of colonial territory and the outside world.' Explaining continuity in this modality of rule over time, he goes on to state, "Most [postcolonial] rulers realized early on that their own interests were served by the same strategy of gatekeeping that had served the colonial state."[11]

The paired history of Customs in both the colonial and imperial realm make it evident that Customs regimes are an implicit—if not fundamental—feature of the modern state apparatus in the global north as well as global south, both overlooked and sorely undertheorized. The reach and continuity of Customs regimes over time and space point to fiscal administration (territorially based forms of commercial extraction, to use Tilly's terms) as a key pillar of modern state sovereignty. Combining force and bureaucratic authority, territorial dominion and claims to movable wealth, Customs embodies modern sovereignty's middle range, standing between the self-regulating subject of late modern governmentality and the *dramatis personae* of monarchal absolutism. Straddling the divide between the sovereignty of self-discipline and the despot, Customs, in short, wields a powerful brand of infrastructural sovereignty, to draw again on Mann's (1986, 2008) formulation.[12] With the systematic analysis of Customs regimes largely neglected by scholars due perhaps to the sheer ubiquity of these bureaucratic entities, the reconsideration of a governing structure buried deep in the annals of modern state formation is clearly in order. As we shall see, this is true for reasons as much predictive as retrospective.

The Neoliberal Turn and the Worldwide Revival of Customs Authority

There is another perhaps even more intriguing insight regarding the problematic of Customs and sovereign statehood revealed by historical comparison (and not so easily explained by Tilly's logic). Despite the vastly different conditions and wide temporal arc separating the classic periods of early modern state formation and late modernity in the new millennium Customs regimes worldwide are undergoing astounding efflorescence. Compared to an earlier imperial mercantile epoch strongly devoted to the crafting of national boundaries, intense international rivalry, and the promotion of national capital, this later moment is marked by a worldwide neoliberal turn necessitating participation in global markets rather than the protection of domestic populations and economies. Here, supranational coalitions, multinational firms, and transnational flows and investment are all at the fore. Nevertheless, the late-modern moment is accompanied by a surprising resurgence of Customs regimes and capacities around the globe. Examined through the lens of Ghana, the conundrum of Customs sovereign revival in neoliberal times stands at the very heart of this book.

Specifically, in the context of global capitalism, Customs is by no means a forgotten strain of state authority left to fade and fray but a site of concerted and self-conscious investment by states and international bodies. It is an administrative regime demonstrating surprising global convergence and coordination. In 2008, 98 percent of the world's recognized states contained national Customs administrations. These numbers are growing rather than dwindling at the decade's turn.[13] As in the past, those developments are occurring in the core as well as the periphery. In Europe, even as the expansion and strengthening of the European Union (EU) obviates many other realms of national government (such as national currency), Europe's many Customs authorities remain and their responsibilities are compounded. Likewise, with the collapse of the Soviet Union spawning a plethora of new states, the number of national Customs authorities is on the rise across Europe and Central Asia.[14]

In the United States the trend toward strengthening Customs regimes is evident in the establishment of the enlarged U.S. Customs and Border

Protection agency in 2002, which combines Customs, the Border Patrol, and the Immigration and Naturalization Service. At the same time, free trade agreements elsewhere in the world, from MERCOSUR to NAFTA to ASEAN, all involve the reworking of Customs controls and improvement of Customs capacities if only to facilitate cross-border flows. African states are heavily enmeshed in these trends, not just in Ghana but across the continent. Extant Customs authorities are upgrading, from Mauritius to Kenya, Guinea to Senegal. Customs corps are rapidly rebuilding in the aftermath of state breakdown, as in Liberia, Sierra Leone, Angola, and Mozambique. Regional coalitions such as Southern African Customs Union and the East African Customs Union are revitalizing (Maiko 2004).

Playing a central role in enforcing the shifting terms of political and economic ordering worldwide, Customs authorities around the globe oversee an expanding mandate. This runs the gamut from the monitoring of trade pacts, managing export processing and investment promotion schemes, collecting revenue for other national financial authorities along with Customs own coffers, to coordinating relationships with a host of supply chain stakeholders (importers, exporters, manufacturers, shippers, and logistics providers). It also involves the pursuit of a wide range of protective functions with regard to health or fighting of trafficking and terrorism (WCO 2002b).

Though certainly augmented by the U.S.-led post-9/11 security platform, the extended reach of Customs has both earlier roots and an alternative logic traceable to the mandates of multilateralism emerging in the last decades of the twentieth century (Harvey 2005). Specifically, the worldwide revival of Customs appears to reflect a neoliberal vision of government *minimis*, where states' regulatory capacities are consolidated within a single body geared to the promotion and management of international investments and commercial flows while other arenas of government are cut or streamlined. In this vein, Customs transformations reflect a related global project of standardization and integration inspired by the direct and indirect interventions of a host of international organizations and supranational powerbrokers committed to the tenets of multilateralism. Paramount among them are the World Trade Organization and the World Bank (institutions at the ideological and legal heart of the neoliberal agenda worldwide), adjunct bodies such as the United Nations, World Customs Organization (WCO), and a number of regional hegemons dominated by the United States and European Union.

Differing from and at the same time building on the early modern modalities of state-making described by Tilly (1985), colonial templates captured by Anderson (1991), and the UN-centered post–World War

II and postcolonial model of isomorphic state formation discussed by scholars such as John Kelly and Martha Kaplan (2001), Customs' current global iteration represents a distinctively late-modern and late-capitalist formulation. Indeed, if Jean Comaroff and John Comaroff (2001, 35) are correct in their contention that "[n]ation-states appear, at least in their exterior forms, to be more similar than ever before . . . borrowing from a single stock of signs and symbols . . . and all alike dealing with the impact of the global economy," Customs mandates are once again a site of such convergence. In addition to shared responsibilities premised on the flow of information among national Customs administrations, there are increasingly shared terms of operation followed by Customs officials in all corners of the world, whether in traditional realms of Customs work, such as taxation, or new ones related to security and risk management (WCO 2005a). Further sustaining the effort to craft Customs into a single professional and epistemic community, there are new modes and norms for training available at home and at regional centers and international Customs academies.

Demonstrating the recursive relationship between market and state building—the profit-bearing flow of goods and the flow of governmental forms and reforms—in neoliberal times, these efforts strongly rely on the input of the private sector, all the while contributing to national capacity and the possibilities of global governance. Private, fee-for-service Customs consultants travel the world, writing handbooks and providing on-the-spot advice to national authorities. Specialized companies sell Customs services to countries lacking the resources to follow the global rules of the game on their own. A host of new technologies, from inspection equipment to online data and trade certification programs, is made available on the market to national Customs authorities for substantial sums.

Customs' Second Coming: Ghana as Neoliberal Pacesetter

Just as Ghana was a showcase for earlier mandates of neoliberal reform in the 1980s, the West African nation is at the forefront of Customs global revival in the new millennium. Ghana stands among the very first states to adopt a whole compendium of Customs initiatives, serving as a trendsetter in the crafting of global norms. Much like international pharmaceutical corporations' targeting of peripheral locations and populations for clinical trials on a biomedical front (Petryna 2006), on a political economic front, with multilateral agencies at the fore, Ghana Customs functions in many respects as a laboratory for the testing out and in fact, shaping of global modalities of governance.

As I allude to above, paramount to this process are the provisions of the WTO.[15] In Ghana as elsewhere, the roots of WTO Customs initiatives can be traced to the General Agreement on Tariffs and Trade (GATT), the WTO's mid-century precursor, which from the start involved standardizing as well as easing trade controls.[16] Though Ghana joined GATT in 1957 on the cusp of national independence, the profound influence of these provisions would not be felt until 1995 with the founding of the WTO. Based on the premise that a single world-trading system depends on the adherence to a common set of rules (i.e., laws), in contrast to GATT's voluntarism WTO agreements—covering nearly every area of international trade including the details of Customs work—are legally binding for all members (Mendoza, Low, and Kotschwar 1999).

Ghana enrolled in this process early on and was among a handful of states to be slated for WTO Trade Related Assistance at the WTO Singapore Ministerial in 1996, the first after the founding of the WTO. The 1996 initiative contributed to the eventual formulation in 2000 of the WTO Doha Round, specifically committed to a host of development-related trade concerns. Four issues closely related to Customs emerged from these two rounds: Agricultural tariffs and subsidies, Trade Related Intellectual Property Rights (TRIPS), Customs Valuation, and Trade Related Capacity Building (known by its shorthand, Trade Facilitation) (Center for International Development 2004). Shaped by this agenda, in Ghana WTO technical-assistance programs emphasize the standardization of procedures and accountability to the private sector. The WTO Customs package makes the replacement of an older system of national preferences by a "fair market" orientation a clear priority. Challenging the bureaucratic proceduralism deeply ingrained in Ghana Customs in favor of a whole new technocratic outlook accompanied by looming deadlines and strong sanctions, they also bring a host of mandates regarding the step-by-step implementation of WTO rules (WTO 2000).

The WTO directives at work in Ghana are closely allied with those of the WCO. Like GATT Also a product of post–World War II nation-building, the WCO is the offspring of the Committee for European Economic Cooperation (the prime European agent in the formulation and implementation of the Marshall Plan), and was founded in tandem with the Organization for Economic Cooperation and Development (OECD) in 1952 (Customs Cooperation Council 1955). The organization's official mission is to "aid and advise the Customs administrations of member states and foster cooperation among them" through the development of common

"Customs instruments" such as agreed upon operating procedures geared to all the major areas of Customs work (WCO 2002a, 2). Joining the ranks of more than a dozen African states, Ghana entered the WCO in 1968 during a decade of rapid membership growth for the organization.[17]

WCO's membership, numbering 174 as of 2009, has grown exponentially over the years, and with it the scope of the organization's Customs instruments. Moving from basic guidelines about the classification of goods (essential to the determination of tariff schedules and therefore the bread and butter of Customs work), more recent WCO provisions stress the imperatives of partnership with international regulatory agencies and the sharing of information across national borders by Customs authorities (WCO 2005a). Though compliance with WCO initiatives remains voluntary in contrast to those of the WTO, they nevertheless serve as a form of "soft-law" (Maurer 2007) with global reach and attracting both peer-sanction and value-added on the international playing field. What's more, the growing reliance of the WTO on the WCO's technical expertise to aid in the application of WTO rules has made conformity with WCO instruments all but required for the 148 states sharing membership in both organizations.

Building upon the WCO's established expertise in the formulation of a common Customs knowledge base (via indexes, databases, explanatory notes, and the like), in such a context the impact of the WCO in Ghana and elsewhere has grown substantially. Augmented by an array of educational tools and capacity-building projects formulated over the past decade—a veritable cottage industry of Customs reform—WCO endeavors exert sizable influence over the formulation of a singular global Customs regime. Ghana, as a result, despite its status as a contracting party to only a few of the WCO's nearly twenty formal instruments and agreements, is a recipient of all sorts of WCO-sponsored training programs as well as a vast array of Customs communiqués. Endeavoring to bring Customs operations up to par in addition to imparting specific knowledge and skills, these investments exert an ideological pressure on officers and the wider administration to be up-to-date and outward-looking. Tacitly geared to entice the support of the WCO's many African members in the organization's Brussels-based commissions, elections and policymaking fora (WCO 2005a), they also induce the necessity among Ghanaian Customs officials to cultivate ties to players on the international Customs stage, further extending Ghana Customs' scope beyond a strictly national ambit.[18]

Putting "fast-tracked" developing countries such as Ghana at the fore of global Customs agenda, the World Bank has likewise pursued a wide range of self-declared "Customs Modernization Initiatives" since the early 1980s and the dawning of the neoliberal era (De Wulf and Sokol 2004a, 2004b). Between 1982 and 2002 the World Bank pursued nearly 120 programs of this kind worldwide, many with multiple components. Typically embedded in a variety of grant and loan instruments, these reforms are part of the Bank's conditional lending regime, once again making Customs reform (or at least implementation efforts) obligatory.[19] A frontrunner in the Customs modernization race, over the years Ghana alone has been the target of forty-seven World Bank wholly or jointly sponsored Customs projects, many of which are showcased in World Bank literature (DeWulf and Sokol 2004a, 2004b). Decisively impacted by a "good governance" agenda that has gradually come to saturate the neoliberal political platform (and World Bank governance initiatives more generally [World Bank 1993]), many of the Bank's Customs programs target Customs internal operations.[20] They address audit practices, human resource systems, and workplace organization via detailed evaluation and oversight of operations through experts-in-residence, public surveys, and self-assessment instruments.

Positioning Ghana at the front of the international Customs development curve, notable among the World Bank's many Customs initiatives in Ghana is the move toward the privatization or outsourcing of Customs services to foreign firms. Labeled "management contracts" in World Bank parlance, this strategy has been tried in a handful of African and non-African settings. Typically carried out by multinational enterprises with a history of involvement in international trade logistics, in Ghana these initiatives encompass the very fundamentals of Customs work, from the all-important collection of Customs duties to communication between Customs and just about any person or business with goods to move across national borders.

In some cases, such as Indonesia, Angola, and Mozambique, nearly the entirety of Customs operations are conducted or managed by private operators. In others, like Ghana, private firms are involved in key areas of Customs operations such as inspection and valuation. A similar system is in place in Ghana's West African neighbors: Senegal, Niger, and Benin (Blundo and Olivier de Sardan 2006, 101). In a much wider group of states, private companies and consultants serve in advisory capacity. This is the case of Mauritius, for example, where a Canadian Customs consultant currently serves as the Director of Customs (see Hirschmann 2005). All of these arrangements are financially lucrative for the private entities in question. Paying a 1 percent cut of the value of every transaction they process along with other user fees, they amount to many millions of dollars annually. Yet as they cede state authority to foreign commercial interests, such privatization directives can only be uneasily injected into the national Customs apparatus.

Very much in keeping with its longstanding promotion of mega-projects, the World Bank's Customs initiatives in Ghana also involve investment in major Customs infrastructure, from the renovation of port facilities to the provision of (or at least partial funding for) information and communication technology on a grand scale (Engelschalk and Minh Le 2004). Situating Ghana on the cutting edge of global Customs innovations, this includes the financing of a huge x-ray cargo scanner capable of screening full cargo containers to avoid the time-consuming and corruption-prone task of physical examination. Ghana's scanner was one of the very first on the African continent, and indeed the world, at time of installation. A precedent followed only years later by major world ports, this investment alone placed Ghana at the operational fore of Customs modernization.

Finally, all of these multilateral initiatives have a variety of bilateral counterparts, contributing labor, capital, and political clout, and reflecting the influence of the organizations leading members. The United States, via USAID and U.S. Customs and Border Protection, is a major player on this front, relying on an extensive plan of training, advising, and disseminating information (Nathan Associates 2002; USAID 2001, 2005a–c).[21] They are carried out by U.S. Customs delegations and consultants and clearly convey U.S.-specific preoccupations, whether global crime pre-9/11, or global security in the post-9/11 context.

It bears notice that in Ghana all of these interventions are occurring alongside much more publicized processes of political renewal that make up the official liberal-democratic face of neoliberal reform. The highly trumpeted political agenda is founded on the orthodoxies of democratization via the designation of national executives and legislative representatives through electoral politics. Seeking to counterbalance the rebuilding of national institutions, it also involves the promotion of decentralized participatory rule carried out by district assemblies (Crawford 2009; Green 1998; Gyimah-Boadi 1999; Nugent 2001). These more publicized initiatives stand in sharp contrast to the expansion of Customs bureaucratic might by decree and arcane international agreement. Echoing Gledhill's (2004) notice of the persistent might of neoliberalism's political backstage, the retooling of Customs' massive administrative edifice, as we shall see, thus stands as a shadowy—yet insistent—partner to the battery of electoral benchmarks celebrated by the public, the press and the donor community and typically considered emblematic of Ghana's twenty-first-century neoliberal political face.

Customs Regimes and the Premises of Early and Late-Modern Statehood

The examination of Ghana's Customs authority through a dual historical and comparative optic brings a wide array of insights to the fore regarding the conditions and character of neoliberal sovereignty in Ghana and more broadly. Of singular importance is the recognition of the fiscal-administrative authority embodied by Customs as an enduring attribute of sovereign statehood evidenced in imperial core and colonized periphery of the modern state system. More than a minor feature or epiphenomenon of the modern state apparatus, Customs emerges as integral to the state's fundamental capacity to rule over both fixed and movable persons and property. This observation reveals the lasting relevance of modern sovereignty's infrastructural and largely bureaucratic underpinnings, different from either the assignment of sovereignty to the personage of a supreme ruler or a conception of sovereignty as diffused among self-regulating governmental subjects. Here we have a middle ground of sovereign authority, quotidian yet unabashedly present via an array of political agents and proscriptions.

Affirming this central point, equally remarkable is the vitality of Customs' authority, not only over geopolitical space but over the long temporal *duree*. The foregoing account makes evident Customs' capacity to embody both the continuities and transformations of the modern state form, at once responding and contributing to epochal shifts in international political economy. Regarding grand historical narratives, much is suggestive here. Might this convergence signal parallels rather than discontinuities in the conditions of early and late-modern state formation? Of, for instance, the shared centrality of fiscal discipline as mode of governance and commerce as a mode of accumulation? Or the complex refiguring of territorial boundaries and the position of bureaucratic agents as prime repositories of legitimate authority in both eras?

There is also the question of the specific political functionality, in the spirit of Tilly (1985), of the designs of late-modern Customs regimes, such as the kinds of international and domestic relations and rivalries they serve, and the alternative configurations of authority they foreclose. Does Customs' revival signal the ascendance of common modes of bureaucratic coordination between states and within—of the fusion of internal and external relations, war-making and state-making by another name? Might it suggest the growing primacy of the protection of multinational firms and the privileging of efficiency over accountability via the outsourcing of state-based extraction? Is Customs' resurgence contributing not to the deterritorialization of the state but to the enhancement of specific commercial/territorial nodes as sites of governmental concentration?

Closer to my roots in anthropology and African studies, the comparative frame can be pushed in another direction as well. As I've already suggested, while it is valuable to analyze what is perhaps a decisive global phenomenon, it is equally important to specify the conditions of the global and set the history of the core and the periphery in dynamic relation lest we naively contribute to a sense of their inevitable, *sui generis*, formulation and momentum. Though it is popular to argue that weak states of the periphery are swept up in global processes because of their vulnerability, one alternative is to consider the institutional features that make peripheral states both amenable to and agential of particular sorts of reform. Namely, in the example of Ghana, the longevity and embedded might of Customs authority, preserved from an earlier era and continually renewed through the postcolonial period (pace Cooper 2002), puts Ghana at the vanguard of Customs worldwide revitalization in the present. In this case of "theorizing the global from the periphery," an African example, typically considered a latecomer to neoliberal globalization, comes to serve as a pacesetter, foreshadowing transformations both profound and wide-ranging. Taking the form of the clinical trial, in the world of biomedicine this relationship is well appreciated. However the "bio-available" body (Cohen 2005) is by no means the only experimental site within the less developed world and indeed exists within a wider context that might be termed "sovereign availability."

With these observations in mind, the story to follow thus operates on several registers. On a basic level the goal is to present the Ghanaian story in its specificity and nuance—what the field of anthropology typically glosses as the local variation of the global (Marcus 1998). But this optic also gives voice to a different sort of theorizing from below. Rather than treat the specificities of the Ghanaian case as aberrations, they are taken to expose the hidden, contradictory, and/or unacknowledged priorities and principals of so-called global norms (see Ferguson 1994).

Finally, my analysis is strongly informed by yet another analytic turn, moving beyond treating Ghana as an effect of, alternative to, or diagnostic of "the global neoliberal." Rather, the Ghanaian case is shown to be a causal force—a space for the formulation and refinement of designs occurring or slated to occur in other national sites. In this regard, I argue that Ghana and its Customs bureaucracy stand as a paradigmatic rather than unique case of statecraft and sovereign reconstruction in neoliberal times, bringing to the fore what may be elsewhere pending, nascent or submerged. These processes can best be understood from a perspective that puts anthropology (specifically the anthropology of the state) into a new sort of dialog with political economy, a move for which I take my inspiration from William Roseberry's 1989 seminal cross-disciplinary work of nearly two decades ago, *Anthropologies and Histories*.

Building on the historical and institutional perspectives explored here, the next chapter examines the theory and method necessary for such an analytic project.

TWO

Anthropologies of the State: Marrying Ethnography and Political Economy

Comparative Perspectives on Neoliberal Sovereignty

If recognized for its true position at the vanguard of neoliberalism's advance worldwide, the global reform of Customs points to a profound alteration of the conditions of state sovereignty in Ghana and more broadly. In its paradoxical configuration, both expanding and limiting state authority, Customs' revival in Ghana shares a striking resemblance with other forms of sovereign restructuring considered characteristic of the neoliberal turn in more industrialized corners of the world.

Supplanting earlier contentions suggesting an inverse relation between state authority and neoliberalism's varied global dispensations (pace Strange 1996), according to more recent portraits of global political-economic reordering "there is no retreat of the state, but a changing balance of public and private authority within the state, hence a changing form of state embedded in structural market transformations, as opposed to a decline as such" (Underhill 2000, 118; see also Trouillot 2001). While other studies highlight developments in the realms of finance, international law, and industrial organization, these regulatory arenas are closely aligned and intertwined with Ghana's Customs mandates. They are also a backdrop against which the case of Ghana's Customs Service presents novel departures and developments and thus

Fig. 2.1 Ghana Customs poster, circa 1990. Courtesy of Ghana Customs, Excise and Preventive Service.

compel the rethinking and refinement of prevailing theoretical and comparative claims and investigatory methods.

International relations scholar John Ruggie stands as a leader in this sort of conceptual revisioning of sovereignty in neoliberal times. Examining the contours of post–World War II economic regulation, Ruggie was among the first to recognize a growing trend toward the "unbundling" of sovereignty (1993, 171). The term refers not so much to the breakdown of the sovereign state but a breaking apart, where certain attributes remain salient or even gain new relevance, while others, namely the state's exclusive territorial claims and the trappings of interdependence sovereignty, are suspended or reduced in import. In the case of Customs reform, we see a similar effort to break down the prohibitions of border control. Rather than supplanting the state's territorial claims through non- or extraterritorial arrangements as in Ruggie's formulation (173), Customs reforms evince an alternative mode of territorialization, asserting exclusive authority to foster and regularize flows across the nation's frontiers and the global market more generally. In such arrangements, the sovereign importance of place and the "sovereign importance of movement" do 'not appear to be in competition, as Ruggie suggests, but go hand in hand (174). Here, too, Customs oversight of movement across its territorial and other boundaries, formally termed "interdependence/territorial sovereignty," is enhanced rather than undermined (Krasner 1999, 11).

The insights of sociologist Saskia Sassen (1996, 2002, 2006) likewise make a crucial contribution to the theorization of neoliberal sovereignty relevant to contemporary Customs reform. Sassen, focusing on transnational financial flows and related trends in banking and commercial law, shows that the signature dynamics of neoliberalism are in fact singularly dependent on the operations and stability of national level institutions, leading to concerted investment in their standardization and strengthening.[1] Sassen specifically points to the role of state institutions in securing the conditions for capital mobility and the cultivation of market relations via banks, commercial dispute mechanisms, and the provision of information, infrastructure, and enforcement. As in the case of Customs' continuing oversight of commerce, from this perspective state sovereignty—that is, the capacity of the state to make and enforce rules as well as delimit the rulemaking of others—remains of critical importance.

According to Sassen, under such arrangements the substance of state sovereignty is substantially reoriented, becoming progressively "denationalized," that is, less driven by national priorities and increasingly geared to the facilitation of transnational economic processes (2000, 228). While

Sassen (2002) does rightly point to the embedding of sovereignty in a range of institutional and regulatory realms outside the state, a process she identifies as the "decentering" of sovereignty, claims of denationalization may not fit the case of Ghana Customs. Rather Customs reforms in Ghana reflect a distinctively "internationalist" turn, with participation in multilateral organizations and the adoption of global standards aggrandizing Customs as the bearer of the state's "international legal sovereignty" (Krasner 1999, 11) and allowing national level institutions to gain status and recognition in a supranational realm.

The notion of a reconfigured sovereignty where both the ends and the means of state power are reordered is further developed by anthropologist Aihwa Ong (1999; 2006) who identifies a differentiated or "graduated" sovereignty emerging in the context of East Asian industrial restructuring. In this setting, governments operate in highly uneven ways, with different categories of persons, industries, and locations being subject to greater or lesser authority, to render the nation-state a mosaic of "zones of special sovereignty" (Ong 2006, 100). Providing an intriguing parallel with the privatization of Customs operations, under these circumstances states cede power to corporations who ultimately come to control particular populations and territories. But in the situation of Ghana Customs, the core functions of governance regarding the regulation of persons, revenue, and territory, not just those ancillary governing functions surrounding the operations of manufacturing, are being outsourced to private and indeed multinational firms. Here, the state's right to resist the incursions of other states or organizations in internal affairs, or "Westphalian sovereignty" (Krasner 1999, 11), is considerably impaired. Nevertheless, Ghana's engagement of global Customs reforms at the same time substantially augments Customs' domestic sovereignty by bolstering Customs' domestic capacities and renewing its public presence.

Simultaneously enhancing and undermining Customs' sovereign writ in a manner unprecedented or unexamined in other domains, the ultimate impact of these innovations on sovereign restructuring cannot be determined without on-the-ground exploration.

Anthropologies of the State: An Alternative Approach to Neoliberal Sovereignty

Not only do the unique conditions of Customs restructuring remain unexplored, but the largely political economic assessments of neoliberalism's varied sovereignties recounted above, though insightful, also leave unanswered a host of questions about the human dimensions of sovereign restructuring. It remains to be seen how sovereignty is known and experienced, not just prescribed, but instantiated in consciousness and practice—what the Comaroffs term "the ontological conditions of being under millennial capitalism" (2001, 2). What's more, the programs and pressures of sovereign transformation must be understood and internalized, not simply by the state's minions (or even its proxies), but by the state actors fundamental to neoliberalism's deeply technocratic vision. How are the modalities of neoliberal rule struggled over, and indeed brought into being, through the everyday spaces, personages, and practices of rule—the offices, checkpoints, registries, inspections, calculations, enumerations, laws, claims—that stand for government? What ways of knowing and being are engaged, mobilized, forgotten, or undermined? In short, what are the implications for the lived experience—and "experiential contradictions" (Comaroff and Comaroff 2001, 2)—of sovereign power? As international relations theorists Thomas Biersteker and Cynthia Weber (1996, 11) argue in their seminal volume *State Sovereignty as Social Construct*:

We need to [devote] adequate attention to the ways that the practices of states and non-state agents produce, reform and redefine sovereignty. . . . Rather than proceeding from the assumption that all states are sovereign, we are interested in considering the variety of ways in which states are constantly negotiating their sovereignty.

Driven by these concerns, the remainder of this chapter proposes a distinctively ethnographic approach to the problem of neoliberal sovereignty bringing the insights of the anthropology of the state to bear on the highly objectivist depictions of sovereign restructuring discussed above, which form the predominant explanatory frame. While pursuing the close reading of political economic circumstances suggested by established approaches, the proposed ethnographic diagnostic expands and reworks prevailing theorizations on several fronts. Notably, in the framework elaborated here, an examination of the state's entanglement in a complex of social relations is used to challenge assumptions regarding the structural imperatives of governance. Depictions of the instrumental logics of governance are similarly complicated by a consideration of the state's ideological and affective rendering, and, finally, claims of epochal transformation are supplanted by a concern with the ongoing layering and uneasy interaction of distinct historical agendas.

The Governmentalization of Sovereignty

Regarding the first point, the theoretical and methodological innovations proposed treat sovereignty as a social relation—expressed and experienced not through force or the threat of violence alone, but much more routine and consensual forms of rule. As Janice Thomson, a leading proponent of critical sovereignty theory, cogently articulates, "State control is a function of capabilities defined much more broadly than simply in terms of coercion. Monitoring, surveillance, prevention, and other proactive, sophisticated means of controlling behavior are at the state's disposal" (1995, 224). According to this logic, transformations in sovereignty are neither guaranteed nor singular in form, but wholly dependent on the day-to-day inscription of new political and economic arrangements and orientations. Such an approach to sovereignty is deeply informed by Michel Foucault's notion of governmentality (1991). Foucault understands governmentality to be a form of sovereignty (rather than an alternative to sovereignty as some read Foucault to argue) distinctive to the modern state that is grounded in disciplinary tactics and techniques rather than solely dependent on outright force or a divinely ratified right to rule (Foucault 1979, 1991).[2] In the words of Aradhana Sharma and Akhil Gupta:

Such an analysis of state formation does not simply assume that the state stands at the apex of society and is the central locus of power. Instead, the problem becomes one of figuring out [if and] how "the state" *comes to assume* its vertical position as the supreme authority. (2006, 9)

Focused on the multiplicity rather than singularity of governing strategies, quotidian rather than extraordinary practices of rule, and self-monitoring as much as external surveillance, a governmental theorization of power allows for the location of the core of sovereign authority in the practices of administration. Shrouding the display of force in processes of classification, inspection, documentation and the commutation of all material forms to a single arbiter of value, Customs undoubtedly engages this mode of rule. Indeed, Customs stands as a stark example of Marxist historians Philip Corrigan and Derek Sayer's contention that "Administration is as much a part of the sinews of legitimated power as the monopoly of the means of physical force (with which of course it is inextricably intertwined)" (1985, 10).[3]

State Agency and the Sociality of the State

Most research on state power that employs the concept of governmentality considers how administrative tactics are experienced by those whom
the state rules over (see Gupta 1998; Ferguson and Gupta 2002). In the
research discussed in this book I double the focus to include state agents
as well as state subjects (see also Herzfeld 1997, 2005)—the personages
behind the practices of disciplinary rule.[4] Such an agential orientation,
addressing not only how state representatives enact power but the specific ways they configure, replicate, and renew their ability to rule, makes
it possible to trace how the aura of sovereign ultimacy is sustained and
internalized by those considered to be its source. While anthropologists
studying localized communities and parapolitical domains have come to
recognize that "sovereignties are saturated with 'ways of life,'" to quote
Caroline Humphrey (2004, 435), they have struggled to recognize the
state as the prime locus of such life forms. My approach thus differs considerably from both this vantage point and the well-known scholarly
evaluations of neoliberal sovereignty outlined in the first section of the
chapter in which the state functions as a conceptual focus but is largely
treated as outside the purview of sociological inquiry. Although there is
ample consideration of the shifting contours and experiences of citizenship in the work of Ong (1999, 2006) and Sassen (1996, 2000, 2006) for
instance, state agents largely disappear as a site of investigation, with
private agents—managers, consultants, experts, and so on—posed as
stand-ins. Yet if the conventional locus of state authority is indeed disappearing, how this happens and is experienced needs to be considered
rather than assumed.

A revitalized anthropology of the state, taking state agents into account, understands state practices to be "every bit as local in their materiality and social situatedness as any other" (Ferguson and Gupta 2002,
992). This perspective makes it possible to trace how the state is configured as a field of power in its own right, as much as a force operating upon
others. As Thomas Hansen and Finn Stepputat remind us, "The state not
only strives to be a state for its citizen-subjects, it also strives to be a state
for itself" (2001, 6). Although an issue of perennial significance, it is particularly salient in context of persistent and externally induced change,
as in Ghana. In the Ghanaian setting, as described in chapter 1, the very
source and logic of authority are being altered yet the imperative of rule
remains, especially for gatekeeping institutions such as Customs which
stand as an enduring arbiter of both infrastructural power and sovereign

order. Here again the case of Customs illustrates Hansen and Stepputat's critical observation that "most contemporary societies remain governed by yesterday's administrative structures" (2001, 29–30).

Attention to the agency of state actors brings to bear Biersteker and Weber's fundamental insight that "sovereignty [is] negotiated out of interactions within inter-subjectively identifiable communities" (1996, 11) without falling into the trap of treating the state as a necessarily unified form. We cannot forget that states are replete with contradictions, among them the fact that representatives of different state bodies pursue diverse and at times conflicting objectives shaped by their distinct position within a wider governmental apparatus—not to mention their personal outlooks, social ties, and trajectories. The divide between bureaucratic actors and those they act upon is necessarily shadowy (Herzfeld 1997). Characterized by social proximity, "state authorities and the private users of its services share not only the same locations but also the same normative arena, the same education and the same type of activities" (Blundo and Olivier de Sardan 2006, 82).

State functionaries are thus simultaneously positioned as bearers of the law and as citizen/civilians, endowing them with multiplex affinities and interests. Hence, a bureaucratically rendered sovereignty—such as that which forms the foundation of Customs authority, old and new—is necessarily refracted through multiple vantage points within and beyond the state. The resulting expressions of authority are always to some degree social-relational rather than solely rule-bound even as they contend with the proscriptions of a Weberian (1968) bureaucratic rationality inherited from the modern polity's colonial predecessors. Paralleling the case of the colonial "pilgrim creole functionaries" captured by Benedict Anderson in *Imagined Communities* (1991), bureaucratic consciousness is shaped in a wide social field not always directly related to governing.

State Legitimation and the Techno-Politics of Rule

A fully anthropological approach to the state equally recognizes that sovereignty is deeply entangled culturally as well as socially and involves the production of meaning and ways of being and knowing. Such a cultural orientation offers an important alternative to more strictly political economic approaches which privilege the instrumental over the experiential dimensions of state authority and hence fail to address the fundamentally ideological character of sovereign power and its transformation. As James Scott makes evident in his treatise on the production of modern

forms of government, *Seeing Like a State* (1998), even the apparent technicalities of rule (how to count, code, classify, look, touch, tax, document) are grounded in distinct epistemes and ontologies: specific ways
of imagining the world and one's orientation within it. Consequently,
the technical grounds of state administration serve as a critical means of
ideological engagement central to the manufacture of consent as well as
the articulation of dissent for state agents and subjects alike. Indeed, this
is a key feature of what Timothy Mitchell (2002) describes as the "techno-
politics" of modernity.

Informed by these insights, the ethnographic representations in the
chapters that follow attend to the practical dynamics of Customs reforms—the technicalities of how, when, and by whom they are actually
put into practice—along with their cultural and ideological entailments.
This includes the examination of specific forms of knowing upon which
technical routines rely, the ways in which these knowledge frames are
disseminated and reproduced, as well as the ways in which they are challenged and recast in the course of application. Attention to these processes is absolutely essential for understanding how state power—and
hence, the specter of the sovereign—claims a presence in everyday life,
at once tacit and tangible.

My ethnographic investigations of Ghana Customs are additionally
concerned with another aspect of sovereignty's conjoined instrumental
and ideological rendering. The day-to-day techniques of rule are deeply
bound up with the state's legitimation project, what Phil Abrams (1988)
describes as the public reification of state power as coherent and purposeful and somehow supreme (in my view, a conception of sovereignty
by another name). Of particular relevance to this project are the means
through which both innovations and established forms of government
practice are presented as necessary or self-evident, whether by dint of
force (or its threat), moral argument, or distinctively practical rationales.
Articulated by bureaucrats and civilians, politicians and policymakers
alike, such legitimations are central to the rendering (some might say the
mystification) of sovereign power as both an intimate part of everyday
life and somehow logically superior to it. Indeed, touching on a key point
of interchange between rulers and ruled, a concern with the day-to-day
discourses of legitimation draws attention to the inherently popular
character of state sovereignty. Discussed by the founding theorists of the
modern state, they include a Hobbesian notion of sovereignty centering
on the knowing surrender of populace to the Leviathan, a Rousseauean
conception of sovereignty as the expression of popular will (Philpott

2003), and a Marxian-Gramscian claim that state authorities and their public necessarily inhabit a common cultural ground (Corrigan and Sayer 1985; Roseberry 1994).

From Tactical to Structural Approaches to the State

Setting my sights on the routines and points of view of state agents, I partake of an analytic strategy recently revived by other anthropologists of the state in Africa.[5] Gerhard Anders's (2002) study of Malawi's civil service comes closest to mine in terms of method as well as findings, though focused on the bureaucratic operations within the capital rather than the center-periphery relations of interest to me. Sharing the same British bureaucratic legacy as Ghana and affirming the historical underpinnings of extant patterns of rule, Malawi likewise demonstrates a pattern of bureaucratic integration geared to the protection and interlocking of administrative networks.

Based in Francophone West Africa (Niger, Senegal, and Benin), Giorgio Blundo and J. P. Olivier de Sardan (2006) similarly seek to capture the "state from below." Providing a close reading of local administrative practice within specific sectors of the state, their work is primarily concerned with uncovering the social and cultural logics of government corruption.[6] In addition to comparing corruption in the legal, health and procurement sectors, one essay in the collection (Arifari 2006) addresses Customs operations. Oscillating between event analysis and discussions of the tie between everyday norms of governance and the wider social order, the authors devote less attention to the implications of corruption for the structural contours of state administration and authority—something my study fully pursues.[7] Historically minded, they do however share my concern with the continuities between colonial and postcolonial bureaucratic structure and practice, hinting at the impact of international interventions. Attuned to "the fact that the *official* African state is a Western-style state is also part of the "real state' and must be taken into account in the analysis," they likewise take seriously the formal guidelines and logics of state practice (Blundo and Olivier de Sardan 2006, 109).

Janet Roitman (2005), based in Cameroon and situating her study within the wider Chad Basin, also documents the "real politik" of local level practice. Much like my research, fiscal controls are central to her analysis of state function as well as dysfunction. Roitman vividly portrays the shared moral and social worlds of state officials (including Customs officers) and smugglers in this multinational border zone and the contending regulatory regimes they both protect and exploit. Perhaps symptomatic of the weakness of Cameroonian and neighboring state governments and the overarching regional orientation of Roitman's research as much as her of analytic predilections, Roitman's investigations, in contrast to my own, occlude a concerted examination of the historical or institutional development of Customs or other national authorities. Stating "the reconfiguration of power on the continent today is a less a matter of new practices of the exercise of state power than novel ways of negotiating the changing world economy or managing extroversion" (2005, 177), Roitman does note the impact of liberalization on the rise and popular acceptance of illegal cross-border trade. With other ends in mind, the specific policy interventions, chain of causality and overall implications for the neoliberal project are not addressed by her.

Sidestepping not only international political economy but a concern with state authorities' projection of autonomy and coherence (cf. Abrams 1988), these latter works refrain from systematic consideration of state agents' immersion not only in society at large, but in specific bureaucratic apparati that delimit their identities, capacities, and aspirations, and in which they maintain a vested interest. Straying from these otherwise innovative studies and driven by a prevailing concern with state sovereignty, my aim in contrast is to bring bureaucrats and bureaucratic institutions into the center of the ethnographic picture without losing sense of the state in its totality, however fragile, fragmented, or illusory (cf. Abrams 1988). Thus besides attending to the microtactics of rule pursued by Customs officials across Ghana's frontiers, I keep close watch on the dynamics of political aggregation and structuration: namely, the way individual acts shape and are shaped by prevailing institutional orders, histories, and political economic conditions. Thus I situate my ethnographic observations of Customs officials and operations in relation to Customs' overarching bureaucratic edifice and the wider field of executive, technocratic and administrative power (whether public or private, national or supranational) with which Customs struggles and co-exists.

Because I consider both modern and late-modern state making to be an international project as much if not more than a national one, setting my research apart from others, my approach is strongly attuned to the interventions and imperatives of multilateral organizations and international bodies. Although these determinations may be more obvious in the case of Customs due to its inherently international mission, I argue that this orientation is applicable to nearly any realm of the state knowingly or unconsciously mired in the pursuit of international standards. Most easily recognized in colonial and decolonized states, and now showing a heavy hand in context of post–Cold War transition (Collier 2005, Dunn 2005) and supranational integration (Shore 2000), this dynamic is inherent to modern bureaucracy (pace Weber 1968). The way it is managed has great bearing on the always tenuous project of state sovereignty.

Epochal Perspectives versus Historical Outlooks

Such a combined ethnographic and political economic perspective on sovereignty does important historical work. The fusing of ethnographic detail with the tracking of macroeconomic and policy reforms makes it possible to complicate the impression of unencumbered epochal change proffered by most discussions of sovereignty in neoliberal times. In turn, the historical processes (whether communal, national, or global) that inform large-scale shifts in the ordering logics of political and economic life are brought to the fore. The inscription of political economic reforms, no matter how radical or all-encompassing, are necessarily informed by past, current, and emerging structures and struggles—a contention overlooked in most studies of neoliberal sovereignty which put the inexorable force of transformation at the heart of their analysis.[8]

As mentioned in the opening chapter, the turn to history advocated here is about more than simply attending to the specificities of situational variation and the "local" subversion of the "global." Rather, it is to argue that the epochal itself is historically determined: that is, the epochal is situated within a broader set of historical processes which shape both its formulation and unfolding (see Roseberry 2002). Namely, it is essential to recognize that neoliberal imperatives are not original but part and parcel of a wider genealogy of intervention and reform. Specifically, in the case of Ghana and other African polities, neoliberalism is built upon the never fully realized imperatives of imperial and developmental state building. Hence, neoliberal efforts necessarily encompass and do battle with already established institutional practices and paradigms. Sullying the possibility of any new or pure starting point, these legacies both give birth to neoliberal solutions and undermine their totalizing realization.

This observation is particularly salient to understanding the neoliberal project within postcolonial and transitional states such as Ghana, which by very definition are and have been the target of successive programs of political and economic reconstruction. Because each of these programs has left behind its own traces, the *status quo ante* here is thus less about a pre-existing order than a situation of multiple macrohistorical trajectories already existing in an unsettled relation. By the same token, we need to treat the epochal itself as historical in a dialectical sense: with the efficacy and reproductive possibilities of reform, however comprehensive, shaped by the internal contradictions and dynamics of reform programs as much as the specificities of context and conjuncture. As we shall see, both types of historical condition bear upon the field of large-scale political-economic interventions in unexpected yet systematic ways. Neither entirely situational nor entirely preconceived, these trajectories and determinations provide a critical basis for both case-specific and comparative understandings of sovereignty in neoliberal times.

The Public Life of the State

My focus on the inner workings and historical trajectory of a single-state bureaucracy is by no means an effort to set the life of the state apart from public life. It is crucial to recognize that state functionaries like Customs officials are an integral part of everyday sociality. Not only do they share the same background and aspirations as the general public, given the sprawling nature of Ghana's state apparatus—conforming to what Blundo and Olivier de Sardan call the "oversized state" (2006, 60), a large sector of the public is or has been engaged in forms of governmental employment, many of them sharing the fiscal-bureaucratic orientations of Customs.

Even if one is not in the state's direct employ, in Ghana the fiscal-bureaucratic enactments of national and local government are ever present. In small rural communities tax collectors are fully visible in public space, issuing tickets and receipts to lorry drivers and market vendors. Despite the retrenching of significant numbers of state personnel, there remain agricultural extension agents who visit farmers in the fields to check on production practices and yields and regulate credit markets for agricultural inputs. Livestock too are counted and registered by representatives of government veterinary authorities.

In the late 1990s, my friends living on the outskirts of Bawku complained to me about the difficulties of recent rural electrification and the hassle of convincing officials of the State Electricity Corporation to raise high-tension wires to their homes and the subsequent monthly bills, and they also dug into their belongings to reproduce vestiges of older fiscal regimes in the form of copper taxation receipts from the colonial period. Indeed, not only was tribute a central part of Ghana's precolonial imperial age driven by the expanding states of Asante and Songhai, it remained a definitive feature of the colonial encounter with highly localized forms of tax collection calculated per household, per head, and on the basis of personal property (such as bicycles) crucial to British pursuit of what Berry (1993) calls "hegemony on a shoe-string."

Building upon this history, ordinary living in Ghana is deeply entwined with the bureaucratic maneuvers. State bureaucracy abounds, from the recording of births and deaths, to school enrollment, certification for national exams and national service, vaccinations, voter registration, national identity cards, and more. Holding much in common with the logics of Customs work, many of these activities require tips, payoffs, and the purchase of application forms in addition to admission fees and the display of credentials and records of past bureaucratic encounters. Contributing to the quotidian nature of these orientations, the persons who execute the duties of the state are typically well known in the community due to their relative wealth and assumed access to the levers of influence further up the bureaucratic chain of command. In a region where the avid cultivation of social ties is a fact of life, individuals readily pursue and maintain relationships with state officials who inhabit their social orbit, whether friends, kin, or others with whom they share associational ties.

Ghanaians from all regions and walks of life also rub shoulders with Customs officials on a regular basis. The number of people involved in cross-border movement and commerce cannot be underestimated. A large majority of Ghanaians are or have been involved in trade and long- or short-term migration and travel at one time or another, necessitating movement across national frontiers. Along with Customs border posts, roadside checkpoints and ambulatory task forces abound and Customs officials regularly surface in markets across the country searching out prohibited and uncustomed goods. Ghanaians from all classes regularly travel through the subregion and across continents. Even the airport cannot be considered the purview of the rich alone. As described in later chapters, transnational travelers span the class spectrum. Many Ghanaian nationals who leave the country and periodically return do so because of low educational attainment and opportunity at home and are far from elite in upbringing or lifestyle, no matter how well dressed they appear at the airport's Arrival Hall.

For these reasons it is incorrect to assume that state bodies such as Customs stand outside the realm of everyday experience. In Ghana as elsewhere in Africa, the state, like kinship and culturally based affiliation, is a realm of sociality holding remarkable historical depth and persistence. The modern state-building project has been at work in Ghana since the eighteenth century. Exhibiting many twists and turns, it has been continually augmented but never abandoned. The state, I argue, is a formative space of sociality at least as crucial to social existence as the family, community, or kin group. It is a world in which all Ghanaians are deeply entangled and which requires mastery of distinct modes of self-presentation and communication. Accompanying Ghanaian friends and colleagues to government offices, I was tutored in modes of address and approach, the proper way to pen letters of introduction and speak to receptionists and officers in charge, how to accept invitations and request services, all with a formality and deference strikingly different from the more casual and egalitarian American ethos I was accustomed to. As I note throughout the text, these relationships ceaselessly shift between formality and friendship, personalism and the assertion of stark power differentials.

Despite these realities, in the scholarship on Africa as well as the broader field of political anthropology the treatment of the bureaucratic domain is remarkably underdeveloped, oscillating between unrealistic legalistic descriptions of rule-bound order and anecdotes of gross bureaucratic self-interest, inefficiency and culturally motivated subversion. Yet, with few exceptions (pace Hasty 2005a, 2005b), the distinctive sociality of the state remains largely unexplored. Like Nader's (1972) injunction to "study up" in an effort to understand where and how power lies, this task is at the crux of the book. But rather than treating Customs officials as a distinct fraction of the ruling class, I consider them a professional or epistemic community with cross-cutting ties and interests. Who are the individuals populating this realm? What are the values and interests driving them? What formal and informal norms do they generate and follow? Most of all, how are these ways of being constituted in practice? How do they come to be known, understood, and reproduced? What purpose, direct or indirect, do they serve? Because these features of the bureaucratic realm in Africa remain for the most part a black box in the academic literature (and are thereby misconstrued in much policymaking), the chapters that follow make a concerted effort to give primacy to the persons, practices, things, and epistemes that make up the state apparatus. At their core, these depictions reflect a broader endeavor to bring bureaucracy back into the study of the African states and sovereignty. This is not about keeping society out, but a purposeful attempt to capture the sociality—ordinary and extraordinary—of the modern state's fundamentally bureaucratic project in all its endurance as well as fragility.

PART TWO

THREE

Histories and Tactics of Territorial Sovereignty: Thinking through the Border

Introduction:
Sovereignty and the Border

In this chapter I open up a central concern of the book: the relationship among territorial sovereignty, territorial border zones, and the wider project of state reproduction before and after the institution of neoliberal reform. I do so through an overview of the history and operations of the Ghana Customs Service at Aflao, Ghana's most active land frontier.

Territorial sovereignty—the even extension of power and control of entry and exit throughout a bounded territorial domain—is considered a defining feature of the modern nation-state. International borders are classic sites from which to comprehend the extent and limits of territorial sovereignty (Donnan and Wilson 1999; Sahlins 1989). Articulating a widely held belief regarding the priority of border control in the constitution of the territorially sovereign state, Steven Krasner, a leading voice in the International Relations field, suggests: "If a state cannot regulate what passes across its boundaries, it will not be able to control what happens within them" (1999, 13).

Operationalizing this perspective, much recent scholarship from the field of political economy, as mentioned in the preceding chapter, has abandoned the assumption that the state's territorial sovereignty is inherent and borders, in turn, secure. These works instead highlight the challenge posed by supranational associations, multinational corporations, transnational capital and the overarching neoliberal project to states' territorial claims (Panitch 1996; Ruggie 1993; Strange 1996). Though cast in somewhat different terms, the perspectives put forth by the growing body of border scholarship combining the approaches of anthropology and cultural and literary studies (Alvarez 1995; Anzaldúa 1987; Rosaldo 1993) offers an intriguing parallel to the insights of international political economy. Also calling into question received understandings of territorial sovereignty, research carried out in this tradition offers a vision of territorial boundaries as sites of transgression and instability, their coherence undermined by the pitched resistance of social actors to state impositions and exactions.[1]

Though sharing in the critique of monolithic conceptions of territorial sovereignty coming out of both schools, my examination of Customs operations at Ghana's Aflao frontier over the long duree brings into focus an alternative theorization of borderlands and their relation to territorial sovereignty in the neoliberal present. In this chapter I develop a series of arguments. First, calling into question the arched dichotomization of both state and society and state and market behind the political economic and sociocultural optics, the Ghanaian case, rather than highlighting struggles *against* the border, brings to light the very struggle *for* the border—a struggle occurring as much *within the state* as between state and society, neighboring polities, or global forces.

In this assertion, I share Catherine Boone's (2003) recognition of the centrality of peripheral regions to determining the tenor of African states. But rather than suggesting that the political conventions of rural communities are historically distinct from the central models and places of national governance, I argue that border areas such as Aflao vividly encode and assimilate the very history of the state, in all of its contradictions and iterations.

Peter Andreas (2000) provocatively explores this perspective with regard to the U.S. border, and such a reanchoring of border politics within the wider context of state administration is particularly apt in the contemporary African setting. Despite the questionable origins of colonial boundaries, the government of Ghana and the Gold Coast before it demonstrate an ongoing investment in the state's territorial integrity, whether during the early phases of European intervention, at independence, or in

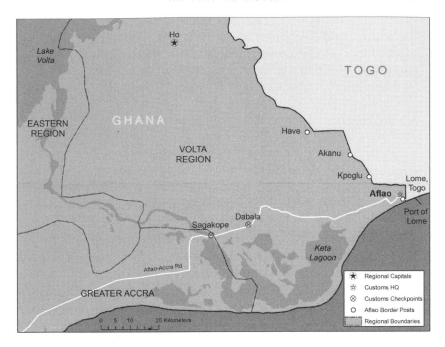

Map 3.1 Aflao substations and regional trade routes.

the present.[2] Upholding Cooper's contention regarding the fundamental gatekeeping character of African state (2002, 5), the geographic contours of Africa's colonial polities have largely endured across the continent (Herbst 2000)—a finding that suggests that even the least-resourced states are invested in the production and regulation of territorial boundaries and may be particularly so. From this vantage point it becomes possible to refute the prevailing assumption that the insecurity of Africa's territorial frontiers is necessarily the result of the absence of state authority and the failure to project infrastructural might rather than the outcome of state engagement (see also Roitman 2005).

Proving the above contention, the history and ethnography of Aflao reveal the entrenched presence of Customs officers and installations in the lives and livelihoods of the residents of Aflao's border zone along with the reciprocal contribution of borderlanders to the reproduction of the state's territorial limits. A close examination of Customs operations at Aflao points to the border's historical embedding and details the territorial frontier's encoding of the unsettled legacies of the Ghanaian state more generally. In this setting, as we shall see, neoliberal strategies of territorial control operate amidst a multilayered political landscape calling forth the designs of earlier regimes—colonial and postcolonial, nationalist and socialist, militarist and populist—coexisting in unsettled relation. Though a dilemma shared by all polities to some degree, in Ghana such political-territorial disjuncture is all the more complicated by the country's colonial heritage, inspiring the persistent pursuit of internal and external reform, much of it focused on the "techno-politics" of infrastructural control (Mitchell 2002).

These initial observations undergird my second argument regarding what can be called the "double life" of territorial rule. On the one hand, territoriality is deeply embedded in the frontier zone and the experiences of those who cross over, reside by, and manage the border. On the other hand, territorial sovereignty remains fundamentally a national political project. Giving lie to the contours and contradictions of the wider state apparatus, sovereign authority is made manifest at the frontier in the personages and practices of state officials, but does not originate there. This optic thus calls for the theorization and investigation of borders and territorial sovereignty as forms conjoined yet distinctive. From this vantage point, the border is not a reflection of territorial sovereignty but a space to reflect on the project of territorial sovereignty. An "effect" of territorial sovereignty as well as a host of other determinations, at the border such diverse refractions are already in play. The life of the border thus provides an opportunity to think through the forces—both distant and proximate—behind these effects: their origins, aims, strategies, and contradictions, and the extent to which they have been realized, resolved, or reordered. Borne out of the differential unfolding of a common history (like the refraction of a ray of light from a common source), the distinction between the border and project of territorial sovereignty opens up a political (and analytical) space within which border agents play a central mediating role.

Finally, the third argument gleaned from research at Aflao suggests that the processes of intrastate contestation and territorial refraction mentioned above, inherent to the territorial aspirations of the modern state, although not attributable to the neoliberal era are nevertheless intensified by it. Generating new frictions in the state apparatus, the expression of state authority at the border zone in neoliberal times is ever more geared to the management of mobility rather than outright exclusion or enclosure. However, instead of the complete evacuation of state controls, as many proponents of global borderless world predict, in Ghana we witness the rolling out of state interventions via a battery of specific governmental reforms. Inciting the trial of new policies and practices and the perpetuation of older ones centered on the management of flows, Customs authorities find themselves mired in a host of strategies of "territorial unbundling" (Ruggie 1993). Some well institutionalized, some not, they offer an array of solutions to the partial renunciation of full territorial control. These politically motivated articulations of territorial sovereignty—much more than the generalized conditions of economic liberalization via the intensification of cross-border flows—at once undercut and overwhelm state capacity. Posed atop an already unsettled governing apparatus characteristic of the postcolony, their staying power and coherence are highly uncertain.

Highlighting the distinction between the nation-state's claims to territorial sovereignty and the actualities of rule, under such conditions the border shows itself to be a site of an expansive functionality. In contrast to the precarious political dynamics standing behind the process of territorial reform, the communities surrounding the frontier embrace the opportunities afforded by the neoliberal turn. Participating in numerous forms of cross-border trade, official as well as unofficial, they are also the prime providers of the knowledge and services necessary for both public officials and private actors to navigate the border zone. State officials at the frontier likewise cobble together arrangements of rule from the detritus of policy, both old and new. Often profitable and systematic, and always multifunctional, the borderland hence stands in contradistinction to the unsteady and ever more historically parcelized sovereign aspirations of the wider state apparatus at the same time it is built from them.[3]

Customs and the Ebb and Flow of the Aflao Frontier

Along Ghana's 1,300-mile frontier, the national state's ongoing quest for territorial control is evident in the continual trial of new programs and projects. In such a climate, the border line may be more visible in some locales than others, yet the aura, if not the presence, of the state is deeply sedimented throughout. Though physical demarcations are often in disrepair and state regulations routinely transgressed, given the ongoing projection of state authority along the border zone, the border is acknowledged nonetheless

This is amply true in the vicinity of Aflao, located on the southernmost edge of Ghana's eastern boundary on the shores of the Atlantic. Aflao is one of the busiest official border-crossings in the West African subregion (Le Vine 2004; Sakyi-Addo 2005). Two hundred kilometers (120 miles) from Ghana's capital city, Accra, and adjacent to Togo's capital of Lome, which begins at the border's edge, Aflao is also the gateway to Benin, just 60 kilometers down the road, and Nigeria 120 kilometers beyond. Aflao is the site of extensive cross-border traffic. The local residents who cross the border regularly include: schoolchildren, office workers, traders, bureaucrats, religious practitioners, and the informally employed whose lives and livelihoods occupy the two sides of the Ghana-Togo divide. There are as well a wide range of Ghanaians—from consumers and petty entrepreneurs to large-scale business people—drawn to Lome to shop due to Togo's free-port status, and countless traders and transporters engaging in a more extensive commercial circuitry spanning Africa's entire Atlantic coast, from Nigeria in the east to Cote d'Ivoire and beyond in the west.

At this active economic frontier, traffic exhibits predictable patterns that reinforce the distinctive features of Ghanaian and Togolese political economy. Though similar in geography and cultural makeup (Geurts 2002; Herskovits 1967; Rosenthal 1998),[4] the different experiences of colonial rule and subsequent political and economic history in these neighboring states enshrine their contrasts. Ghana was a British colony; Togo bears the legacy of first German and later French administration. Ghana, the first sub-Saharan African nation to achieve independence, has moved through a succession of socialist, military, and democratic regimes, while Togo's modern political history is characterized by a consistently authoritarian form of one-party rule with an overlay of electoralism and the ongoing receipt of French political support and economic aid (Walker 2003).

Informed by these enduring distinctions, a wide range of overseas imports from Togo's free port in Lome move across the border into Ghana. There are expensive textiles, specialty foods, and other high-end European wares, as well as secondhand clothes, cloth and suiting material, kitchen items, shoes, processed foods, cars, scrap metal, and appliances and manufactures of all sorts from wherever they may be sourced at cheap rates, China included (Sylvanus 2006). Togo-made goods that fill basic needs, such as klinker (the main raw material needed to produce cement) and animal feed, also cross the border to Ghana. Nigerian goods move into Ghana through this overland trade corridor as well, bringing low-value, high-volume goods like the ubiquitous black polythene bags, too cheap to ship or send by air.

If "Lome 'dresses' Ghana," as is often said, "Ghana 'feeds' Lome," sending agricultural produce and products of local industry across the border: vegetables, dried fish, salt and red pepper, chewing sticks (toothbrushes), and *alata samuna* "black" soap. Industrial goods, such as plastic

Figure 3.1 Early morning foot traffic, Aflao border. Customs clearing agencies, business centers, and foreign-exchange bureaus can be seen in the background. The portable drinking bar in the foreground, arranged for business the previous evening, will soon be disassembled.

and aluminum ware, and Unilever products like washing powder, also cross the border from west to east. Overseas imports that have landed in Ghana, such as propane gas and petrol for which consumer prices in Ghana are heavily subsidized and export is restricted, similarly make their way to Togo. They are typically smuggled through clandestine exchange networks that complement the illicit movement of textiles and clothing from Togo to Ghana and form part of a vast underground economy recognized by the state but escaping its control.

Despite these transgressions, at Ghana's Aflao border post, like other official points of entry and exchange around the world, the specter of the governmental intervention and oversight looms large.[5] Marked by an elaborate architecture of barriers, gateways, office blocks, and guard posts, the border is flanked by the officers and installations of a watchful state. Here, state power is dramatized through interviews and inspections, the checking of bodies, bags, and documents, and excessive emblematization by means of flags, tags, titles, oaths, posters, insignias, and uniforms. Aflao's official border-crossing is distinguished by a massive ceremonial arch topped by a black star, a symbol of national unity originated by Nkrumah in the fight for independence. Resembling Black Star Square in downtown Accra built to commemorate Ghanaian independence in 1957 (Hess 2000), this is just one of many ways the state's administrative center claims a presence at the frontier.[6]

In addition to Customs, the border post hosts state agents of manifold stripes and functions, including officers of the Ghana Immigration Service, the Bureau of National Investigation, and the ministries of Agriculture, Trade, and Health. Of all the state agencies at Aflao, however, Customs has the heaviest presence, with the greatest number of personnel, the most responsibilities, and the most extensive installations. The Aflao Customs Collection employs nearly 300 officers (287 in 2003) and is the largest of the Ghana Customs Service's seven frontier posts. The Aflao Collection oversees the operations of six substations (Have, Kpoglu, Akanu, Denu, Dabala, and Dzodze), each regulating official and unofficial entry points extending thirty miles northward. This is supplemented by numerous checkpoints and patrol zones inland and along the border as well as the coast line extending from Aflao to Keta and the Sagakope Bridge, forty miles beyond.

Holding power at once domestic and international, fiscal and territorial, coercive and consensual, Customs is the state's most visible representative at the Aflao frontier. Customs officers within the Aflao Collection are responsible for the oversight of all cross-border flows and the assessment and collection of tariffs and duties as well as state and public security. These duties involve the scrutiny and documentation of all persons and property (including currency) crossing the border, the apprehension and deterrence—by force if necessary—of anyone who contravenes national laws and international agreements, and communication with other Customs offices and relevant government and international bodies.

The pervasive presence of Customs at Aflao comes as no surprise given Customs' longstanding role in Ghana's and Gold Coast political and economic history. As mentioned in chapter 1, the roots of Customs administration in Ghana can be traced to 1839 when a group of British merchants were mandated to collect duties on all goods and merchandise coming into Gold Coast settlements. These tariff ordinances would generate the bulk of the revenue necessary for imperial expansion, laying the foundation for the formal imposition of colonial fiscal and administrative authority in 1885 and the establishment of the Gold Coast Customs Service (Anim-Asante 1988, 9). With the ranks and responsibilities of Customs officers growing throughout the colonial period, by independence in 1957 Customs was among the largest and longest-lived bureaucratic orders within the new nation of Ghana.

Figure 3.2 Ceremonial arch flanking the Ghana-Togo border.

Mirroring this larger institutional history, at Aflao the presence of Customs along with the contours of the border line and adjacent border post are firmly incorporated into the local landscape. The region, referred to by geographers as the trans-Volta, was an early site of imperial intervention and subsequent colonial rule. According to Nugent, the pre-eminent Anglophone historian of the region, "The British first defined their southeastern border in 1874. The arrivals of the Germans in 1884 necessitated a formal partition of the interior over the following decade" (2002, 3 n. 12). Acquisition of land for Aflao Preventive Station was completed in 1913 (Gold Coast Land Registry 1913). As is visible in a photograph from the Bodleian Library, as early as 1920 an official border post had been established in Aflao with barrier and gate, Customs office, flagpole, and a retinue of guards. In much of the southeastern tier of the area, the boundaries of Togoland changed after the German defeat in World War I, moving from German to British and French hands. Aflao, at the edge of original German claim, remained in the British domain throughout: "To all intents and purposes, the present borderline is the same as that which was demarcated by the Franco-British Boundary Commission of 1927–29" (Nugent 2002, 4).

Over time the boundary has become the organizing feature of the region's sociocultural and political economic fabric. In 1934 the Gold Coast Comptroller of Customs noted in a letter to the Colonial Secretary: "Aflao is a very important Preventive Station and its importance is likely to increase with the years" (no. 1204/31), thus winning approval of his request to expand the government station, despite the high cost of land (Colonial Secretary's Office 1934; Gold Coast Comptroller of Customs 1934). Demonstrating the longstanding incorporation of the boundary (and the battery of controls centered upon it) into the surrounding community, in these transactions local interests held sway, determining both the price and the location of the frontier post. This sentiment is apparent in the comments of officials from the colonial government's Land Department.

The District Commissioner, Keta informs me that the claimants price is high partly because they are annoyed that their ancestors gave their land free to Government and partly because land on the strip between the lagoon and sea changes hand at absurdly high prices. The claimants also state that this is the last bit of family land remaining to them. (No. 3099/Lands Dept/Accra, 1207/31)

It is evident that even as resistance to colonial rule took shape elsewhere, Aflao residents were more interested in capitalizing on the border than contesting it. This point is well illustrated in the vignette below, drawn from a 1941 report of the Chief Customs Collector for the area.

I am informed that a man at Agbosome has his "own" gang of police. These men make themselves look as much like the Preventive Service as possible by dressing themselves in black singlets, khaki knickers, a large fezz [sic] and carry a stick. They patrol the bush at night in the hope of coming across smugglers who, thinking they are Preventive Service Constables, will drop their loads and scatter into the bush. They then take possession of the goods. (Wilson 1941)

Today in no uncertain terms the town of Aflao represents the border. In southern Ghana, to speak of "going to 'the border'" is to make a trip to Aflao, and a trip to Aflao implies a visit to or across the frontier. At Aflao the presence of the border is inescapable. It is the point around which the lives and livelihoods of the town's residents revolve. Like the inhabitants of the Benin-Nigeria boundary zone described by Flynn (1997), they are "borderlanders" through and through, with distinct mores, identities, and political economic standing. Nearly everyone is in one way or another involved with the frontier, either crossing the border or servicing those who cross it and profiting from their proximity to and intimate knowledge of its physical features and the manifold regulatory fields surrounding it, including the conventions of Customs administration. In a region saddled with decrepit infrastructure and shrinking opportunity due to environmental decline as well as government betrayal and neglect, "working the border" provides one of the few routes to economic survival and gain. This sentiment is expressed in a proverbial description of Aflao in the Ewe language: *"Aflao flalala, kpoklikpo deve, tsimadzamadza gake baba didi ame"* translated as "In Aflao, even without rain, there is mud to make man slip and fall." Alluding to the original arrival of the Ewe in Aflao where they confronted inexplicable hardship (falling and slipping in the mud without rain) it is understood to say "no matter how hard the situation is in Aflao, the Ewe people remain and prevail."[7]

In Aflao the territorial border and its attendant personnel, structures, and regulatory orders, far from being a foreign construct or imposition, have been wholly assimilated into the fabric of life. These adaptations are marked by a spectacular division of labor and realms of novelty and fine-grained expertise. Even before the gates open at 6 a.m. the border's vast service economy, licit and illicit, is already in motion. The vehicles waiting out the night at the car park, along with those arriving before dawn, line up to exit as their passengers alight and make their way to the Departure Hall. Stalls, tables, and work spaces are dis- and reassembled according to the tempos of the border and the needs of its personnel, whether resident or transient. There are those who provide food and drink, and other means of physical reproduction. At dawn, business at the tea and egg stands is in full swing, the *akpeteshi* (a local gin distilled from palm wine) and Schnapps sellers and prostitutes are closing up after a long evening's work, and the chewing stick and snack vendors have begun their perambulations. Medicine, kola, and tobacco sellers lay out their wares, while barbers, nail-parers, hairdressers, and shoeshine boys ready for business. The border's beggars and infirmed set down their mats and wait to receive travelers' loose change. The Lotto doctors, gamblers, and Ludo players, "those with nowhere to go and nothing to do" in the words of my research assistant, drug addicts and the mad, as well as researchers, make a place for themselves amidst the border traffic.

Recording these rhythms, my notes from an early morning visit read as follows:

6:30 a.m. at the border. It rained during the night and the air and ground are still wet. The border is already mobile, but quietly so. People cross one by one and a few large trucks are lined up waiting to go through the gate. The Malian beggars are just arriving.

One, umbrella, teapot and prayer beads in hand, tries to find a dry spot for himself on the damp sand where he will sit for the rest of the day. Two Lagos cars are parked in front of the gate waiting for the officers to inspect the contents of the boot— the ubiquitous rice bags—before they proceed to Accra. Pushcarts loaded with onions, okra and garden eggs (the produce of Ghana) are wheeled across the border from Ghana to Togo and those with head loads follow. The shoe vendors are already around, the same ones we saw yesterday evening. Do they sleep here? Porters and *goro*-boys are sweeping last night's dust and garbage and goat droppings, that same sound of a broom on a hard floor that is heard throughout Ghana. Three buses from Cote d'Ivoire are lining up to cross the border on the way to Nigeria. Children come to Ghana from Togo to attend school, wearing dark brown uniforms. Ghanaian children, wearing khaki, cross in the opposite direction for the same purpose.

Shipping containers turned mini-marts line the roadside approaching the border. They are stuffed with imported goods: soaps, soft drinks, candy, and the brand-name processed foods often difficult or expensive to purchase in Ghana. With wares identical to those sold in Lome, these shops provide a way to take advantage of the economic benefits of the border without the trouble of crossing it. Behind these temporary sales points are more permanent structures built of wood and concrete block to house communication centers, typing pools, Customs clearing agencies, and foreign exchange bureaus. Employees and clients of these businesses as well as other passersby are served by chop bars and drinking spots erected between and behind them.

Providing a related set of logistics services, unregistered money changers (sharing the vague appellation of "Hausa"), their calculators famously rigged to compute less than the rate they display, operate out-of-doors near the bus station. They are joined by the ranks of young men who selflessly volunteer to help the traveler for a tip, but whom only the most desperate or naïve dare to trust. Here too are an array of transport services, from school-age boys and teenagers pushing handpainted carts to uniformed porters officially licensed to carry goods from one side of the border gate to another. Sometimes one and the same, there are equally organized but typically more clandestine couriers who cross the border post's departure and arrival gates dozens of times a day. Most female, they conceal their wares on person and in parcels for a price, enabling travelers and traders to avoid Customs duties and other state controls. They deliberately appear nondescript, highly impoverished, or "otherworldly" (like the many women who bear the garb, jewelry, and body markings of vodoo priestesses [Rosenthal 1998]), and hide their wares under their skirts, tied on the back like a baby, or inside head loads.

Even in the midst of the Aflao border's crowded byways, it is not un-usual to see a group of women in a state of "economic" undress, unload-ing the goods they have smuggled across the border. Another entry from my field notes records such an event:

In one incident I witnessed, a woman peeled off 8 bath towels from under her skirt. Another woman removed about 6 yards of men's suiting material which was folded and wrapped around her waist. She then reached under her skirt to free a parcel con-taining several sets of baby outfits which she had tied around her thigh. She removed another from her calf which she had tightly folded and then wrapped with rope and attached to her leg with some foam for padding. Another courier in the group pulled off the cloth she had tucked above her breasts and around her waist to reveal a slip into which she had placed several packages of baby dresses. In addition to the textiles concealed on the body, all sorts of provisions were hidden in the women's head loads. From her basin of beans, a woman fished out about a dozen or more tins of tomato paste which she then repacked in their original box. The same was true for some bags of pasta and candies and even Omo detergent that was hidden in a head loaded bag of rice and reassembled in the correct box for resale.

The vast complex of clandestine transport across official and unofficial entry points spans the entire length of the border and the whole of the inland route from Aflao to Accra, Accra to Kumasi, and beyond. These strategies of economic mobility suggest that the border and the attendant battery of state regulation are ineffectual yet at the same time, affirm their reason for being. Even Aflao natives who have since moved away or are not immediately present at the frontier claim the border as their own and involve themselves in cross-border trade and transport between Aflao and a new place of residence, on both a professional and periodic basis. They are the border's experts, handlers, detractors, and investors. Though all these roles are chaotic in their density and variety, they are nonethe-less routine, providing a predictable order to the frontier.[8] So invested are Aflao's residents in these activities and the economic opportunities they present, they would likely sustain the border even if it were abandoned by its official overseers within Customs and other state bodies.

Customs officers, in turn, operate amidst these persons, practices, and social networks. Borderlanders form the backbone of Customs officers' survival, both personal and professional. Border residents cook, clean, and shop for officers during their twelve-hour shifts. Serving as Cus-toms "auxiliary" or "civil personnel," to borrow a term from Blundo and Olivier de Sardan (2006, 103), they are their prime informants regarding illicit trade and their prime assistants while on post—running errands, filling log books, assisting with inspections, crowd control, and the discipline of travelers, and even accepting "gifts" for them out of view of their colleagues or other authorities. While these relationships are occasionally uneasy due to betrayal or unreasonable demands on both ends, they for the most part maintain an equilibrium beneficial to all parties involved (cf. Flynn 1997). Deeply implicated in this economy of appearances, Aflao residents, in short, have made the border and its regulatory fields their own. Gleaning livelihoods and identities from it and sustaining those of Customs officials, border residents make an essential contribution to the ongoing functioning of the frontier zone, guaranteeing its reproduction day to day and over the long term.

The Architecture of Territorial Sovereignty and the Logics Customs Work at Aflao

Making evident the important conceptual and empirical distinction between borders and territorial sovereignty, while the locus and reproduction of Ghana's Aflao frontier may be secure, the state's claim to territorial supremacy here remains unsettled. In contrast to the locally embedded workings of the border economy, Customs operations at Aflao reveal the instability and inconsistency of the wider governmental apparatus. Indeed, rather than internal or external subversion, the central threat to the coherence of the state's territorial project at the frontier is in many ways the state's own political history. Ghana's diverse political legacies: colonial, nationalist, socialist, military, populist, and neoliberal— none fully compatible or fully realized—are encoded in Customs practices of the present. In this light, the state's claim to territorial sovereignty at the Aflao border, however incomplete, is equally marked by political excess, an observation undercutting the claims of those who theorize the demise of territorially inscribed statehood brought about by societal transgressions or the ascendance of market logics (Appadurai 1996b; Strange 1998).

At Aflao assertions of territorial sovereignty, neither consistent nor foolproof despite their historical depth, are further complicated by the fleeting alignments of Customs officers. Not only does the administration of each Customs collection rotate officers through a range of different assignments every few months, but it is also Customs headquarters' policy to reassign officers from one collection to another after two years of service. Nodding to the Weberian precept of bureaucratic disinterest (1968), this is meant to limit fraternization between Customs officers and border-zone residents and thereby ward against collusion, as well as undercut officers' claim of "ownership" over a particular job and the attendant personalization of rule. As a result, Customs officers are constantly engaged in the process of learning to rule, a policy interfering with the coordination and effectiveness of their efforts despite its legal-rational foundation.

From this perspective, state operations—at the frontier and more generally—constitute not so much a well-oiled engine of social order as a Weberian optic might suggest, but an assemblage of distinct and sometimes disparate historical and individual imperatives, the workability of their intersection contingent rather than guaranteed. The notion of "assemblage" in the sense developed by Ong and Collier (2005) to capture the temporary social and cultural configurations emerging in the course of global circulation may well be relevant to postcolonial state formations such as Ghana. The application of this rubric to the postcolonial polity comes with the important caveat that here the state form is both figure and ground (Strathern 2002), in motion and in place, endogenous and extrinsic.

State Building on the Border

Customs operations at Ghana's Aflao frontier are marked by a tangible record of agendas that have been officially abandoned or replaced yet continue to claim a presence in the daily routines of border management. The unsettled layering of Customs' political logics is vividly illustrated by the spatial and tactical features of Customs installations at the Aflao border. Indeed, over the course of my research, Customs operations at Aflao confounded any notion of the border as the site of any singular logic of control. Despite earlier moments in Ghanaian history marked by various forms of border closure—whether the outright denial of passage brought about by failing political relations between Ghana and Togo, as occurred at several periods during the 1980s and early 1990s (Owusu 1994), or periods of the border's militarization when movement served as prompt for systematic violence and harassment (Nugent 2002) — the border post was little marked by official practices of exclusion.

By the millennium's turn, Customs work at the Aflao frontier post was increasingly geared to the management of mobility, drawing on long-established forms of *laissez-passage* as well as a variety of newer strategies for organizing and making claims upon cross-border flows. Sparked by the shifting political economic environment as well as the deliberate (oft-times mandated) rearrangement of political and economic policies

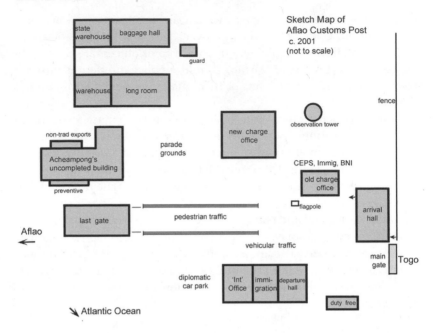

Figure 3.3 Sketch map of Aflao Customs Post.

and outlooks, this orientation is at least partially attributable to various forms of neoliberal influence and intervention, from the global circulation of more and cheaper commodities and declines in profitable productive opportunities to a host of international pressures and obligations, as detailed in chapter 1. These strategies and unsettled histories are most obviously encoded architecturally.

At the border, where the state seeks to inscribe its authority in terms that are fixed, functional, and well ordered, architecture serves as a highly efficient means for the display of state capacity. Reflecting the modern state's quest for domination through strongly technocratic modes of representation (Mitchell 2002; Scott 1998), this dynamic (along with its limits) is acutely evident in the various spaces of rule making up the Aflao border post. They include an Arrival Hall, old and new Charge Office and Office block, a Customs Yard housing a Baggage Hall, Long Room and Customs Warehouse, Last (or exit) Gate, an International Office, Departure Office, and Duty Free Shop.

While some of these structures are remnants of the colonial era, most were erected in the postcolonial period. Starting with Nkrumah's intensive "state-building" campaign inspired by a socialist and largely Soviet model of infrastructural glorification (Hess 2000, 47), this same pattern was pursued by other leaders in his wake.[9] While much of the state's architectural efforts were sited in the capital and regional centers, major border-crossings such as Aflao also received a share of infrastructural investment.

Arrival Hall

Taken in sequence, the first point of entry for persons entering Ghana from Togo is the Arrival Hall, built around the original frontier post. Less a building than a passageway, the Arrival Hall consists of a dark and cramped corridor not more than twenty feet long divided by an examination table. In the 1980s era of Rawlings' populist-militarist regime, the space was manned by border guards who subjected anyone who dared to navigate this official point of entry, and any wares they attempted to carry, to virtually unrestrained scrutiny, with all persons and baggage searched and all commercial goods stamped by Customs. In the post-military/neoliberal age, border-crossers navigate a densely packed and extensively (but incompletely) surveyed point of entry.

Customs officers are posted at the entrance and exit of the Arrival Hall and along the walls. Officers sit on tall stools and hold wooden sticks or metal rods that allow them to poke travelers' parcels or prevent movement. Setting their gaze above the heads of travelers, they watch for suspicious persons and parcels to be singled out for quick interrogation and subsequent direction to the more specialized offices within the border post. In the cramped and heavily trafficked space of the Arrival Hall it is common for officers to interact with travelers with a mien of disinterest while demanding regulatory compliance (along with discretionary tips). But due to their fleeting nature and the high volume of traffic, interactions between Customs officers and travelers in the Arrival Hall are generally impersonal, whether with regard to Customs officers' self-presentation or their treatment of those who cross the border.

At the far end of the Arrival Hall is the office of a supervisory officer separated by a bilevel door that can be open or shut without notice. The post is distant enough from the center of the action to allow the senior officer to gain perspective on traffic trends, yet close enough to call both anomalous officers and travelers to his or her attention. The supervisor also provides the first line of documentation for those entering the country, issuing permits and official forms to travelers. The office is filled by a massive desk covered with Customs manuals, bound volumes of Customs law, forms, registers, stamps, and seals. Set apart from travelers and junior officers, the individual manning this post represents the larger regulatory edifice of the Ghanaian state, both eclipsing and backing up the command functions of the junior officers stationed in the main part of the Arrival Hall.

During my research, the Arrival Hall supervisor sought not to stem the tide of cross-border traffic but to normalize it. For the first few months of my study, for instance, he was preoccupied with apprehending what appeared to be an unusually large number of TVs carried through the Hall, ostensibly for Customs officers—according to those who carried them. He was also involved in an unending battle to stop the coordinated surge of groups of clandestine couriers (described above) during periods of already high cross-border traffic—a strategy that worked to buffer them from apprehension by Customs personnel. Enforcing the broad legal provisions of Customs administration pertaining to the carriage of dutiable, declarable, controlled, or prohibited goods, these interventions accomplished a generalized form of social sorting rather than the intensive individualization or apprehension of goods and travelers (Lyon 2003). Given the crush of traffic through the Arrival Hall, Customs officers could accomplish little more than this "normalizing" function, imposing a rudimentary order with only limited sanction on those entering the country via Aflao.

Beyond the Arrival Hall stands the old "Charge Office" built in the 1930s. A modest office block of just a few rooms, this is where the officer-in-charge (OIC, in Customs parlance) of the entire Collection (typically holding the rank of assistant commissioner) was posted for many decades. Close to the road and the Arrival Hall, from this perch the head officer could easily be approached as well as easily watched as he trained his own eyes on border traffic. A visible and immediate statement of Customs authority, the accessible presence of the OIC conveyed an image of power concentrated in a person, superior but not remote and well aware of the material realities of the border's ebbs and flows, who could engage in the commutation and negotiation of Customs rules. When I first arrived at Aflao in October 2000, the Charge Office was still in use by the OIC, although a few months later it had been given over to clerical workers and the head officer relocated to a brand new administrative complex out of the direct path of cross-border traffic. Despite this shift in the locus of Customs ultimate authority at the post, the flagpole remained in place next to the old building and the flag, raised each morning and removed every evening to the notes of the Customs bugler, a remnant of colonial ceremonial.

Last Gate

Upon exiting the Arrival Hall and passing the flagpole and former Charge Office, travelers may go one of two ways. If they have nothing to declare (or seek to appear as such), they move through a final round of checks at the "Last Gate," called *agbadovianu* or "little shed" in Ewe. If they are transporting items of commercial value or any type of restricted goods, travelers proceed—sometimes voluntarily but also under official order—to the main Customs Yard or Charge Office, 200 meters inland from the beachside border post.

The Last Gate, made of plywood, two-by-fours, and battered zinc sheets, consists of a roofed, open-sided channel fifty feet in length. Containing a collection of weathered examination tables, like the Arrival Hall, it is a decrepit structure. Customs officers stationed at the Last Gate operate through an intensely visual economy. At the Last Gate traffic thins out, allowing Customs officers a better look at border-crossers and the goods they carry. One officer explained, "Most of the work entails the inspection of baggage, panels, head loads and the like, but little or no inspection of persons [i.e., no body searches]. There's too much traffic to do that." Another, new to the post, affirmed this logic, "Although it is my first day, I can already recognize people. I saw one man cross the gate three times in two hours so I stopped him to inquire why." He later stopped another man with a pushcart to inspect his documents and his wares. When the vendor was found to be carrying more than declared on his baggage receipt, the officer unpacked the excess goods and told him to return to the office for additional duty payment. (Of note, this breach represented as much a contravention of law as a disjuncture in the informal norms of Customs operations. When Baggage Hall officers and traders strike a deal to underdeclare goods, it's necessary for the Baggage Hall officer to send a message to the last checkpoint to let his or her colleagues in on the deal.)

The same opportunities for visual examination at the Last Gate also allow for greater sociality than permitted at the Arrival Hall, playing on, but also turning around widely held cultural conventions of personalism. In fact, sociality is itself a criterion of evaluation and those whom officers know and see day-to-day selling clothes, food, radios, and so forth, typically pass through the gate with ease. Equally personalized though much less amicable, border-crossers who are liable to smuggle or cheat are often the target of Customs officers' abuse. Agatha, a junior inspector who frequently rotated through the post, did not hesitate to call the many women

Figure 3.4 Customs officer at the Aflao Last Gate reviewing documents.

carrying head loads over for inspection, going so far as to forcibly pull them back to her examination table, slinging epithets along the way.

On another occasion an officer stopped a man carrying two pairs of jeans and confiscated one pair, suspicious of his participation in a popular smuggling practice known as *deka-deka* or "one-one" in the Ewe language. When the man returned a few minutes later to plead for their return, the officer and his colleagues demanded to know the owner of the lot. Trying to turn sociality to their advantage, travelers might plead for an officer's "understanding" on the basis of familiarity or other shared commitment, but without personal ties, few concessions are granted. An elderly Muslim man protested his treatment with the following remarks: "Don't you know me? I served in the Ghana Army for twenty-eight years, since 1962. Who are you? I served this country! What right do you have to stop and search me? I declared myself to you! What right do you have to look in my things when I've declared myself? I am taking my son here to the hospital."

At the Last Gate, the increased oversight of mobile persons is matched by the oversight of specific forms of mobile property, namely motor vehicles. Checks on motor vehicles at the Last Gate follow on the heels of the physical search of vehicles conducted by a group of officers who patrol the last stretch of roadway leading to the border-crossing. Except for diplomatic vehicles, the various compartments of all incoming and outgoing cars are examined, along with the necessary licenses and paperwork, by officers detailed to the open space near the Black Star Arch that marks the border. All foreign vehicles entering the country are then rechecked at the Last Gate for the payment of an "undertaking" fee, which includes a road fund and payment for the number of days the car is permitted to be in use in Ghana.

Vehicle checks serve manifold ends. Vehicles, with their many enclosures, are obviously a major means of smuggling. A topic explored in depth in chapter 5, vehicles themselves are also a prime object of value. Cheap to purchase in Togo, they attract high duties in Ghana, making the temptations for smuggling across the border, and thus the need for checks, high. A holdover from the sumptuary controls of the socialist era, vehicle controls at the Last Gate serve a secondary purpose as much symbolic as practical. In addition to document-checking, here officers record the license-plate numbers of all vehicles coming into or leaving Ghana via Aflao and tabulating the number of vehicles, country of origin, and vehicle type along with a separate list of diplomatic and international organization vehicles passing each day. In an endeavor that can be construed as both extraneous and anachronistic, officers painstakingly write their entries in ballpoint pen in the handruled columns of an oversize (18"×24") ledger book.

This rote act of documentation stands as an important form of bearing witness, less about overt control than the capture and compilation of knowledge about what moves across the frontier. Through these rudimentary statistical practices Customs demonstrates the state's capacity for encompassment, molding what is expansive and dynamic into a microcosm, tangible and moored (cf. Anderson 1991; Ferguson and Gupta 2002). Like the highly personalized exchange between those who cross the border and those who man the Last Gate, this is yet another way the state imprints its authority on mobile persons and things. Indeed, Customs officers working this site are highly conscious of what they took to be the open-ended nature of their authority, adamantly telling me, and whoever else was in earshot, that their jurisdiction extended well beyond the final checkpoint and into the town of Aflao.

Acheampong's Folly

For travelers who do not proceed directly to the Last Gate from the Arrival Hall by dint of choice or more typically obligation, their path across the border requires a detour to the new Charge Office and the main Customs

Yard. Though just a couple hundred meters, the direct route between the roadway and Customs office and yard is blocked by a massive multistory edifice with little apparent official purpose. Reclaiming the spirit of Nkrumah's state-building campaign, it was erected in the 1970s along with a guard tower overlooking the border by Col. I. K. Acheampong's military government (Gocking 2005; Nugent 1995), still remembered throughout Ghana for the many construction projects initiated.[10] Combining a dually bureaucratic and authoritarian vision, the building was intended to house the offices of all state agencies operating at the frontier, but was never completed. Out of touch with the on-the-ground goings-on of the frontier by dint of scale and design, what remains of Acheampong's folly is a largely abandoned concrete shell towering above the rest of the post. Beside the vagrants and travelers who seek shelter and conduct business in its unfinished stairwells and corridors, there are a few makeshift offices, recently cobbled together by the senior officers of Customs Preventive Unit concerned with antismuggling and anticrime activities and the policing of unofficial points of entry away from the border post.

The fixing of the Preventive heads' presence on the ground floor of Acheampong's unfinished edifice speaks volumes for their unsettled role on the post. An alternative source of authority to the assistant commissioner heading the post and with a range of rule lying elsewhere, they are relegated to the Aflao Collection's margins yet at the same time cannot help but evoke its loaded meanings. The Preventive officers' improvised workspace bear plywood doors with nailed-on locks and latches, unplastered walls covered in cheap linoleum and paper calendars to hide the dark damp concrete. Their aesthetics resemble the temporary domiciles of the "land guards"[11] occupying the unfinished homesteads that make up much of Accra's neoliberally inspired suburban sprawl (Yeboah 2003). But while the squatters inhabit a "city yet to come," to borrow a phrase from A. M. Simone (2004), the Customs officers occupying the remains of fallen regimes are much more guests of the past. Standing for a singular and irrefutable vision of state power neither realized in its day nor since, but always lurking in the background, the building is rarely explicitly noted by other Customs officers despite its size and centrality. Working and walking around it, Customs officers and operations domesticate this chapter of Ghana's political history even as they deny it.

Charge Office

Behind this structure is the newly built Customs Charge Office, a large single-story square office block with a grand staircase and an entryway with a long counter for customer service just steps from the front door. The layout and location of this large and newly renovated building is at once more open and less accessible than the old structure near the Arrival Hall. The office of the assistant commissioner at the helm of the entire Aflao Customs Collection is located in the back of the building, facing an interior courtyard. He is joined by the post's second-in-command, now relocated from the Long Room. Though their large and well-appointed offices demonstrate their senior position, the design of the new space shields them from public access and denies them a window on frontier traffic. Indeed, with windows looking north to the Customs barracks rather than east across the border or south toward the border-crossing, the new designs mark a shift in orientation of commanding officers, from monitoring the frontier to monitoring the internal workings of the post itself. This combination of "customer service," predicated on a voluntaristic mode of self-rule, and the "governing of government" (Dean 1999) inscribed in the spatial arrangements of the new Charge office reflects a distinctively neoliberal reworking of Customs authority at the frontier.

Customs Yard

Across a dusty parking lot from the Charge Office is the Customs Yard. A U-shaped compound with a single manned point of exit and entry, this is an exclusive domain of the Customs Service to which access is policed. The Yard was rebuilt in Ghana's postindependence era and is indicative of the new nationalist aspirations of the time, modeled on a colonial template but expanded to accommodate the rising prosperity of the Ghanaian state and populace as cocoa prices and international recognition soared in the early 1960s. Although the country's economic profile has since changed, here Customs continues to execute its core functions of "processing entries": inspecting and classifying goods, determining values, and computing and collecting duties. In the Customs Yard, entries may be processed and goods cleared in two areas—the Long Room and the Baggage Hall—depending on the scale of transaction and nature of commodity. The Baggage Hall is used for the clearance of small-scale consignments while the Long Room is reserved for consignments greater than $5,000 in value. It is also the point of clearance for a specified set of corporate-to-corporate transactions involving multinational firms (such as Shell and Mobil) or Ghana's few large-scale local industries (regarding cement and steel manufacture, for instance).

Although substantial differences exist between the procedures pursued at each site, as will be made evident in the next chapter, Customs work at both locations is mired in the production and circulation of various forms of documentary evidence. If Riles is correct to refer to documents as "the paradigmatic artifacts of modern knowledge practices" (2006, 2), then the Baggage Hall and Long Room serve as the Customs altar to this brand of modernity. At the crux of Customs documentary authority is the Landing Account. With roots harking back to the Gold Coast Customs department in the nineteenth century, this is a portable, handwritten dossier (much like a "blue-book" examination notebook) accompanying every Customs transaction and containing a record of all the steps along the way. Not only does the Landing Account encode individual Customs transactions, a surprisingly resilient administrative artifact, it has endured the shifting orientation of Customs over time, incorporating new sorts of knowledge and procedure into its longstanding form.

Central to the Landing Account's enduring documentary authority is a set of semiotic capacities well suited to the management of mobility (cf. Caplan 2001).[12] As described below, Landing Accounts are widely intelligible symbolic registers that attach names, categories, and codes to material goods and transaction details. The Landing Account is iconic as well because it contains a detailed verbal portrait of things that is considered to encode a true and accurate representation. A tangible record of the co-presence of objects, Customs agents, and the application of Customs rules, the Landing Account is also indexical as it captures a lasting trace of things and their scrutiny by the state. Embodying forms of knowledge codified, correct, and accountable, the Landing Account thus incorporates a multiplex political authority, additive rather than singular in capacity.

The creation of the Landing Account and the work of Customs at both the Baggage Hall and Long Room begin with an inspection of the items a trader or traveler is bringing into the country, followed by the inscription in the Landing Account of the item's physical description. The description is then matched to the appropriate commodity-code drawn from a massive multivolume set of ledgers. Known as the HS Code (for Harmonized Commodity Description and Coding System Code), this index is compiled and updated by the World Customs Organization and a major international tool of coordination among Customs authorities as well as commercial parties of all sorts.[13] A form of "categorical identification" (Caplan 2003, 50), the selected code is noted in the Landing Account and then cross-referenced with the Customs Service's own tariff schedule to determine the proper duty rate, also noted in the Landing Account. Bringing the sumptuary controls of Ghana's 1960s and 1970s socialist experiment into the neoliberal present (despite the pressures of WTO membership and global trading system), tariffs for a host of consumer items remain steep, averaging close to 20 percent, and sometimes more for goods such as textiles and apparel.[14]

Because Customs duties, whatever their rates, are typically *ad valorem* or value-based, Customs officers need to determine value of a given consignment as well. This involves referencing yet another body of documentary evidence. Depending on the method of calculation in use (there are seven standard methods according to WCO), value may be computed from receipts provided by a trader/traveler or from Ghana Customs' own list of standard values (a distinction that will be discussed in detail in the next chapter). Though the latter method has fallen out of favor in both WCO and WTO, in Ghana, harking back to a succession of earlier economic orders based on extensive government control and the limited official circulation of imported goods, it remains the preferred scheme of Customs officials due as much to convenience as political conviction.

In the Long Room, however, a different standard of value with its own form of documentary evidence is applied to transactions, requiring the services of one of the private firms with whom Customs service holds a private "management contract." Unlike the form of value used in the Baggage Hall, the standards used here are not specific to Ghana, but derive from an internationally vetted database designed to respond to real-time changes in the price of goods on the global market. Only partially compatible with Customs' existing clearance procedures, this alternative valuation method requires the incorporation into the Landing Account of several additional sheets and forms to verify the source and outcome of any valuation ruling.

Once all the information is collected, all taxes and duties are computed with the aid of a calculator or simple mathematical manipulation and the figures entered into the Landing Account. Given the fact that the purchase of goods in Togo entails the use of CFA (the West African *franc* named after the *Communaute Francaise d'Afrique* Currency Union it represents) and Customs' own standard value rates are reckoned in U.S. dollars, this process often involves the additional step of currency conversion, requiring reference to the day's published exchange rates. After these procedures are completed, the Landing Account is stamped with Customs' official seal. The final step in the Landing Account's actualization, the stamp is usually printed with dramatic flourish, held high and meeting the paper with substantial force. Perhaps necessary due to the worn state of the rubber, it equally establishes Customs' active copresence in the construction of the Account.

The Landing Account is then brought to the cashier for the payment of the required duties and fees and subsequently surrendered to Customs.

Figure 3.5 Typical Customs Landing account. Note multiple signatures, receipts, Customs stamps, and perforated identification code.

These transactions result in the production of a series of receipts by both Customs and the bank which signal the official release of the goods at hand. Transit is now authorized, freeing traders and border-crossers to proceed to the Last Gate.

In all of these forms of documentary production, the claims of the state are brought to the fore. The commutation of diversity to conformity is a central feature of Customs rule over the persons and things moving across the frontier. By way of the Landing Account, not only are the vast material diversity of the goods crossing the border converted to a single physical form of representation (the paper document), conformity with international standards and national conventions is also at issue. Further, the very computations recorded in the Landing Account allow for the conversion of material difference into a single form of monetary value. Claimed by Customs, its payment clearly marks the fealty of trader/traveler/border-crosser to the state apparatus, but mediated by "paperwork" it is removed from direct expropriation by the state. In much the same way the diversity of goods are commuted to a standard measure, so too are the diverse persons crossing the border commuted to a common category of state subject through the workings of a uniform process of documentary production.

The receipt, like the Landing Account, also contains an autonomous agency. A "portable token of an originary act of bureaucratic recognition" (Caplan 2003, 51), the receipt stands as a sort of documentary proxy that records past action and establishes possibilities in the future. Legally marking the distinction between "customed" and "uncustomed" goods and, in turn, compliant versus noncompliant state-subjects, the receipt specifically serves as a license for the unencumbered movement of person and parcel between frontier and market. Through this semiotic twist, the receipt serves is an emblem of the sovereign, allowing the state to attach itself to the process of social and material mobility by way of permit.

If the receipt inserts the state into the public lives of private citizens, the Landing Account in its afterlife serves a different role, enlivening the private workings of public actors. For the Landing Account circulates through the backstage of Customs internal administration, enabling surveillance of Customs public representatives by way of audit. The Landing Account likewise provides the basis for the compilation of trade statistics and forecasts, building the Customs bureaucracy's all-important bureaucratic files (Weber 1968). Simultaneously accounting for the state's own history and that of its subjects, the looking back enabled by this documentary regime provides the foundation for Customs continued mandate in the present.[15]

Garnering resources, authority, and international recognition, all of the forms of fiscal and material control exercised in the Customs Yard via the surprisingly capacious instrumentality of the Landing Account are clearly "functional" to the Ghanaian state and the wider project of sovereign inscription. But we cannot forget that they are premised on an uneasy integration of multiple modes of rule: the mercantilist/modernist strategies of the colonial period, the socialist-nationalist logics of the independence era, and the internationalist, market-based agenda of the neoliberal. Bulging with information, inserts, and extra pages, the Landing Account reveals Customs' own effort to encompass this multiplicity of governing logics.

"Int" Office

In addition to the structures already mentioned, another set of Customs installations are found across the roadway from the Last Gate. On the surf side, overlooking the beach is the "Int" Office, used during the days of military government in the 1970s and 1980s—what Customs officers and border residents refer to as "Border Guard time" (Nugent 1991). Now known as the "International Office" with the charge of processing diplomatic vehicles and entries, according to current personnel the office was formerly used for "int"elligence and "int"errogation—a triple history that gives the office a multivalent denomination. Bringing this history to life, at present, when persons moving through the Last Gate are found to have uncustomed or concealed goods and appear to be evading the payment of duties, the case is referred to the Int Office due to the limited volume of diplomatic work. Because undeclared goods are subject to penalties reaching 300 percent of value and those who carry them face immediate confiscation of their wares, the aura of intimidation remains and is put to full effect. Adding to the intensity of the encounters taking place here, only two officers man this small office. With one or two well-trained local assistants (typically middle-aged men) to help with paperwork, errands, and messaging, they have the time and autonomy to interview those referred to them and review their documents and case.

Revealing the military/authoritarian foundations of this work space, officers posted to the Int Office have the nearly exclusive discretion to decide whether a potentially transgressive trader/traveler should be let go, taxed, fined, or referred to another part of the post. Officers working here are also the last to sign the documents for goods being held and pending release. While they have a wide discretionary sweep, it is different from what is exercised by the post's officer-in-charge. Where the OIC can affirm or trump the decisions of other officers at Aflao simply by dint of office, the senior officers manning the Int Office exercise a more lateral authority, allowing them to justify their course of action through any number of regulatory fields at their disposal. Thus, they employ a discretion, at least in theory, that is procedurally based, rather than the more personalized and open-ended prerogative of office available to the OIC. The Int Office nevertheless remains a site where authority is concentrated. In some ways subordinate and in some ways parallel to the Charge Office, the status of the Int Office at Aflao reveals the steep but nevertheless unstable hierarchy of Customs authority at the frontier—a symptom of the checkered legacy of the state apparatus more generally.

Departure Hall

Adjacent to the Int Office, circling back toward the borderline and the crossing point between Ghana and Togo, is a two-room block holding the offices of the Ghana Immigration Service. Just beyond that is the Departure Hall, a three-sided concrete structure operated by Customs.

Emulating the tactics of their colleagues in the Immigration Service next door, upon entry Customs officers pursue the most basic of "dividing practices" (Foucault 1979) asking travelers for identification—preferably a passport or national ID card—giving clear account of nationality and country of origin.

Mapped onto these nation-based documentary distinctions (see Torpey 2000) is the assertion of sensibilities and controls largely embodied in form. Just as the transgression of state authority works through the body, as in the case of smuggled goods concealed on the private spaces of the person, so too does state enforcement. These optics are evident in the remarks of an officer stationed here: "When I was at Departure Hall, after a while I could figure out who was going and coming from where and why. Even before I saw the documents, I knew who Beninois, Togolese, from dress, luggage, etc." Augmenting and extending such biopolitical logics, gender provides the basis of Customs actions and interventions at the Departure Hall. Once travelers leave the Immigration Office, they are directed into separate male and female corridors. Customs officers are likewise divided by gender with male officers attending to male travelers and female to female. The two groups of officers sit in parallel rows, forming a gauntlet of a sort; the women toward the back of the structure where more privacy is afforded and men toward the front, where the transit corridor is open to the roadway.

Conveying the embodied power of Customs, there is an effort to have this area fully staffed at all times with an unbroken line of officers manning each section of the gate, veritably crowding the departure gate with the bodies of Customs officials while those exiting ideally file by one by one. Compared to the crushing weight of the crowd in the Arrival Hall and the sporadic presence of officers who must fight to maintain a space for themselves, at the Departure Hall it is the traveler who must navigate a space densely packed with the bodies and gaze of Customs officers who rule not by standing over the traveler, but by means of total occupation.

This transit zone creates a sort of human panopticon (Foucault 1979), with the state configuring itself as a filter and a consistent force. Officers wearing identical uniforms are lined up in identical chairs and divided by naturalized bodily attributes of gender to convey a common and co-ordinated imprint of power. Here we see an interesting parallel with the dually naturalized and bureaucratized ethnopolitical distinctions which serve to represent categorical or irrefutable positions as described by scholars such as Malkki (1995) and others (Hayden 1996). Rather than only the public serving as the object of such inscription, at the Departure

Hall the power of state agents is conveyed and consolidated through the display of such naturalized divisions. These divisions, and the gap between them, are further affirmed by the inability of Customs officers to comprehend or converse in the native languages of many border-crossers. Typically fluent in English (Ghana's national language) and Twi (the native language of Ghana's Akan elite), Customs officers posted to Aflao often lack knowledge of Ewe, widely spoken in Togo and Ghana's Volta Region. At the Departure Hall, for this, they rely on the assistance of a small corps of select Aflao indigenes who provide translation services.

In actualizing Customs authority and the accompanying distinctions on which it premised, the disciplinary techniques employed by the gauntlet of officers at the Departure Hall are intensely physical. Small changing rooms occupy the rear of the structure adjacent to the women's line and Customs officers readily search personal belongings as well as persons, ostensibly in search of illegal goods (like drugs) or prohibited exports (such as excessive cash). For officers, the play of visual and physical surveillance is critical. One Customs official recounted to me how he had pulled over a man who he found to have marijuana taped around his waist. The officer explained that he became suspicious when he saw the traveler pause to check if officers were busy or not before he went through the hall. Another revealed her suspicions about a female traveler because she carried a suitcase full of men's clothes, most of which were brand-new.

Duty Free

The sort of somatic regime exercised at the Departure Hall in which "the political apparatus [operates through] a sensual realism" (Linke 2006, 212) is oddly aligned with another. A few steps beyond the Departure Gate is Aflao's very own Duty Free Shop. Unattached to nearby structures and affiliated with Customs only through the official licensing of its private proprietor, Duty Free makes its home in a glossy white shipping container with the feel of a mobile home. Deriving its power from the lure of pleasure and fantasy in contrast to the terror and intrusion of the Departure Hall's embodiments, the Duty Free shop is set apart by its ice-cold air conditioning, carpeting and dust-free interior. Hermetically sealed, the structure in many ways resembles the products it carries: top-shelf liquors, wine in bottles and boxes, and aseptic cartons of tropical fruit juice, exported, processed abroad and now finding a way back to its region of origin.[16]

At the Aflao border, where most buildings are made of wood or crude cement block and are subject to the corrosive effects of time, resource depletion, and the harsh sea air, Duty Free seems to be moored in a different world, adhering to the standards of a far-off international order. Another example of the way borders spawn a diversity of governing sites and logics, entry into the shop immediately evokes a realm of luxury consumption and corporate and transnational capital free from state exaction. But seen "in" rather than "out" of place, Duty Free is equally reminiscent of Aflao's containerized mini-mart phenomenon, in an upscale sort of way. With its contents and discounts nationally and internationally sanctioned, it stands as a prime example of neoliberalism's official mimicry of informal means of market engagement, both in competition and compatible with them. One sign of "the border for rent," like Customs' "management contracts" it also stands as a paean to a wider specter of privatization infiltrating the governing process and claims to state sovereignty in Ghana.

Conclusion

From this overview of the history and operations of Ghana's Customs Service at the Aflao border, it is apparent that state installations at this frontier are fully assimilated into local livelihoods, landscapes, and identities. Given the long record of state-society accommodation in this locale, rather than treat the border zone as a space of resistance to or breakdown of state authority—as is often assumed in the field border studies—the case of Aflao suggests instead the importance of looking to the border to comprehend the character and constitution of state power within Ghana as a whole. The border from this vantage point is by no means a simple reflection of political ideals. Rather, it is a space where ideals are both put on display and take on a life of their own, operating in unexpected ways as they hark back to the wider history of statecraft.

In light of such an optic, at the Aflao Customs post it is possible to trace the diverse and at times disparate legacies of the Ghanaian state, whether colonial, nationalist, socialist, military, or late-capitalist, developing over close to a century of border administration. In their totality the installations making up the Aflao Customs Collection encode the variegated history of the frontier as they evoke (but never fully encompass) the twists and turns of the Ghanaian polity more generally. Stemming from diverse historical projects as well as their shifting purposes in the neoliberal

present geared above all to the management of mobility, Customs operations employ an array of means for exercising power over persons and
things. Some complementary, some divergent, they respond not so much
to the call of the border but to the call of the state and stand in contrast
to the sort of localized accommodation and flexibility created by borderlanders at the frontier, although they rely deeply upon them.

In the stratigraphy of rule that constitute Customs' territorialized
claims to sovereign statehood, the residues of past and current regimes
operate individually and in combination. In the very location of the
border post, the rigid hierarchy of Customs ranks, and the manifold
symbolics of rule—from uniforms, to flagpoles, bugles, rubber stamps,
Landing Accounts, and ledger books—the inheritance of the colonial
state is inescapable. Carried forward, these designs cannot be seen as entirely separate from the directives of the nationalist era, also rooted in
extensive emblemization and architectural rendering of state power and
the modernist administrative logics of documentation, statistical representation, sorting, and standardization. Yet remnants of the national-
izing impulse are also evident in the personalistic strategies tried by state
agents and subjects alike at Aflao's Last Gate or the now fleeting presence
of the post's officer-in-charge.

The legacy of socialism is equally apparent in Customs operations at
Aflao, from the imposition of sumptuary controls via car registration and
close policing of imports to the continued reliance on internally generated standards of value distinct from market price, and duty schedules
designed to provide protection for state-run industry (though, ironically,
few are left). So too does the specter of Ghana's military past remain present at the border post, plainly revealed in Acheampong's grand architectural folly, the guard tower no one dares to climb, the unofficial offices
of the Preventive Unit, and the ambiguous nomenclature and operations
of the Int Office with its capacity to translate any claim on person or
property into law.

That which connotes the neoliberal exists side by side and within these
strategies and spaces. Some are formally scripted and legally prescribed,
whether the privatization of exchange controls, the "renting out" of
the border as a duty-free shopping spot, the adoption of international
commercial codes, or the turning of the post's higher administration
to the "government of government." Others appear more inventive or
organic in form: the Preventive officers commoditized refashioning of
abandoned office space, the panoptic regulatory arrangement crafted by
officers at the Departure Hall.

Taken together, these logics and loci of governance forge a form of territorial rule that neither holds cross-border flows nor the state in place. Thus the case of Aflao suggests that despite the proliferation of state installations and interventions at the frontier, the achievement of sovereignty is always incomplete, both unfinished and unstable. The changeable nature of territorial sovereignty can be attributed only in part to the inherent challenge posed by governing that which is mobile—a problem states have, to some degree, managed for centuries (Ruggie 1993; Torpey 2000)—not least of which, modern African states, from the start cross-cut by highly durable social and material circuits. Rather, in nations like Ghana, these tensions are exacerbated by the country's postcolonial condition. The problem lies not in the intransigence of local political conventions and elites (pace Boone 2003) or the artificiality of the boundaries imposed by colonial regimes—a liability that border residents have turned to their advantage. Instead, it stems from the postcolonial state's very susceptibility to reform, ever invested in "fixing" the state, in the full sense of the term.

The etiology of this overarching reformist agenda is multiplex. On the one hand, it is rooted in internally generated struggles over political opportunity and vision—centrally, the proper mode of overcoming the state's colonial past—a dilemma complicated at the border, where the colonial legacy looms large The reformist impetus at play on the frontier is further engaged by external efforts to guide, "right" or otherwise "jump-start" late-developing states. As a consequence, the border stands as a record of the state's unfinished projects, some complementary, some divergent, none foolproof in scope or effectiveness. Hence, in spaces like Aflao, though the boundary line has been long settled and its reproduction virtually guaranteed by the investments of border populations, territorial sovereignty—the state's articulation and realization (however partial) of a transcendent vision of border management—remains out of reach. In the neoliberal context it is this dynamic of political reform, of retooling and replacing the institutions of the state—much more than the play of the market—that most alters the conditions of territorial sovereignty. Foreshadowed here, the political terms and outcomes of this process will be made glaringly evident in the proceeding chapter.

FOUR

The Sovereignty of Good Governance: Bureaucratic Contests and the Recentering of Power

Introduction:
Governing Aflao in Neoliberal Times

Against the historical backdrop of Customs operations presented in chapter 3, this chapter provides a closer look at the ways neoliberal prescriptions engage national political struggles to alter the expression and bearing of Customs sovereign writ. Also drawing on observations from the Aflao land frontier, the chapter specifically probes the changing tactical and spatial configuration of territorial rule accompanying neoliberally inspired good governance initiatives, whether those tied to anticorruption and antipatronage platforms or the overall effort to purge the state of older military bodies and proclivities.

At Aflao, the working out of good governance directives above all heightens the strain between Customs administrative headquarters and Customs officers and operations at the frontier. Such tensions between Customs' center and periphery are further complicated by the new political hierarchies that come with the privatizing impulses of neoliberal reform. Rather than generating greater political transparency as their proponents claim, these moves undermine established modes of accountability and re-endow the authoritarian potentials of state executives. The result in a reconfiguration of power in a manner both top-heavy and dispersed that confounds neat notions of sovereignty—unbundled, graduated, denationalized, or otherwise.

As discussed in chapters 2 and 3, scholars and policymakers tend to share the assumption that neoliberal reforms pose a challenge to territorial expressions of sovereignty due to the acceleration and enlargement of cross-border flows, the lifting of myriad state-based exchange controls, governmental deference to international standards, and the supplanting of state enterprise by private and multinational firms outside the state's regulatory ambit. In the case of Ghana, rather than the outright renunciation of control over that which crosses and circulates within national frontiers, we see a more complicated scenario at work where territorial sovereignty is substantially restructured but not necessarily reduced. Specifically, at Aflao, neoliberal interventions worsen the perennial strain between Customs' administrative center and officers and operations at frontier stations, ultimately shifting the locus of the state's territorial controls away from the border to a range of alternative spaces, less public or permanent. Largely defying the predicted results or pathways of reform, the outcome is a process of sovereign readjustment in which the border is no longer exclusively sovereign or the exclusive representation of the state's territorial claims.

A prime example of the inherently uneasy relation between the principles of hierarchical subordination and infrastructural or networked power dually characteristic of the modern state (Mann 1986, 2008; see also Agnew 2005), Ghana's neoliberal transition brings to the fore the pan-modern paradox of territorial sovereignty. A phenomenon deeply relevant but by no means restricted to the postcolonial polity, according to the conventions of the modern state borders are considered the instantiation of the power of a centralized administration. Signaling the state's outer limits, territorial boundaries are thus always authorized elsewhere. At the same time borders are loyal to the center, they must also represent it. But for a border's representation of a center to be deemed credible, it must also be construed as somehow autonomous or originally endowed. Hence, within the territorially sovereign state, national boundaries are the center's subsidiary, proxy, and equivalent, a relationship that is inherently tension ridden. While this discord applies to all forms of representative rule (cf. Boone 2003), it is dramatized at the territorial frontier where the paradox of delegation is both extreme and critical given the border's object of representing the limit and extent of the state's reach to

Figure 4.1 Customs officers at work and rest, Aflao substation. Un-uniformed Customs assistants are in the background. An importer (with headwrap) stands besides the Customs desk.

citizens, noncitizens, and other political entities alike. As we shall see, the neoliberal milieu restages this drama such that processes of bureaucratic delegation are intensified and hierarchical authorities both split apart and supplemented.

At Ghana's Aflao land frontier, of particular significance to playing out of the paradox of territorial power is the "second-generation" neoliberal turn to good governance (World Bank 1992). Despite the rhetoric of decentralization, these directives inspire the consolidation of power within centralized administrative apparati. In Ghana and many other African states this is boldly evident in the concerted focus on the re-endowment of the offices and officers of the executive via electoral processes (from actual elections to voter registration and party politics) as well as their attendant license to implement and enforce policy prescriptions (Lindberg 2006). The renewal of executive authority is further amplified by the concomitant promotion of select bureaucratic realms concerned with fiscal matters, Customs included. These hierarchical arrangements are complemented (as well as complicated) by the neoliberal tendency to cultivate parallel authority structures, both inter- and multinational, public and private in standards and stature, to carry out executive responsibilities in tandem with state-based institutions.[1]

Ghana Customs is caught at all "ends" of such reform. Given Customs' status as the state's most significant revenue authority, Customs' central administration has gained status and recognition as a leading edge of economic restructuring, with a new political profile and enlarged mandate. Driven by the political winds of the day, Customs' central administration is equally charged with cleaning up Customs' wider bureaucratic apparatus. Yet, reflecting the extensive and highly technical "trade-related" economic platform on which neoliberalism is built, it is Customs officers at the frontier, much more than those at the Head Office, who are responsible for carrying out a host of new and expanded responsibilities. These activities are at the very foundation of the neoliberal economic agenda and address the details of export promotion and import flows, tariff reductions, free trade agreements, and global standards of business practice along with the overarching mobility of persons, capital, and currency. Rather than a simple transfer or reallocation of power, what results is a situation of multiple and conflicting endowments at the territorial frontier. Proliferating instead of streamlining the modalities and spaces of rule, as we shall see, these shifts divest the border of a certain or exclusive sovereignty.

Below I sketch these processes as they play out in three realms of Customs operations at Ghana's Aflao frontier: Administration, fiscal control, and Preventive work.

Case 1: Administrative Discipline and the Excesses of Good Governance

As Ghana's ruling National Democratic Congress (NDC) party geared up for the 2000 elections, the winds of reform blew hard. Not only would the election force J. J. Rawlings, the twenty-year incumbent, to give up power even if his party emerged victorious, there were now a host of opposition parties, politicians, and platforms to contend with, each espousing its own vision of national renewal (Smith 2002b). Adding to the mix of reformist discourse was a new articulation of the neoliberal ideal, this time focusing less on a singular economic fix than the signs of good governance (World Bank 1992). This was a recipe in which accountability and anticorruption were central figures (Hasty 2005b; West and Sanders 2003). According to this outlook, efficiency and transparency were to be at the top of the political agenda and any sort of secondary interests, what might be described as the politics of politics—cultivating patronage, catering to sectional interests, and building a power base—were to be shunned entirely (Lindberg 2006).

WARNING

IF YOU CONCEAL OR SMUGGLE,
YOU MAY HAVE TO PAY A PENALTY
OF NOT LESS THAN
THREE TIMES
THE VALUE OF THE GOODS...
IN ADDITION TO
PAYMENT OF THE TAXES.

FURTHERMORE

THE ITEM WOULD BE SEIZED
AND FORFEITED,
AND YOU MAY ALSO BE LIABLE
FOR CRIMINAL PROSECUTION.

Smuggling is a crime.
SHUN IT !

3

Figure 4.2 "Smuggling Is a Crime." Antismuggling notice from Ghana Customs Guide. Courtesy of Ghana Customs, Excise and Preventive Service.

Touting such a model of governance, the NDC government, and with it, the press and the public, made Customs a target of administrative rehabilitation. Considered a bastion of corruption and cronyism, this was a bureaucratic realm both donors and the public believed was sorely in need of cleanup (Toye and Moore 1998). In a widely circulated 2001 report on perceptions of a cross-section of Ghanaian businesses and citizenry sponsored by the World Bank and carried out by the Center for Democracy and Development, a leading political consultancy, Customs was found to be the most corrupt government agency. In light of these allegations, Customs was made the target of a reform agenda all its own, augmenting the wider reorganization of the state's revenue agencies already underway.

As much political as economic in scope, these efforts included the outsourcing of a select group of Customs operations to a private multinational, insistence on firm adherence to standards of international bodies such as the World Trade Organization, World Customs Organization, International Civil Aviation Organization, Interpol, and others, and a hefty dose of administrative restructuring geared to improving accountability and transparency within the Customs Service. At the center of the latter stood the separation of Customs revenue and managerial functions, the improvement of Customs public image, and a new mission as "trade and investment facilitator" as opposed to Customs' longstanding and largely disciplinary ambit of tax collection and policing—all goals sketched in the succession of Customs "Corporate Plans" (Integrated Solutions 1999). These reforms, in ways intended and not, would have sweeping implications for division of labor and distribution of authority within Customs at Aflao and within the organization as a whole.

At the fore of the broader project of bureaucratic restructuring was the appointment of a new Customs commissioner in 1999. Although it was not unusual for appointees to rotate out of the commissioner's office every two or three years, this case was remarkable for the selection of an a leader with limited professional experience in Ghana, let alone Customs. The son of a healer and petty trader, the commissioner-elect was a man of Ghanaian (specifically Ga) descent who had left the country in the 1970s, a period of political and economic decline when Ghanaians with professional and educational ambitions sought opportunities elsewhere. He earned a B.A. in the United States and remained there to pursue a law degree, finding employment in Washington, D.C., where he specialized in corporate finance and tax law. Compared to any internal candidates for the post, this individual appeared fully in step with the all-important Washington Consensus touting commercial opportunity, administrative efficiency, and global harmonization of governmental and business practices (Williamson 1993).

Despite his substantial time abroad, like many other professionals the commissioner-elect had stayed in touch with Ghanaian friends and family, including J. J. Rawlings and first lady Nana Konadu Rawlings, his classmate at the elite Achimota Secondary School, long a way station for would-be power brokers. The commissioner-to-be embodied the proclivities and life-course of both an old and new elite and captured a turning point in Ghanaian political style and principles. In the mid-1990s, he found himself posted to the Board of Ghana's Ministry of Finance. After overseeing the 1996 inaugural celebration he won further recognition from the Rawlings family with a presidential appointment to the post of Customs commissioner in 1999. This was an opportunity he embraced, along with the other successful migrants lured back to Ghana not only by material promise, but by the possibility of political and professional relevance (Manuh 2002). At the millennium's turn, such a potential seemed all the more obtainable after two national elections, the apparent recession of military rule, and a fifteen-year trajectory of economic growth. Here was a figure perfectly suited to the task of neoliberal housecleaning—at once a political loyalist and a political outsider who could "talk the talk" and master the technical details of reform. Moreover, because of the commissioner's long absence from the country he was locked out of the larger grid of power and thus remained beholden to his benefactors despite his worldliness and international credentials. This made him a figure with a very broad and very narrow appeal, a situation rendering him politically safe for those at the pinnacle of the Rawlings regime but at political risk for himself.

Augmented by Customs' existing authority structure and his own sense of mission, once the new commissioner assumed his post, his staunch pursuit of a reformist agenda was felt in all corners of the service. Enshrined in practice and historical precedent, the distribution of power in Customs is strongly centripetal. With authority surrendered to those at the top, the commissioner holds the ultimate prerogative to interpret, augment and contravene Customs law. If a fine is imposed on a trader or goods seized, the commissioner may legally and officially amend or nullify these charges. Equally, the commissioner is authorized to grant exemptions from duties and taxes as specified in PNDC law 330, section 26, 330 (Ghana Customs 1993, 18, 114): "the commissioner in accordance with provisions of the Investment Code 1985 or any other enactment for the time being in force grant exemptions from duties and taxes as specified in the Code." Such a configuration of authority within

Customs underwrites both hierarchy and a sort of "infralegality," with an internal or parallel code of conduct emerging out of the official organizational and legal structure.

This play of power within Customs is highly normalized, finding expression in the battery of "Commissioners Orders" containing explicit instructions on how to implement and interpret policy distributed to all of the country's Customs collections each year. Received at Customs collections without forewarning and often commanding radical shifts in the norms of customs work, the "Orders" take immediate effect and must be implemented without deliberation or delay. Each year officers at Aflao, like everywhere else, were also subject to decisions handed down from headquarters regarding promotions and job assignments. Collections were also expected to provide detailed financial accounts to headquarters each month, including information on the major items of trade passing through the station, the number, value, and major items of transaction passing through each station, and the revenue earned. These sorts of administrative oversight were no doubt necessary to managing a sprawling bureaucratic apparatus on the scale of Customs.

The wedding of such entrenched hierarchies with a new sort of neoliberal activism would dramatically heighten the commissioner's oversight at the Aflao frontier, further unsettling the inherently tense relationship between Customs headquarters and border stations. Building upon the conventions of centralized oversight and intervention already in place, the new commissioner in his "Maiden Address" styled himself as "an action-oriented administrator," intent on "correcting indiscipline" in the Service (Ghana CEPS 1999b). Soon after he came on board, Aflao along with a host of other collections became the target of surprise visits by official delegations from Customs' Accra headquarters—the commissioner included. Indeed, such "unannounced visits to ports and stations by management" were among the recommendations contained in one of CEPS' succession of corporate plans that were readily realized (Integrated Solutions 1999, 26). The *Customs Newsletter* put out by Customs public relations office highlighted the commissioner's new visitation policy in a commentary titled "New Wind Blowing over CEPS" (1999a, 1):

Within a brief period of two months—March and April—a lot of changes have taken place in the Service . . . This relatively short period has also witnessed for the first time in our long history, a Commissioner taking time off his busy schedule to visit seven Collections, namely KIA, Tema, Accra, Aflao, Ho and lately Kumasi and Sunyani. The visits are aimed at creating an opportunity for him to meet and interact with staff, know the problems on the ground and share their anxieties.

This official commentary, however, fails to expose that many of the visits were unscheduled, leading to a climate of suspicion and insecurity rather the bridging of gaps between Customs higher-ups and officers on the ground at the various frontier stations, as recommended by Customs corporate consultants. Although Customs headquarters did concede the frequency of unannounced arrivals, attributing them to "poor communication" infrastructure (Ghana CEPS 1999d, 46), the uncertainty surrounding these visits worked to keep officers on their toes, giving headquarters a sort of immanent presence at Customs far-flung frontier stations. More than an impetus for renewed self-regulation, these visits made frontier officers targets of the forthright exercise of disciplinary authority by the commissioner and his entourage. Facing surprise inspections at their work sites, officers at Aflao were under pressure to mobilize resources to properly receive higher-ups on short notice—not always easy given the high volume of border traffic and an arduous system of twelve-hour shifts. Upon the arrival of the commissioner's delegation, officers would be expected to assemble immediately and perform military-style drills—whether or not they were otherwise engaged in official duties, in the barracks, or on break. They might also be expected to immediately open their books and desks upon the request of visiting superiors.

In contrast to the fleeting claims exercised by border officials on cross-border traders and travelers discussed in chapter 3, the commissioner's visits sought to induce a type of territorial enclosure, however temporary. Here we find a clear parallel with the techniques of administrative encompassment described by Ferguson and Gupta (2002) for central government oversight of local social-service providers in India. In the Indian setting, "The most important mechanism was the surprise inspection by a host of visiting superior officers . . . surveillance of surveillance . . . a kind of recursive regulation" (985). In Ghana similar managerial tactics are in play not among middling social-service agencies but within the most powerful echelons of state administration, bringing together those at the bureaucratic apex with the rank-and-file. Excepting the surprise element, these tactics are also curiously akin to the royal pilgrimages described by Geertz (1983) within pre- and early modern states in which an otherwise unbounded realm of rule is physically mapped by the body of the ruler.[2] Effective even if unknowing, here the commissioner crafted a synthesis of disciplinary surveillance and sovereign display borne out of a neoliberalism's recharged rule of law as much as older colonial and precolonial conventions of political ceremonial.

This confluence of intragovernmental tactics was given further force by their amalgamation with headquarters' newfound concern with Customs officers' comportment. Also a hallmark of the new commissioner's reign, this included attention to the minutia of officers' dress, along with punctuality and neatness (Ghana CEPS 1999e, 2). In his first public statement, the commissioner enjoined his fellow officers "to insist on the strict use of the uniform by personnel of all ranks." The details of these orders were circulated to all collections:

1. It has been observed that the turn-out of some officers of the Service is improper and tends to bring the Service into disrepute.

2. As a Para-military Institution, regulations concerning dressing shall be strictly enforced.

3. The following instructions shall serve as a guide to the turn out of officers: a. Officers shall at all times, when in uniform wear the head-dress except when they are in the office or at a meeting. b. Under no circumstances should an officer tug [sic] his head dress under the epaulette or belt loops, in a pocket or in a hand bag, unless in the office or at a meeting. c. Officers leaving their office to the general court (i.e. within the CEPS compound) shall be properly dressed and be in head-dress. d. It would be improper for an officers in uniform to be seen at any location outside the general premises of CEPS headquarters, Station, Post, etc. without a head-dress or uniform accessories (i.e. badge, prescribed belt, pair of boots or shoes). (3)

At Customs headquarters and stations throughout the country, officers commented to me about the new requirement to wear uniforms, head gear, and ID tags bearing their name and an official Customs employee number at all times. An old but little-enforced aspect of Customs work, the dress code was lauded by officers of all ranks for enhancing their dignity and recognition and providing a source of order within the Service. In a culture where self-presentation is considered a direct gauge of self-respect and social worth and dress has long functioned to publicly mark social status (Allman 2004), the commissioner's admonitions were taken seriously. Handwritten signs reminding officers "to be clean, neat and correctly turned out" were affixed to the mirrors in the halls and staff rooms of various collections. When old uniforms wore out, officers purchased the appropriate shades of blue serge with their own money to bring to the tailor's even though the Service was supposed to provide ready-made uniforms for them free of charge.

Although the dress code was a source of pride, it made Customs officers vulnerable to a host of new sanctions tied to a close monitoring of the body. Customs employees complained not about expectation of professional appearance—a premise they generally agreed with—but the violence and impracticality of enforcement. Despite its popular support, the implementation of the dress code was shot through with the taint of personalized and in many ways arbitrary rule in which both the ruler and rule-breaker were singled out as outside the law, the ruler above it, without any obligations, and the other below it, without any protection (Agamben 1998). One senior officer vividly narrated to me his encounter with the new Customs commissioner on a visit to headquarters.

When he arrived at the head office, the officer realized that he had forgotten to wear his name tag, which the Commissioner had made a mandatory part of the CEPS uniform. When the Commissioner saw him, the officer received a severe reprimand, which was to him far out of proportion to the offense. According to the officer, the commissioner declared, "I will put your name in my book," like a school master disciplining his student. Contrary to the more common Ghanaian practice of keeping passions [but very much in line with American tendency to "let it all hang out"], whether anger or affection, at bay in public, the Commissioner yelled at him so loudly that employees on the next level of the building could hear. When the officer got ready to leave, those around him asked what happened to so infuriate the boss. Upon explanation, the witnesses confided that the Commissioner had lashed out at others for the same offense.

Months later, the discomfort and embarrassment of the incident still lingered in the officer's mind. He mentioned how he continued to feel demeaned by it and how such admonition threatened his own authority over those he supervised. As he put it: "If a senior can receive such a harsh and public rebuke, how will he be able to ask his juniors to do anything and receive their respect?"

In another incident related to me, on a surprise visit to a checkpoint on the road between Aflao and Accra under the auspices of Aflao Customs, the commissioner saw some Aflao officers wearing the black T-shirts. Although they were not part of their official garb, they were considered a necessary part of their uniform by officers and regularly worn to prevent the oil used to clean and upkeep their weapons from staining the official issue shirts and jumpsuits. Despite their neat appearance, practical necessity, and universal adoption, the commissioner loudly and aggressively threatened to dismiss the officers donning the black Ts.

Producing what might be termed "the terror of transparency," in these cases we see the extensive elaboration of policy providing the basis for the exercise of excessive power through "on the spot" intervention. Though not entirely foreign to Customs' already steep hierarchy, magnified by the commissioner's exacting personal style and professional distance from the arcane practicalities of Customs operations (Plange

2001), under conditions of reform this tendency was legitimized anew. Here, the employment of the rhetoric of personal accountability that was fast becoming a benchmark of the neoliberal mindset allowed for a sort of liberal authoritarianism in which the already wide berth of Customs centralized controls was further enlarged and their sanction intensified. In this setting, as in others (Blundo and Olivier de Sardan 2006, 67), the local appropriation of the power-laden discourses and policies of good governance set the stage for their subversion.

In such a climate the expanded reach of the commissioner and concomitant threat of dismissal accompanying his mandate to clean up Customs ranks were taken seriously. Soon after the commissioner's appointment and for the duration of his reign, Customs officers throughout the Service found themselves the target of a rising number of interdictions, investigations, and dismissals. Dismissals, representing only a fraction of a much wider field of internal disciplinary measures, numbered only 10–20 annually for most of the 1990s, but rose to 50 for 1999 (the commissioner's first year on post), followed by 40 in 2000. Officers at Aflao were highly sensitive to the threat of suspension and the expanding oversight of headquarters that came with it. Referring to the high rates of interdiction, the chair of Aflao's Junior Staff Association asserted with little irony, "Half my mates are 'in the house,'" going on to say, "[Among officers at Aflao] fear of interdiction is at the forefront. Fear is always there, part and parcel. The moment news gets to the head office, there will be interdiction without any query." Others suggested that any news of wrongdoing "filters to Accra very quickly," and that "the Commissioner could dismiss an officer through a phone call." Affirming this sentiment, a senior officer with many years of experience in the country's main frontier stations confided that there was a "feeling on the ground of being 'surrounded by witch hunters' because the Commissioner has planted people all over. There are some officers you can't converse with [because you] don't know how it will be construed."

With the incentive for independent decision-making reduced by the overarching climate of suspicion, the tendency of frontier officers to refer decisions to headquarters, already widespread, took on a renewed importance.[3] In the case of seizures, for instance, a well-connected officer in Customs investigative branch explained:

Nowadays, the head of post or collection where goods are seized will prefer the goods to be sent to Accra even though he has the legal authority to determine or at least enforce the penalty. This is because they fear their decision may be misunderstood and they themselves would be subject to disciplinary action.

Because the commissioner had the authority to waive or override rulings of inferiors according to a statute long a part of Ghana's Customs law (PNDC no. 330), such a referral up the chain of command was something cross-border traders often lobbied for and found increasingly likely. Here the triumph of private economic interests over strict trade controls— a hallmark of the neoliberal project—was made a reality, but not through a route that anyone might have expected. It was of course by no means new, but under the cleanup exercise it was accentuated rather than extinguished.

Despite this liberal attitude toward the public, no Customs officer, regardless of record or stature, was spared the commissioner's exactions. One senior officer who earlier held a high-ranking position at the country's main seaport in Tema (one of the most attractive assignments in the whole of the Customs Service, to be discussed in detail in chapter 6), recounted how he found himself under investigation just a week after receiving an award for superior performance. In response to rumors circulated by junior officers, he was summarily dismissed and sat at home for three months without salary. In a sign of the commissioner's untrammeled discretionary authority, but also the extreme fluidity of the situation, after securing an audience with the commissioner he was able to re-enter the service. Although the original charges were never dropped, he was given a post as the head officer of a small substation in a rural backwater on the eastern frontier under the Aflao collection.[4]

The strong pull of the Customs administrative center on frontier stations, along with the overall liability of power in the context of political transition, is evident in a fantastic story of dismissal and reinstatement that preoccupied officers at Aflao Collection during the course of my research. In this case Aflao's officer-in-charge, holding the rank of assistant commissioner (AC) (just two ranks down from commissioner in the Customs hierarchy), was interdicted and suspended from work for several months. Here, the Aflao AC found himself the target of a panoply of centralized controls in which the commissioner was deeply entangled but not supreme. In September 2000 the AC, already under assault due to the vast scope and frequency of headquarters' administrative override, heard rumors of a possible interdiction ordered not by the Customs commissioner, but by the Customs managing board based in the Ministry of Finance. The interdiction was neither finalized nor publicized until November when he received two letters, one calling for interdiction and the other withdrawing the order. The AC was then ordered to send both letters back to Accra and to ignore their contents. Shortly thereafter he received another notice of interdiction, this one less strongly worded. This was accompanied, again, by acknowledgment from the commissioner that this was by order of the CEPS Board and not in line with his own opinion.

The interdiction, according to the details of the board's letter—as told to me—stemmed from a case at the AC's former post involving a truck he ordered seized after learning that it had entered the country without the payment of the required duties. The truck remained under seizure in the Custom Yard for more than nine months. Finally someone came to claim the vehicle, producing the documents proving that duty was paid. However, because the documents were dated just a few weeks prior, they confirmed, in the AC's view, the legal grounds of the original seizure. With this in mind, the owner and the AC haggled over the terms of release without coming to any agreement and the vehicle remained CEPS property. However, one day, in the AC's absence, his second-in-command (2I/C) released the vehicle. Attributed to a tipoff from the 2I/C to the CEPS board, this incident was used to explain the AC's interdiction several months later while he was working at an all-together different location.

Revealing the forceful yet surprisingly amorphous order of the upper echelons of Customs hierarchy, while the AC disputed the details of the case for suspension, as a lawyer, he was even more skeptical of the board's jurisdiction to interdict and possibly dismiss him. After appealing to the commissioner and the Investigations Department at CEPS headquarters for a fair hearing and even approaching the country's newly formed Special High Court for Administrative Justice (a fast-track court established as part of Rawlings's government investment in administrative transparency [Hasty 2005b]), the Aflao AC decided to take the matter into his own hands and take the CEPS Board to court. Based on a 1998 law passed by Parliament, the independent CEPS Board, the boards of Value Added Tax Directorate (VAT), and the Internal Revenue Service (IRS) were to cease operation, effective immediately. In their stead a single administrative board overseeing all three revenue agencies was to be established. Attesting to the endurance of older state institutions despite their formal nullification in the wake of larger projects of political reform—a type of shadow statehood (cf. Reno 1998) —while the VAT and IRS boards were disbanded, the CEPS board was not. In January 2001, just days after the new President and Parliament were sworn in, the court ruled in the AC's favor arguing that the board had no legal mandate to exist and therefore could not issue orders. Exercising notable independence, the judge found this a clear-cut case, challenging the board's assertion that it had "unfinished business" and justification for its continued authority and operations.

Despite the AC's victory and rapid reinstatement, the incident and attendant allegations had substantial bearing on the tenor of Customs administration at Aflao. Dramatizing the distance between officers and headquarters, there was an overall uneasiness about where the Customs "center" stood but also exactly who stood for the center: the board, the court, or the commissioner? This uncertainty was made all the more tangible when the commissioner himself was placed on involuntary leave just a few weeks after the longstanding opposition party, the National Patriotic Party (NPP), emerged as the victor of a nationwide election, replacing the NDC government under whose chairman, J. J. Rawlings, he was appointed and personally affiliated.

At Aflao all of these dynamics came together to provoke a "turning inward" in which the AC sought to buffer Aflao officers and border stations from headquarters exactions, effectively rejecting the entitlements of Customs hierarchical authority for the more base opportunities of infrastructural power (cf. Agnew 2005). This response, however, was as much about networking among Customs personnel as between Customs and the public. A key feature of the AC's move was the implementation of an administrative self-help plan. Blurring otherwise sharp distinctions in rank, the AC instituted an open-door policy, encouraging officers to come to him with their complaints and concerns, even soliciting suggestions from junior officers with longer experience at the post. In an effort to avoid sharing all but the most serious disciplinary issues with headquarters, the AC put investigatory and dispute resolution procedures in place within the post itself, relying on the collaboration between the AC and head of the Junior Staff Association (JSA). In such arrangement, if a senior officer came to AC with a concern about a subordinate, the head of JSA would be asked to hear his/her side of the story and represent them in discussion with the AC.

This strategy of administrative self-rule on the part of Aflao officers can be construed as a sort of bounding or quest for authority parallel to that of headquarters in which the accountability of frontier officers is devoted to the post. This shift found an uncanny reflection in the design of the new Charge office sketched in the preceding chapter. Boasting a grand entrance way and a long counter for customer service in the front, the offices of the AC and 2I/C were located in the back of the building facing an interior courtyard. Shielding those leading the post from public access, the new design sustained a shift in orientation from monitoring of the frontier to monitoring of the inner workings of the post itself.

Discussion

With respect to the territorial rendering of rule under the impetus of neoliberal reform, in this example we see a commissioner compelled by a neoliberal mandate of good-governance in combination with personal political ties, a strong dose of bravado, and wide-ranging legal license. In the face of these forces, Customs officers at the Aflao frontier were subject to the intense scrutiny and exactions of Customs central administration. Propelled by the rhetoric of accountability and transparency borrowed from a neoliberal playbook already well situated in public policy and discourse, the commissioner's reach at Aflao was "scaled up" in all sorts of ways: from greater presence on post, to the oversight of the minutia of dress and comportment and a rapidly rising numbers of disciplinary actions. Legitimizing and enlarging the concentration of power, these directives provide compelling evidence of the way good governance and other anticorruption initiatives—contrary to their explicit goals—both utilize and augment the authoritarian leanings of the bureaucratic apparatus. These directives also deepened the fissure already existing between Customs administrative center and border officers and installations and increased Customs' already steep hierarchy, providing little room for negotiation or power-sharing. In response, Customs officers at the Aflao frontier sought to protect their turf by cooperating across ranks and asserting a hold on concerns otherwise the purview of the head office.

These administrative dynamics set in train a certain "dis-integration" of the frontier zone with power drained from actual border agents and channeled to Customs headquarters. While Customs officers at the frontier sought to protect whatever authority remained "on post," their resulting preoccupation with internal administrative matters worked to turn them away from the day-to-day operations of the frontier. But this was not a simple siphoning of power from the border zone to a single centralized authority. Although somewhat less pronounced, these adjustments went hand in hand with a notable disintegration of Customs administrative core apparent in the uncertain distribution of authority among the Ministry of Finance, the Customs Service, and various governing boards, and further sustained by the political dispossession of the commissioner as his patrons and party fell out of electoral favor.

Case 2: Fiscal Discipline and the Paradox of Delegation

At Aflao the heightened tensions between Customs administrative center and border agents incited by neoliberal initiatives are not restricted to issues of management, comportment, or administrative style. They also very much affect the technical details of Customs operations. This is glaringly evident at Aflao's main Customs Yard, which is devoted to Customs core revenue functions: the computation and collection of various tariffs, taxes, and duties. Taking place in the Long Room or the Baggage Hall, the execution of these operations takes a markedly different form in each location, once again revealing the patchwork of governing logics within the postcolonial state. Nevertheless, within the Customs Yard as a whole, as in the realm of Customs internal administration, we see the unfolding of a contest between center and frontier. But this is less a simple struggle between Customs headquarters and Customs outposts and more one between a battery of service providers and regulatory authorities. Depleting the frontier of authority, this arrangement would intensify and complicate the hierarchies to which Aflao officers are held, altering the configuration of sovereign power, territorial and otherwise.

The Long Room

As outlined in chapter 2, Aflao's Long Room is immersed in formalized procedure and the hierarchies that come with differential power.[5] The vast 40×40-foot space is divided into separate reception and work areas by a two-foot-high wooden counter, as much a barrier to interaction between those clearing goods and Customs officials as it is a place to exchange documents and information. The main work area, in public view, is tightly filled with half a dozen or more wooden desks for junior officers involved in processing Customs claims. A bank of private offices occupied by senior and supervisory officers takes up the far side of the room, overlooking the exterior of the yard. Demonstrating the significance of the Long Room to the larger operations of the border post, until the recent building of a new Charge Office, one office was conventionally reserved for the chief collector, the Collection's second-in-command. Another is for the principal collector, the third highest of the Collection's many ranks.

At the millennium's turn, the implementation of a host of new directives focused on efficiency, professional accountability, and adherence to international standards would bring the hierarchies of the Long Room to the fore. Among them was a series of measures put in place shortly before I began my research in 2000 that targeted Customs clearing agents and received strong support from Customs officers. Clearing agents work within private businesses known as Clearing Agencies and are employed the world over by individuals and firms to oversee the submission and processing of Customs entries. The larger and busier the point of importation or export and the larger or higher the value the consignment, the greater the likelihood a Clearing Agency will be used. Clearing agents are involved, for example, in nearly every transaction at Ghana's Tema Harbor, typically geared to large-scale transactions, both import and export, and at Ghana's Kotoka International Airport's cargo sector, which focuses on high-value goods due to the expense of air freight rates. Submitting the bulk of entries at Aflao's Long Room, clearing agents here work for importers involved with the movement of bigger and more costly consignments as well as corporate transactions.

Aflao's Clearing Agencies—with names like Cargo Care, Door to Door, Silver Lane, and Supermight Shipping—form a mini-office park occupying a bank of cottages and storefronts lining the road to the frontier crossing, with the beach behind them. They are staffed or directed primarily by middle-aged men who are long-term residents or natives of Aflao. The work requires literacy in English and sometimes French as well, a basic understanding of Customs regulations, and rudimentary business skills. Work as a clearing agent is considered by many as an attractive vocation, providing the opportunity for financial gain and carrying the connotation of a white-collar professionalism. During the heyday of Ghana-Togo trade, when Togo had more to offer and Ghana was in greater need, work as a clearing agent was quite lucrative. My research assistant spoke with fondness for his youth when his father, a clearing agent, drove a Peugeot sedan, was always well dressed and provided treats for his young sons. He compared his memories to his father's current situation, facing quiet days with little business in a now-weatherbeaten office and the shell of his burned-out car permanently parked behind Customs Yard, a bitter reminder of better days. Now that profits have fallen and the competition is stiffer than in the past, as younger men with new ties and technological skills enter the profession, the work holds the promise but little of the prestige or profits of the past.

Complicating a profession already in the throes of adjustment, by the early part of 2000 Customs established a host of new requirements for clearing agents throughout the country. As a prerequisite for licensing, each agency's director and all other agents on staff would now have to register with Customs, attend Customs-sponsored seminars in Accra, and pass an examination. These policies were made known through an extensive public information campaign in the daily papers announcing new requirements and the dates and venue of the exams and seminars. Playing the politics of reputation-making, this public information campaign included the broadcasting of the agencies and agents who conformed to the new standards, and those who failed to make the grade. With the new plan in place, only registered and licensed Clearing Houses and their designated agents could represent clients to Customs authorities.[6]

Customs officers clearly felt threatened by the many clearing agents working the Long Room, with their in-depth knowledge of Customs procedures, familiarity with local economic actors and economic conditions, and a strong sense of entitlement due to their status as borderlanders (Flynn 1997; Nugent 2002). They complained that clearing agents announced tariff rates to them even before the Customs officer had finished the necessary paperwork and often refused to go through the necessary steps for their entries. One officer explained to me, "The agents will say, 'Who are you? You just came. This is the way things work here.'" His colleague concurred: "Some are so well connected that they will threaten to report you to Accra." In an effort to restrict the access of the many agents who challenged their status and expertise, Customs officers at the Long Room embraced the new agenda of credentialization imposed on them by the commissioner, posting a sign on the door stating, "NO one w/o ID tag can enter." They sought too to limit entry to those carrying out specific business only, claiming there were too many unauthorized visitors in the Long Room and questioning the wisdom of opening up Customs offices to the public.

Despite their efforts to harness the new licensing requirements and affirm an older system of ranking where Customs was clearly on top, there were other areas of administrative reform stemming from a similar push for professionalism that Customs officers at the Long Room found entirely problematic. Subverting Customs officers' expertise and necessitating their fealty to other persons and places, this applied to a set of new arrangements regarding the inspection and classification of goods and the determination of their value. This was boldly evident in the attitudes of the many junior officers in the Long Room involved in the compilation of Landing Accounts. Typical to Customs administrations around the world, the Landing Account, as discussed in chapter 3, is compiled for each transaction and contains a verbal description of the goods coming into the country drawn from documentary evidence, physical examination, and international commodity codes and records. Landing Accounts also include the consignment's value, applicable duty rates, and the amount owed and paid to Customs.

In a country such as Ghana where the government derives the bulk of revenue from Customs duties (figures average 40 percent), the terms and accuracy of product classification, tariff category and valuation make a critical difference for national coffers. Historically, the Ghana Customs Service used a list of fixed values known as Commissioner's Values. Ostensibly based on market research, Commissioner's Values were in actuality a generalized and largely outdated list containing rough estimations of the going price with select markups and markdowns serving as de facto system of import controls.[7] However, in 2000, as a condition of much coveted membership in the World Trade Organization (an organization concerned with trade and also, if we recall earlier the moniker, GATT, with tariffs), Ghana Customs had little choice but to institute a new valuation scheme based on the notion of Transaction Value (Chalfin 2006; WTO 2007).

Transaction Value, steeped in the valorization of market-based knowledge, is supposed to reflect the "price paid or payable" rather than fixed or standardized values—a distinction paralleling that between free floating or "real" versus fixed exchange rates. This "true" value is determined through documentary evidence of all the transactions surrounding a commodity's import—from manufacturer invoices, purchase orders, and receipts to records of bank transactions—rather than the Customs commissioner's decree or generalized market research. Transaction Value emerged as standard for all WTO members in the mid-1990s when GATT was transformed into the WTO. Developing nation members such as Ghana were given a five-year window to use the new mode of valuation.

Further undercutting the authority of Customs officers in the Long Room, by 2000 Ghana faced the immanent expiration of the WTO derogation and had no choice but to conform to the new regulatory order. According to the new system, records provided by importers, traders, and manufacturers were to serve as the standard of value, not state preferences or Customs professional knowledge-bank. Even more upsetting to Long Room officers' position in the established professional hierarchy, the assessment and application of the new value scheme was to take place in Accra, not in Aflao. Adding insult to injury, clearing agents, already at odds with Customs officers, were to be the vector of this displacement as it was now their duty to travel to the capital to have values computed and verified. More problematic, not just for officers at the Aflao Long Room but for Customs authority more generally, the very computation of Transaction Value in Accra was to be overseen by a private firm formed by an alliance of a Ghanaian company and multinational rather than the Ghana Customs Service outright. Indeed, the company, known as GSBV, not only made the call regarding the proper value, but also earned a 1 per-cent processing fee computed from a combination of cost, insurance, and freight (known in the import-export world as "CIF") on all transactions.

While Customs officers at the Long Room were still responsible for a preliminary document check and the inspection of goods, their authority over importers as well as clearing agents was supplanted by the newfound mandate of GSBV. Because of the delay in clearance introduced by the necessity of a trip to Accra—about seven hours drive round-trip from Aflao and difficult to accomplish in one day—Customs Officers became the target of clearing agents' as well as importers' complaints about the rising expense and bureaucratization of clearance. Officers at the Long Room faced admonishments and constraints and found themselves in-creasingly obligated to agendas and authorities beyond the localized domain of Aflao and even the Customs Service more generally. Despite the fact that Long Room officers took advantage of any opportunity to impose their authority on clearing agents and importers, their actions had little effect.

The Baggage Hall

Though the Baggage Hall shares the Long Room's overall mission of valuing and classifying goods and computing and collecting duties, an entirely different set of dynamics was set in motion here by the modali-ties of neoliberal reform. Elevating the discretionary powers of Customs officers and strengthening their ties with traders and borderlanders alike, rather than an emptying out of Customs power to render their work mere routine without the bite of rule as in the Long Room, the Baggage Hall emerged as one of the last bastions of Customs authority at Aflao.

The solidarities taking shape in the Baggage Hall are reflected in and in many ways facilitated by the much more intimate arrangements of the Hall when compared to the Long Room. Located across the Customs Yard from the Long Room in a cavernous room meant for storage, here there are no counters or divided offices, just a single looming space with four or five desks and chairs nearby for each client to sit in while working out his or her case with a Customs officer. Similarly mitigating sharp differ-ences in rank, the officer-in-charge sits within the same room. Customs operations here are concerned largely with a high volume of relatively small-scale commercial transactions—consignments greater than 20 kilo-grams in weight and less than $5,000 in value. Baggage Hall traffic, as a result, consists primarily of individual traders plying portable and easy-to-sell consumer goods: textiles, suiting materials and ready-made clothes, jewelry and shoes, baby wear, hairpieces and cosmetics, and household items.

Compared to the Long Room, Customs officers in the Baggage Hall hold substantially greater regulatory license to determine the terms of clearance. While the traders moving through the Baggage Hall are responsible for paying the 1 percent inspection fee, GSBV agents make only very occasional appearances and no trips to Accra for authorization are required due to the small size and value of most consignments. Likewise, as mentioned in chapter 2, Commissioner's Value rather than Transaction Value is still in use here. And because most purchases are informal and accompanied neither by invoice nor receipts, officers have a much freer hand over classification, valuation, and even quantification, allowing them considerable opportunity for negotiation with traders.

Despite the appearance of relative autonomy and subscription to older conventions of rule, the Baggage Hall is by no means immune from the policies and pressures of neoliberal restructuring. During my research, Customs officers here struggled to make sense of a host of new terms of tax collection coming with neoliberal reform. Tied to trade, investment, and the possibilities for accumulation, the structure of tax regimes is an abiding concern of neoliberal agendas. The reduction of duties is integral to "freeing trade" and lowering trade barriers and stands as a central plank of neoliberal tax reform, as is evident in the WTO founding Uruguay Round Agreement (WTO 1994). In lieu of indirect taxes gleaned from trade, subsidies, and price fixing, governments are expected to improve the collection of direct taxes such as income tax, bolstering revenue, and cultivating a sense of individual economic worth and accountability (Sahn 1996). Although the Government of Ghana revamped the Internal Revenue Service to mixed effect over the course of the 1990s (Durdonoo 2000; Younger 1996), the reduction of indirect taxes has proven an even more tenuous endeavor. In 2000 import duties for most items were reduced 5 percent, from 25 to 20 percent, only after much public protest and complaint.[8]

Mitigating any real effects of this rather conservative tariff reduction, after the publication of Ghana's national budget in both 2000 and 2001 Customs was made responsible for the computation and collection of a series of new taxes and fees. Providing apparent conformity with neoliberal designs in the strict realm of accounting, the real effects on pocketbooks of consumers and merchants were much more in line with the exactions of the past. At Aflao and other border stations for instance, Customs officers were required to impose a 0.5 percent Export Development and Investment Fund Levy, 0.5 percent ECOWAS Levy, 12.5 percent VAT, and 10 percent Special Tax designed to protect Ghanaian companies, along with the aforementioned 1 percent inspection fee—all in addition to the usual import duties. Adding to the frustration of Customs officials who could no longer claim they "paid" for Ghana's government, a good portion of the funds collected were no longer officially counted as Customs revenue, being the due of other state bodies and Customs a mere agent in their pursuit.

While these sorts of delegated responsibility from an accounting and administrative standpoint undercut Customs' national standing, in practice, in the Baggage Hall at least, they worked against their intended effect to provide an enlarged ground for Customs officers' influence. Specifically, because the numerous new taxes and fees placed a heavy burden on the many small-scale importers moving through the Baggage Hall, Customs officers' decisions and discretions became all the more significant to traders' livelihoods. Indeed, the negotiation of these exactions and commutations provided a basis for a newfound solidarity among Customs officers, importers, and borderlanders. Namely, as Customs officers realized that the strict application of the new duty and tax schedule would force nearly every trader to smuggle goods through the bush tax-free or give up trade entirely, a system of discounts emerged. These concessions kept traders and Customs officers in business and fueled a shared sense of resentment of those in the Ministry of Finance responsible for the new charges.

These sympathies were clear in the remarks of a senior officer with years of experience at Ghana's main frontier stations who was currently serving as the Head Officer in the Baggage Hall:

Taxes went from import and sales tax to five different charges: import duty, special tax,VAT, Ecowas levy, and the inspection fee. This is causing a lot of problems because it creates a tremendous burden for the trader and now prices are escalating as well.

His junior colleague concurred:

There is a problem with special tax (and other taxes) since they are leading to increased smuggling. The government should reduce the tax to promote legitimate trade. Importers demonstrated against the special tax, yet the higher ups are sitting down at the office. They don't know what's on the ground. We are on the ground.

Although the taxes and fees could not officially be waived, it was possible for Customs officers to employ classification codes and valuations that lightened the duty burden for a trader yet still conformed to the parameters of the law. Providing mutual benefits for Customs officer and cross-border trader, these arrangements muted the strong hierarchies typical to Customs work (cf. Blundo and Olivier de Sardan 2006, 83). For example, a woman came into the Baggage Hall with several dozen children's outfits made in Asia. Once the full duty was calculated, she realized she could not pay and started to cry. Soon enough she had worked out an arrangement with the Customs officer allowing the goods to be reclassified at a lower duty rate. The junior officer overseeing the transaction explained because the goods were of inferior quality, rather than children's apparel he would classify them as children's vests and pants (underwear), which attract a 5 percent duty, significantly less than the 20 percent duty applied to apparel. He made a point of indicating the poor quality on the Landing Account as he looked over the goods together with his supervisor. In other transactions, similar attempts were made by traders and officers alike to classify woven leather shoes as sandals, sandals as bath shoes, polo shirts as T-shirts, and the like.

In addition to taking advantage of the ambiguities of classification in order to reduce duties, officers were also prone to undercount or mismeasure goods, allowing for a couched form of misdeclaration by skipping a dozen here or there, not fully unpacking a trader's bag or carton, or using broad categories of measurement (a full arm's length instead of meter) when measuring cloth or suiting materials. Though these actions were carried out in terms of official categories and in conformity with Customs' official mandates, they were nevertheless tied to a system extralegal emolument as Customs officers expected to be tipped for their services. Officers would carefully monitor turn-taking to ensure equal distribution of benefits, garnering as little as 5,000 cedis (less than $1 at the time) to somewhat larger amounts per transaction. They could all readily gauge how much they should receive depending on volume and value of transaction. I observed one officer getting up from her desk, saying, "It's my turn," to her colleagues. As I sat with three junior officers at the Baggage Hall, they chatted casually about how much they could make in tips from each transaction: "If it's only three dozen, you can't expect more than 5,000 cedis."

The interactions between traders and Customs officers in the Baggage Hall were characterized by a distinct sociology and division of labor that cultivated and reinforced a specific sort of political order. Most of the traders coming through the Baggage Hall hailed from Kumasi and Accra or further-flung locations elsewhere in the country. Unlike those who

Figure 4.3 Customs assistants at Aflao Baggage Hall measure textiles in preparation for duty calculation. Most of the bales behind them contain similar items.

resided in Aflao's Volta region or had friends and relatives there, for traders with few local ties it was risky and difficult to tap into local smuggling networks. As a result, they were left with little choice but to run the risk of having their uncustomed goods seized en route to their destination or bringing their goods through the Customs post at Aflao.

These "far-flung" traders were not entirely alienated from local networks. Many of them were escorted to the Baggage Hall by a set of locally born "hangers-on." Described as "*goro* boys" (the Hausa word for kola nut, used throughout the region to denote a "tip") these were young men eager to tap into Aflao's commercial wealth any way they could. Many of them were literate and they might help a trader fill out the paperwork necessary for clearing goods and advise about the proper "dash" to Customs officials, all in return for a small payment. While some of these young men were dismissed by Customs officers at the Hall as "petty thieves" and swiftly booted from the premises, another set was allowed to hang about and were typically assigned specific duties by the Customs officers.

When my research assistant expressed his concern about the presence of un-uniformed men filling out paperwork, the officer confirmed that they were working for Customs as clerks, and not goro boys, explaining," "The boys have entrenched themselves here; they come here for their livelihood. Some are okay. Though they used to be goro boys, they are school leavers and we realize that they have skills." Another officer expressed his concern that "the boys are noisy and can easily capitalize on the ignorance of illiterate traders." Yet shifting from a pragmatic to a moral stance, he went on to state:

Customs tried to sack them several times but they have their economic needs. If the CEPS officers try to dismiss the boys, they bring politics into it, calling Customs "veran-dah boys" [an epithet for political stooges, borrowed from Nkrumah days]. Instead, we're trying to organize them into weekly groups. They are a nuisance. We already have porters, but on humanitarian grounds, we can allow them.

These young men were the ones given the time-consuming and physically taxing job of counting and packing and unpacking traders' wares, a few of them allowed to log information in Customs registry. Customs officers would look on from their desks, more involved with interviewing traders, consulting with colleagues, and doing the intellectual work of assessing the appropriate values and classifications to assign to a given set of goods based on their detailed knowledge of Harmonized System classifications, duty rates, and Commissioner's Values.

Though these arrangements engendered a type of sociopolitical ranking with local assistants standing above stranger-traders and Customs officers standing above the locals, they were infused with a surprising sense of inclusiveness: goro boys being incorporated into the Customs agenda, strangers being incorporated into the culture of the border, and Customs officers sharing a common ground of concern with their compatriots, strangers to the border much like themselves. Despite the ease with which these contraventions could be labeled as corrupt, as Blundo and Oliver de Sardan remind us, they indicate the infusion of Customs' official charge of ensuring civil order in terms disinterested and depersonalized with a morally based understanding of public life (2006, 46). Even the seeking out of Customs categories at once commensurate with the needs of traders, the nature of their goods, and the logics of Customs' classification and valuation reflected a possibility of parity, "blurring the boundaries between the statuses of Customs enforcers and Customs users" (a tendency Arifari [2006, 191] also notices in his francophone West African research), no matter how fleeting or poised upon power relations that are clearly unequal in the official scheme of things.

Compared to the Long Room, the Baggage Hall was much more a site of mediation and Customs officers there were active interlocutors of economic rules devised by parties beyond their control. Though, like their colleagues in the Long Room, they had to contend with policy decisions in which they had no say, the fact that they could negotiate on the spot gave the officers in the Baggage Hall more authority, not less. Indeed, the very possibility for "proximity"—from the physical layout of the hall, to the social relations forged, to approximation of more reasonable duty schemes—made the Baggage Hall a sort of refuge or relic of an imagined and increasingly unattainable reality, its possibilities renewed and memorialized at the same moment.

Discussion

Like other areas of Customs work at Aflao, the process of Customs clearance—in many ways the "bread and butter" of Customs operations— was fundamentally impacted by neoliberal policy. Altering the scope and extent of Customs authority in both spatial and instrumental terms as in the case of administrative reform, these shifts had significant bearing on the territorial dimensions of Customs' "effective" sovereignty. They took the most dramatic form in the Long Room. These changes added new levels and strict standards of oversight and brought a new system of rank in which Customs was largely disadvantaged. Customs officers faced a wide-range evacuation of power in which their functions and authority were usurped by other bodies, clearing agents included, despite the official enlargement of Customs' license to direct and discipline them. A similar sort of demotion pushing Customs officers as well as Customs expertise to the wayside, in this case both *de jure* and *de facto,* was additionally and probably most dramatically evident in the use of fee-based inspection companies, private and foreign in origin.

Through these arrangements not only did the private companies replace Customs authority at the frontier, but also they displaced it, moving the very locus of control away from the border and into Accra. Lacking a strict form of centralization and contributing to a sort of hierarchical diffusion of authority, private operations were not located at Customs headquarters, but elsewhere in the city. The private firm thus constituted a parallel form of authority alternative to that of the state, garnering international clout and resources in a manner as much entrepreneurial as political. Customs exercise of power at the Aflao Long Room was reduced to a managerial role related primarily to the examination of goods, and while it was by all means visible and tangible, it was largely ancillary.

The varied socialities expressed in the Baggage Hall versus the Long Room in the case of Aflao clearly complicate more generalized claims about the emerging parity between Customs officers and cross-border traders (pace Roitman 2005). Compared to the Cameroon example, the Ghanaian situation suggests that alliances and animosities of the borderlands are neither universal nor situation specific, but structurally circumscribed, and thereby reflective of distinct institutional missions and positioning within a wider political-administrative hierarchy. Specifically, in the case of Ghana Customs they reflect a response to efforts to share Customs' central authority with the private sector, all the while placing the day-to-day burden of reform on border officials.

In contrast to the Long Room, Customs officers operating out of the Baggage Hall confronted an alternative set of dislocations in the face of neoliberal intervention. Though significant, they are much less stark than the rearrangements of the Long Room. Rather than dividing or distancing, they allowed for the mediation or mollification of stark distinctions of rank, policy, or purview. This was apparent in the "plus ça change, plus c'est la même chose" nature of the revenue reforms adopted in the Baggage Hall. Although the inspection fee was paid by traders, inspection company personnel were rarely present. Similarly, while duties were commuted under the mandate of freeing trade, the new tax and fee schedule more than made up for the loss. Customs, likewise, was given new revenue responsibilities, but the gains were subdued by the fact the fees were for other state agencies.

The strategies devised by Customs officials at Aflao's Baggage Hall to hold these claims at bay did nevertheless affect the distribution of power in the frontier. These adjustments took the form of new relations of patronage and cooperation and harnessed the possibility of personalism offered by the spatial and transactional conventions of the Baggage Hall. In terms of the territorial dimensions of these arrangements, we see Customs officials ceding power to border residents, both cultivating the distinctiveness of the border and undermining Customs' unique claim to it. Customs officers' relations with traders also resituated their authority, stretching their affinities away from the frontier or the exclusive domain of bureaucratic authority, whether with regard to the frontier or Customs' administrative center, and into the vast public realm of the nation-state. In the Long Room we see a form of spatial and political diffusion in place, but in the case of the Baggage Hall, it is much less about hierarchy or exclusion and geared instead to the forging of horizontal ties.

Case 3: Preventive Work and the Hidden Dynamics of Demilitarization

In addition to the fixed installations clustered around the point of border-crossing, Customs officers stationed at Aflao are also invested in a wide-ranging field of operations encompassing the entire border line and extending beyond it into the southern tier of the Volta Region. In this setting, Customs' Preventive wing prevails. Like other arenas of Customs work, in Prevention, adjustments and inconsistencies are widespread and much intensified by the manifold requirements of neoliberal good governance. Indeed, through the vantage point of Preventive operations it becomes possible to take stock of the checkered history of neoliberal intervention in Ghana: the succession of strategies, compromises, and quick-fixes signifying the making of neoliberal regimes.

Preventive officers effectively constitute Customs' anticrime unit, involving themselves in the policing of unofficial border-crossings, the importation of prohibited goods, and the carriage and sale of uncustomed items—activities all falling under the broad rubric of smuggling. Nowhere are the contradictions, enlargements, and incapacitations of Customs' mandate during the neoliberal era more perceptible than with regard to the charges and ambiguities surrounding Customs Prevention.

Customs involvement in Preventive work has a long and uneven history starting with the Gold Coast Preventive Service dating back to 1897 (Anim-Asante 1988, 26). After the Customs Preventive Branch was reorganized in 1960 and its role restricted to the frontier stations only, just a few years later Preventive operations were entirely excised from Customs and handed over to the police in the form of a dedicated Border Guard Service. In 1972 with the rise of General Acheampong's military regime, the Border Guards were incorporated into the army, becoming the fourth wing of the armed forces (Nugent 2002, 249). When J. J. Rawlings, espousing his own brand of militarist populism, assumed the position of head of state in late 1979 and 1981 (both times via military coup), he took a multimodal approach to border control. Involving the army and police in addition to the Border Guards, Rawlings also enlisted the newly formed revolutionary organs—namely People's Defense Committees—in border patrol, endowing them with the specific mandate to apprehend and punish smugglers (Nugent 1991, 75).

In 1984 the Border Guards were disbanded and their personnel were absorbed into military. In line with Rawlings's populist tendencies, a new paramilitary unit, the People's Militia, came on the scene (Nugent 1991, 77). Tied to a much broader turning point in the strategies and philosophy of Rawlings's Provisional National Defense Council (PNDC) party manifest in the regime's' unexpected embrace of neoliberal directives, it was at this moment in the mid-1980s that Customs resumed the mantle of Preventive operations. This was marked by the extended, eighteen-month training of nearly 300 Customs recruits at the Kamina Army Barracks located on the outskirts of the Northern Region capital of Tamale in 1985.[9] By 1986 Preventive work was fully reinstated into the Customs program. Customs, at the same time, was converted from a mere department under the Ministry of Finance to a full-fledged "Service" and officially recognized as a state security agency (Anim-Asante 1988, 41). These shifts coincided with Rawlings's adoption of the full-plank of loans and conditionalities of the World Bank/IMF Structural Adjustment program, a move establishing Ghana as a frontrunner of neoliberal reform in Africa and worldwide (Rothchild 1991).

Customs' readoption of the Preventive mandate at this time would set in motion a number of processes, many of them neither orchestrated by nor apparent to the organizations behind the new protocols. Although inspired by the ostensibly demilitarizing and political downsizing impulses that were part of the World Bank and IMF structural adjustment package, they effectively *remilitarized* the Customs service. While Customs had long maintained a military slant in its strong and pervasive hierarchy and system of offices and ranks modeled on the army, a point officers frequently mentioned to me when explaining the Customs organization, these tendencies were given new substance. Not only were former military and paramilitary personnel brought into the Service, the Customs corps as a whole was familiarized with weaponry and military skills, and an older fashion of military style garb reintroduced to all ranks.

In short order, a dedicated training academy offering the same courses as Kamina Barracks was established in the mid-1980s at Kpetoe, 20 miles north of Aflao and 150 miles from Customs headquarters in Accra. Located in the Volta Region, considered to be Rawlings's home territory, this military-style installation was just a few miles from the oft-contentious Togo border. The establishment of a Customs academy at Kpetoe made the mastery of military maneuvers—included the handling of weaponry and drills under the instruction of current and former army officers—standard fare for all Customs trainees. The new training regimen qualified all Customs officers, not just a specialized corps, to perform Preventive work and to incorporate these outlooks and skills into any endeavor. Contributing to this possibility, Customs was now qualified and called upon to serve as a sort of National Guard in conjunction with other security agencies to provide oversight at local polling stations on election

Figure 4.4 An ex-army officer in the employ of Customs Preventive wing leads Aflao Customs officers in military-style drills.

days, help contain national emergencies, and participate in all sorts of civic ceremonies and displays. Indeed, during the 2000 elections, these activities took both a more and less public turn, with Customs officers officially dispatched to polling places around the country to guard against violence and other improper behavior, along with more furtive delegations of politically connected Customs officials to select frontier posts (Aflao included) in case of emergency.

Customs' hiring policies further reflected these militarist tendencies despite the swelling rhetoric of good governance and democratization. It is well known that Customs' 1992–93 recruitment brought large numbers of demobilized People's Militia members into the service. Once a key organ of Rawlings's revolutionary platform the militias were now an embarrassment to a waning military regime on the cusp of democratic elections. But as loyal soldiers to Rawlings's cause, numerous militia members with prior professional credentials were rewarded with lucrative bureaucratic posts, where their lack of experience was of little concern to those making the appointments.

For more promising candidates already ensconced in networks of power and patronage, a post in Customs Service offered a fast and apparently legitimate track to political influence as well as economic success in a new political era. In fact, a cadre of individuals rapidly ascended through the Service because of this background, giving them noticeable presence in the higher echelons of Customs administration and putting them at odds with those who had entered Customs on the basis of a wholly different set of qualifications.[10] We see a clear illustration of the contention that in the context of acute change or successive transition, "power brokers, bureaucrats and administrative personnel of the past," and, I would add, their clients, "are left in situ or succeed in finding less visible ways of to keep their hands on the levers of authority" (Comaroff and Comaroff 2001, 35). During my research, the tale of one ex-militia member who entered Customs as junior officer and rose to the ranks of AC in less than a decade was much discussed after he was arrested on charges (never verified) of hiding a cache of arms at his home shortly after Rawlings's NDC was voted out of office (*The Independent* 2001, 1). One of the Preventive heads at Aflao in 2001, a former military officer, was still convinced that Customs was under the army when I interviewed him, telling me "once a soldier, always a soldier," and explaining that he was a soldier "attached to Customs." Thus, while the rest of government performed to the tune of the neoliberal order, purging its militarist roots, these actors and inclinations found a new home within the Customs Service.

Here we find an interesting point of comparison between the workings of Cameroonian and Ghanaian borderlands. While the border region of Cameroon is marked by soldiers and ex-soldiers known as "douaniers-combatants" taking over the work of official Customs officials (Roitman 2005, 162), in Ghana in contrast, we see military logics claiming a greater hold on the formal organs of the state through means that are not necessarily illegal but are in many ways underhand.[11] In both cases however, we witness the wedding of violence and bureaucratization. What Roitman calls the "pluralization of regulatory authority" in the Chad Basin (2005,151), in the Ghanaian setting could be more accurately labeled "regulatory supplementation," and was considered both an opportunity and a burden by Customs officials.

Despite the pervasiveness of these influences, Aflao Customs officers' enactment of their Preventive mandate, though occasionally forceful, was equally reticent. Customs officers felt uneasy about the extent of their power and frequently mentioned their orders to "shoot to maim," not "shoot to kill," when describing the challenges of Preventive work. Equally problematic, the Preventive wing was severely underresourced and Preventive officers complained over and over again about the lack of logistics and man power. Not only did they lack proper offices (note, their makeshift perches in Acheampong's unfinished edifice discussed in chapter 3), the first of the three Preventive heads who circulated through the Aflao border post during my research stint lamented the poor state of Customs' canoes and the broken outboard motors meant to power them, making Customs little match for the seaborne smugglers moving their goods along coastal waters. Officers assigned to Preventive rounds complained about being dispatched to the bush without access to food or water where they were easy prey for snakes, mosquitoes, and smugglers, and lacking any means of transport, shelter, or companionship. One senior Preventive officer explained:

Preventive here lacks logistics. We have guns but not enough ammunition . . . only 5 rounds. It's very dangerous and we can easily be killed. The smuggling boys heard of his presence in the bush yesterday and have already changed their mode of operation. They have scouts in powerful motorbikes and bicycles. I only have access to a small red Toyota Corolla—a confiscated vehicle—to check my offices in the bush or on the beats. Preventive only has 1 Nissan pick-up and that is for the petrol task-force.

Although officers went on patrols in pairs, one's partner could be a kilometer away, far out of sight or earshot. Officers assigned to Preventive rounds all articulated a sense of being asked to undertake a task at which they were incapable and sorely at risk, and stories of being shot at by smugglers, fellow Customs officers, or even the Togo army could all be found in the national media.

Giving voice to a deep-seated fissure between the military, civil service, and professional elements within Customs, the logistical impediments to border policing were matched by many officers' growing feeling of administrative disempowerment in the aftermath of the 1986 restructuring. The move from a Customs Department to a Customs Service and a full-fledged security agency left Customs officers unable to form a union like other civil servants and therefore unable to collectively advocate for better wages and benefits. The new arrangement also left them with paltry "End of Service" benefits consisting of a scanty three months' pay despite an earlier pension option and new risks to which they were exposed in Preventive work. All of this created a situation where Customs officers were politically endowed but administratively unprotected, giving them only a limited incentive to put their power to use.

This situation was further complicated by the lingering claims of former members of the People's Militia and People's Defense Committees to border patrol. Attesting to the layers of political history informing the expression of state power highlighted in chapter 3, many of these individuals were never reassigned and continued to guard their posts long after their units were dissolved. When I toured the various "pillars and beats" defining the Ghanaian side of the frontier, these aging ex-revolutionaries could be found wearing faded and torn fatigues, sitting in battered tents. While they might share their turf with Customs officers, it was one they were considered to hold the rightful claim. Already in difficult circumstances and with few sources of protection and assistance, Customs officers were hesitant to challenge their prerogatives.

Creating a further disincentive to the forceful exercise of state power by Preventive officers at the frontier, rising rates of taxation and an overall environment of economic and agricultural decline in the Volta Region left many residents of border areas underskilled and underemployed. This, along with a growing desire for and dependence of Ghanaians on imports more generally, meant that smuggling provided one of few potential paths for gain. As a result, Custom officers were left with little capacity to stem the tide of illicit cross-border trade and were at tremendous personal risk to do. Officers could do little on their patrols but bear witness to illicit cross-border traffic. A friend in Customs described how she would sit at her guard post, much like a pillar, for show, present but not engaged, while goods were thrown over the fence in front of her. Others officers were more involved, providing a cover for smugglers and only a very occasional pursuit of transgressors.

Compared to the disablement of state power occurring at the frontier, there were different realms where Preventive officers were less encumbered by borderlanders' superior knowledge, motivations, and manpower. Notably, it was at checkpoints set up on remote stretches of road between Aflao and Accra that Customs' Preventive efforts were most effective. The best known was the Dabala checkpoint—the site of the aforementioned tussles between Customs' head office and Aflao officers over T-shirts. Here, all travelers, whatever the mode of transport, were required to alight from their vehicles and present their bodies, baggage, and documents for inspection. Anticipating these encounters, on public transport just minutes after pulling away from the Aflao lorry park, traders would organize collections to pay to officers at Dabala and other checkpoints in hope of dissuading them from serious examination.

It was always a game of chance, not knowing who would be called to pay, whose goods would be removed, who would be a target of Customs officers' exactions and interrogations. With no other means of transport and far from other authorities or local assistance, traders and travelers at the checkpoints experienced Customs authority as formidable and inescapable. Indeed, this is where Aflao's Preventive forces had the greatest

Figure 4.5 Customs Preventive officer on duty at an Aflao border pillar.

success, seizing goods—concealed and not—from vehicles and travelers of all stripes. Officers recounted how the bus coming back to post from Dabala every Friday evening would be full of goods, such as textiles and apparel, and revenue to return to the post. According to one officer familiar with the routine, at the end of each week they could easily rely on tens of millions of cedis. On an especially good week, they might return with hundreds of millions of cedis worth of goods.

The successes of Aflao Preventive staff at Dabala did not go unnoticed by Customs' central administration. Revealing the ever-present fissures within the Customs service between frontier officers and the administrative center (the uneasy alliance of hierarchical and networked or infrastructural power discussed by scholars such as Mann [1986] and Agnew [2005]), when the Customs commissioner was appointed in 1999 he did not wait long before turning his attention to the checkpoint. Notorious for his surprise visits to Customs border stations, he also organized surprise missions to check up on Aflao officers at Dabala. Preventive officers assigned to the checkpoint described with a mix of humor and resentment the commissioner's exhortations about Dabala officers' supposed "black pot" where they would hide their illicit payoffs: "Dabala is a hot spot. The commissioner was there yesterday. He just tore the place apart, very angry."

In an effort to monitor the checkpoint's activities and perhaps tap into its profits, the commissioner assigned a Task Force from headquarters to specifically work with Aflao officers at Dabala—a move that was considered an outright incursion into the Aflao Collection's domain. Shortly thereafter, headquarters launched a sting operation targeting Dabala officers. Capturing Task Force members in its net (ten were dismissed from the Service) while failing to incriminate Aflao officers, the operation backfired, but not without challenging the purview of Aflao's Preventive unit. Although the Aflao officers escaped charges or internal discipline, they were informed by headquarters that the Dabala checkpoint would be closed down.

When I queried higher-ups at headquarters about the decision, they claimed it was necessary to promote the free flow of goods along the West African coastal highway in accordance with the principles of ECOWAS, of which Ghana is a leading member. Officers at Aflao found this explanation hard to believe since checkpoints elsewhere remained in place. The closure resulted in a significant loss of revenue (official and unofficial) for Aflao and reverberations were felt throughout the border post. One officer complained, rather poetically, "on Friday evenings, the wind blows through [the now empty] bus." Now relocated and effectively demoted, Aflao's Preventive corps found themselves reassigned to the Police checkpoint at the Sagakope Bridge. Once again frustrating Aflao Preventive officers' designs, and further melding fiscal and security mandates (pace Roitman 2005), police officers at Sagakope used Customs' incursion onto their turf to make claims on Customs work, demanding documents and bribes from traders in the name of Customs, whom they claimed were somehow "under them."

Customs headquarters' efforts to assert its authority contributed to the centralization of state power through the fusing of Customs and police power and the concentration of operation on fewer sites, all in the name of liberalization and commercial freedom. Such efforts were, not surprisingly, met by a countermove among Aflao Customs officers. Although according to my sources, the Aflao officers eventually adjusted to the new arrangements with the police, the closure of Dabala proved an impetus to their investment in another form of Preventive operation. Also removed from the actual frontier, these Preventive strategies were more ambulatory in nature than the checkpoints and therefore much less available to surveillance from headquarters and the Customs commissioner. Preventive officers strayed from the checkpoint around Sagakope and tracked suspicious persons and vehicles into the surrounding rural areas and coastal enclaves. One Friday afternoon, a joyous Preventive staff returned to the post, the bus full again after a successful detection of a huge cache of uncustomed items, signaling the pursuit of a new modus operandi. My notes recall the following incident:

We waited for the officers to meet the bus at the state warehouse. The head of the Dabala stores explained that this was a seizure based on a tip-off and the value of the goods were over 107 million cedis, a substantial sum. The goods consisted of poplins, Nigerian and Asian/Levant-made curtain materials as well as imitation London wax prints. They were found hidden beyond the Sagakope Bridge, near where the ceramics are sold on the roadside.

Mr. G and a few others detailed to Dabala were out on patrols and they saw a mini-van/trotro on a small sandy road with only the driver and a few Nigerian/Malian men. When queried, the men said they were in the area to buy sheep and goats. Nearby, the CEPS officers saw several abandoned structures built from flimsy reeds. They decided to look around and asked a young man in the area to assist them. Suddenly, the man "bolted," which heightened the officers suspicions. They continued to peek inside each structure and found the cache of uncustomed goods.

Discussion

What do these shifts in Customs' Preventive operations mean for the arrangements of rule at the frontier? Triggered by the government's investment in projects of democratic reform closely aligned with neoliberal conditionalities, we see the diffusion of militarist arrangements, attitudes, and techniques into Customs operations at Aflao, to uneven effect. A result of new training procedures and a revised mandate, military tendencies—from the carrying of weapons, to the amplification of authoritarian attitudes, and identification with other security bodies—have come to infuse Customs work at Aflao. Yet for a variety of reasons—the lack of logistics, poor conditions of service, the lingering presence of earlier generation of border officials, and the imperatives of unofficial trade in a region beset by economic decline—the Customs' Preventive force at the frontier maintains a presence more passive than forceful, once again drawing attention to the distinction between border installations and the project of territorial sovereignty discussed in the previous chapter.

These dynamics are intertwined with a number of other trajectories of de- and remilitarization. On the one hand there exist coordinated networks of power tied to the higher echelons of state authority which sustain an older paramilitary order in the executive ranks of Customs—a semi-sovereign ruling clique perhaps. Alongside this paralegal authority, the work of Customs Prevention finds other modes of expression in the form of checkpoints, which are situated beyond the physical limits of the frontier. Geographically atomized, these are sites where the expression of state power is concentrated and recurrent, if often unchecked. As claims on these spaces intensify due to the pressures of centralization and concomitant creation of special units and operations by Customs headquarters, an alternative logic and locus of operation has gained renewed import for border officers: Preventive search missions.[12] Peripatetic in form and unpredictable in organization, they evade the predictions of both the public and central administration, even as they mimic them. In terms of the actual effectiveness of Customs operations, the shifting internal frontier they create appears to be more charged than the actual border. Policed by Customs but controlled by border residents, the latter operates as more and more a symbolic space. Nevertheless, at the border and the ever-expanding border zone, Customs' license to rule by force, typically benign yet never entirely at bay, lies beneath the surface, ever pernicious given its mixed motive and unmoored location.

Conclusion

Reflecting the historical underpinnings of sovereign restructuring, at the Aflao frontier Ghana's multilayered political past both inspires and confounds the neoliberal agenda of good governance. The retooling of government, initially conceived as a supplement to an original bundle of economic reforms, has come to hold equal import to those bodies drawing up and funding the neoliberal road map as well as those who follow it. Such interventions, informed by Ghana's multifaceted political inheritance and their own internal contradictions, generate a host of political "side effects" rather different from the promised outcomes. In this environment we see the neoliberal "fixation with democratization," as Comaroff and Comaroff (2001, 1) put it, not only "emptied out of meaning" but filled with a host of ancillary and historically enduring political agendas.

At Aflao, for example, the hidden authoritarian potentials of anti-corruption initiatives, part of a broader enchantment or fetishism of notions and strategies of "good governance" (Comaroff and Comaroff 2001), are magnified as they interface with Customs' already steep chain of command. In such an environment, not only do efforts to "clean up" Customs betray the continued intermingling of technocratic and highly personalized modes of rule, they foster anew the top-down spread of authority and allegation, undermining their purported aims of power-sharing or due process. Justifying the pursuit of emergency powers by the Customs commissioner and his agents, in such arrangements the potential "terror of transparency" is experienced within Customs' own ranks at the frontier and throughout the border zone. Here we see a marked resemblance to the sort of bureaucratic license at work under conditions of political emergency identified by Judith Butler (2004, 61–62), which occupies an ambiguous space between "law" and "lawlessness." Allowing for unexamined and expanding power carried out in the name of moral/political right, Customs headquarters accomplishes a form of administrative sovereignty that comes from being "below the law," that is, temporary or mere procedure, at the same time these agendas are authorized and encouraged by international bodies that stand "outside the law."

The Rawlings government's simultaneous embrace of neoliberal reform and renunciation of the country's military past worked to a similar effect to bolster the state's authoritarian potential. Although specialized paramilitary units and functions were officially excised from the state apparatus in the cause of democratization, rather than disappearing a number of these bodies and behaviors resurfaced in a new guise in Customs. Under such conditions ruling party loyalists found a place within the highest echelons of Customs to shore up the agency's internal networks of privilege, as is common in situations of rapid or successive political transition that comes with the neoliberal turn (cf. Comaroff and Comaroff 2001; Hansen and Stepputat 2001). The absorption of military personnel and outlooks also has a decentralized effect of making Preventive operations—whether military-style training, policing, the use of force, or the criminalization of economic activity—general features of

Customs work. Supplanting the more specialized "professional" aspects of Customs related to the reckoning and collection of duties, the enlargement of Customs Preventive functions both inflate and reduce Customs power.[13] Lacking resources and facing a rising tide of smuggling, Preventive officers are neither especially motivated nor proficient in the Preventive arena. Yet the very shortage of means necessary for consistent pursuit of Preventive actions gives Customs' Preventive operations a rather unpredictable presence on- and off-post.

Customs officers assigned to Aflao's Customs Yard experienced a rather different set of political dislocations and adjustments brought about by the neoliberal quest for governmental streamlining and accountability. Abiding by international agreements, Customs officers at the Long Room have little choice but to surrender their authority to the private firm contracted to verify Customs values. Similarly, Long Room officers find their authority further eclipsed by a newly professionalized cadre of clearing agents whose influence Customs' own licensing requirements had sought to curb.

Customs officers in the Baggage Hall are also forced to contend with the reduction of their authority as they too face a rising burden of obligations to other agencies and agendas in the service of fiscal efficiency. But, maintaining a hold on arcane professional knowledge and skills, officers here, unlike their colleagues in the Long Room, are better able to buffer themselves from the most onerous demands of restructuring. Working out a systematic set of compromises that appear to comply with but do not fully conform to the letter of the law, Baggage Hall officers are able to evade and appease the demands of Customs headquarters and other executive authorities within and outside of the state, whether the new tax regime or inspection and valuation requirements. Shoring up Baggage Hall officers' alliance with and dependence on borderlanders, such strategies work to foster the independence of frontier installations from the claims of Customs' central administration. Their efforts, however, do not signal a disregard of national power structures or ideals. Rather, the strategies of Baggage Hall officers are premised on a shared alliance with travelers and traders from elsewhere in the country that is in many respects nationalist in orientation. Built on common disdain for the unreasonable exactions of Customs and other executive authorities, Aflao Customs personnel use their official positions and knowledge to partake in and cultivate a form of popular sovereignty.

Shaping the means and ends of governance under the neoliberal aegis, all of these dynamics have decisive bearing on the territorial expression of sovereignty. Magnifying tensions within the state apparatus and heightening the perennial struggle between Customs' administrative center and border officials and installations, the border is increasingly rendered neither exclusively sovereign nor the exclusive locus of the state's territorial claims. Specifically, the promotion of programs and paradigms of neoliberal good governance at Aflao spur the movement of state controls away from the frontier proper as Customs officers, as well as representatives of Customs headquarters, pursue increasingly peripatetic, temporary, and emergency strategies of rule. Efforts by the Customs commissioner and others at Customs headquarters to wrest border controls away from the frontier have been met by agents' counterefforts to disassociate themselves from headquarters' grip by focusing on internal administrative matters.

These struggles make the frontier a space of increasing autonomy, but they also undermine the expression and effectiveness of the state authority here. Border officers and headquarters personnel seek new ways to secure their turf in changing times, playing "cat and mouse" with each other as much as with the members of the trading and traveling public who defy Customs injunctions. These tactics contribute to the dispersion of Customs' authority to an array of sites off the border. Whether headquarters' takeover of roadside checkpoints and commissioning of special Task Forces, or frontier officers' adoption of more mobile and temporary strategies of intervention, they render displays of force at the frontier increasingly more symbolic than actual. While Customs officials are by no means absent, in such a climate the day-to-day running of the border is more and more assimilated by border-zone communities, further undermining any overarching expression of state-based territorial authority at the border line.

In this contest between center and periphery, the attenuation of the border's status as a locus of control does not result from the simple siphoning of authority by Customs' central administration. Rather, in the context of "good governance" initiatives, it is matched by a hydralike vertical distribution of power. Working in tandem but also in tension with Customs headquarters are the impositions of new, private international and multilateral regulatory bodies and codes. These agencies are located in Ghana's administrative capital Accra, not at Customs' head office and are only minimally on-site at the nation's various frontier posts. The dispersion of central command is replicated in the uncertain distribution of authority between the Customs commissioner, the Office of the President, and various government ministries and managing boards.[14] The dissolution of a singular or explicit structure of Customs governance is further exemplified by the enduring infralegal alliances of military loyalists, creating a parallel structure of governance at frontier stations such as Aflao and within the wider apparatus of Customs. While these tendencies are not wholly new, they become particularly salient in the context of neoliberalism's explicit agenda of government accountability and reform. What is at stake here is neither a process of recentralization nor decentralization, but a mode of authoritarianism characterized by a multisited verticalization of control where there are multiple centers of authority in a networked, but unsettled relation to each other and to the frontier.

Attesting to both differences in geography and explanatory vantage point, in contrast to the Cameroonian frontier where Roitman (2005, 164) identifies the pluralization of regulatory power on the ground as both a cause and effect of political disorder, in Ghana attention to the history and configuration of the state's wider bureaucratic edifice reveals the splintering of regulatory authority at the higher echelons of Customs administration to spawn competing bodies and claims at the frontier.

From this perspective the Aflao border stands as a figuration of a complex and highly bureaucratic "distributed sovereignty." Like the zones of graduated sovereignty in Asian economic restructuring as described by Ong (1999, 2006), Aflao is a site for the interworking of a variety of regulatory agencies and fields—public, private, local, multi- and international—and the executive and bureaucratic wings of the state. But unlike the sites of special sovereignty identified by Ong, the division of labor here is characterized by overlap, uneasiness, and ambiguity rather than a clear-cut, contractually obliged distribution of authority. This is due to the fact that the frontier, in contrast to the special economic zones Ong addresses, is not a political blank slate but an old space of rule, already invested with meaning, value, and ongoing and indeed irresolvable or "undecidable" political claims.[15] What's more, the sovereignty being reassigned in the context of the neoliberal call to "good governance" is not only economic but overtly political—regarding the way the state rules over its subjects for political ends.

Thus, in any effort to "fix" the frontier (in the multiple connotations of this term), these legacies necessarily resurface and are reengaged. And although territorial expressions of sovereignty may be centered at the border, the actual territorial locus of sovereign authority is unrestricted, in contradistinction to the spatially articulated economic zones at the heart of Ong's theorization of sovereignty. Territorial sovereignty, as we see in the Ghanaian case, is not bound to the frontier. When contested, it spawns satellites and counterclaims, whether fleeting or institutionalized, outright or veiled, rendering the neat distribution of authority untenable. As subsequent chapters make clear, this is because sovereignty, existing in multiple shadowy presences—including the popular imaginary— is never fully the state's to give away.

FIVE

The Properties of Popular Sovereignty: Customs and Corruption, Cars and Democratic Discourse

"Cars! They are the most amazing product of industrial manufacturing Jomo. Is it true the word "manufacturing" is now irrevocably obsolete in English? Anyhow, I was telling you something about cars:

They attract everyone from passionate lovers of the fast life through thieves and burglars to pretty women with the least resistance to the material lure of this world.

Pensioners, social hustlers, not-made-too-good and ageing civil servants in faded, old-fashioned neck ties, drive around in them as do business tycoon, diplomats and big time thieves in impenetrable masks.

The former category of car owners have learnt to be extra careful how they drive, for you cannot help noticing that some people who drive big, gleaming expensive cars tend to be incorrigible traffic bullies who an attitude that always seems to warn the average motorist: Just you make a mistake and hit my smiling queen in the rear or front and you will sell that beat-up tin can of yours for broken bits of peanuts to pay the cab fare to court where you will hear what the police and judge have to tell you!

During the Rawlings administration, our Customs, Excise and Preventive Service seized under law, a large number of cars whose importers had failed to pay duties on them. The seized cars, I was told were being sold at relatively cheap prices to public servants. The car fever caught me then and I spent nearly a year investigating the sale of the seized cars to public servants, an assignment that took me from the CEPS headquarters to the old Publishing Corporation Yard at Tema where seized and "over aged" cars seized from importers are kept. ABUGRI 2001

Introduction: Popular Sovereignty and Mobile Property

The contradictory impact of neoliberal good governance initiatives, at once holding state agents in check and giving new legitimacy to the unbridled expression of state power, did not go unnoticed by the Ghanaian public. Providing a powerful vehicle for the articulation of popular sovereignty, rather, the refiguring of Customs under the neoliberal mantle inspired substantial public outcry. Nowhere are these contentions more evident than in the vociferous debates among private citizens and public officials surrounding the clearance and acquisition of motor vehicles. With cars the most coveted form of mobile property under Customs' command, these debates bring to the fore the grounding of popular sovereignty in the attribution of property rights.

The theorization of popular sovereignty can be traced to the political philosophers of the Enlightenment, from Thomas Hobbes and J.-J. Rousseau to John Locke, invested in the ideal of the social contract. From this perspective, a state is sovereign not because it is imposed from on high or stands outside of society but because it reflects the will of the people; that is, it is both popularly conceived and conceded (Philpott 2003). In this conception the interface of popular sovereignty and property is always doubled-edged. On the one hand, according to a classic Lockean point of view that "the reason why men enter into society is the preservation of their property," the modern sovereign stands as the prime guarantor of property claims, with the state both protecting and delimiting private rights with the consent of the public (Locke 1960). Yet the separation of the sovereign from property is equally central to the expression of popular sovereignty, whether the recognition of property holding subjects distinct from the state, or the capacity of private actors to curb state claims to public or private property forms.

As the preceding chapters demonstrate, state sovereignty has long been founded on claims to "real" or landed property, that is, the state's territorial imperative. However, state sovereignty, evidenced by Customs' command over cars and a host of other consumer items, is additionally bound to the management of mobile forms of property. This chapter uses the controversies over cars to argue that in contexts where territorial controls are in flux and neither solely nor consistently concentrated at the border line, as in Ghana, movable property is equally as important as territory to the reckoning of sovereign authority, especially its popular variant.

Once again revealing the alter-modalities of neoliberal governmental reform, at the millennium's turn Ghana's Customs Service sought to intensify its grip on the importation and ownership of motor vehicles. Triggering public outrage over the lingering influence of socialist and military-era commercial controls on Customs operations, contentions over cars emerged as central to the wider efforts of the public to reclaim the sovereign compact and determine the practical and conceptual terms of state authority. And, in a striking example of neoliberal norms being taken up by the populace even if they are subverted by the state, as we shall see, the ensuing public critique of Customs handling of vehicles utilized the ideals of the market for collective ends, at once checking state power and legitimating private accumulation.

Mobile Property and Elite Power: Pre- and Postcolonial Sumptuary Regimes

The twenty-first-century investment of the government of Ghana in monopolizing the distribution of vehicular wealth should come as little surprise. In Ghana, as in other regions of the world, elites seeking to mark power and protect privilege have long controlled the circulation of mobile consumer goods through sumptuary regulations (Bowie 1993; Earle 1994; Hunt 1996, Wilks 1993). In the region that would eventually become the nation-state of Ghana, the expansion of the Asante empire in the eighteenth and early nineteenth centuries depended on the oversight of trade and the collection of taxes and tributes through control over the circulation of the most valued forms of material wealth via an extensive and highly disciplined bureaucratic apparatus. The goods subject to ruling-class scrutiny included gold as well as a variety of foreign manufactures such as alcohol, cloth, and eventually, firearms (Wilks 1967, 214–16). Although most striking in the Akan court traditions of Ghana's central forest zone, the sourcing of sumptuary wealth and the attendant protocols surrounding their consumption and circulation also involved coastal elites of Ga, Fante, or mixed European and African ancestry (McLeod 1981, 95, 98). Attesting to the link between sumptuary might and political privilege in contexts of political economic transition, members of such groups served as conduits for most of the imported items moving inland and were thus crucial go-betweens in the assertion and containment of European political and economic influence.

The formal creation of the colonial state apparatus in the Gold Coast and its hinterland in the second half of the nineteenth century would similarly depend on the extension of imported consumer items (and/or desire for them), along with processes of commercial rationing meted out by an aspiring ruling class. Once the Gold Coast Colony was established in 1874, it was colonial officials who oversaw the terms of import consumption and circulation. Strongly mercantile in nature, colonial policies enabled the dominance of a handful of trading concerns, among them the French Compagnie Francaise de l'Afrique Occidental (CFAO) and the British United Africa Company (UAC). With these enterprises came distinctive retailing systems featuring a specific array of brands and products, from textiles and guns, to tea, soap, and bicycles.

Despite the desire to break with the colonial past which fueled the drive for self-rule in Ghana during the 1940s and 1950s (Austin 1964), at independence in 1957 many of these conventions were replicated in a new guise. However ardent the government's rejection of metropolitan dependence and intervention, the mobile commodity and the ideals of industrial manufacture and mass-marketing embodied by it remained central to nation-building and the broader state project (Anderson 1991). As Nkrumah's vision of African socialism evolved, the state continued to harness signs of the modern nationhood by way of the commodity. In contrast to an earlier focus on imported goods, although a few European-based private firms remained in place, state-run industries, state stores, state farms, and state brands and territorially confined circulation became the norm (Austen 1987, 212; Hopkins 1973, 277, 278). With a State Gold Mining Corporation, State Footwear Corporation, State Fishing Corporation, and a panoply of manufacturing enterprising (from fruit processing to corned-beef canning) (Killick 1978), these entities served as central symbols of progress and development despite the fact that many items (cars included) were never to be made in Ghana. Import restrictions were imposed and the Ghana National Trading Corporation (GNTC) was established to displace most private importers (Austen 1987, 228, 237, 250–51; Chazan 1983, 48, 166; Killick 1978, 264).[1]

Not surprisingly, given the expansion of global markets at the time and Ghanaians' longstanding cosmopolitan outlook, in the crafting of such an altermodernity the ever-mobile commodity came to serve as a prime battleground between state and society.[2] Consumers continued to cultivate access to a wide range of imported goods from the economies of the north Atlantic as well as neighboring African states. Businesspeople in turn evaded onerous exchange controls through all sorts of informal economic activity, from smuggling and black-marketeering to the sale of import licenses (Azarya and Chazan 1987).[3]

Since Ghana's turn to neoliberalism in the mid-1980s, nationalist enterprises and aspirations of a self-sustaining economic order have been all but jettisoned in favor of unfettered commercial flows, floating exchange rates, foreign investment, and the shrinkage of state services and firms (Rothchild 1991). Yet even as Ghana now crafts its modernity upon a free market, cars are among a restricted set of commodities that remain potent signs of the state. Their significance enlarging as other avenues and targets of state intervention fall by the wayside in the wake of economic reform, these mobile markers of wealth and status have emerged anew as charged sites for the renegotiation of the sovereign compact between government and the public, and thus the mutual rendering of state and society in Ghana, in late-modern times.

Cars and the Modern Nation-State in Comparative Perspective

Setting us apart from nature, the past, and each other, cars may be the technology of daily life that most makes us modern. If cloth can be taken to be the original commodity of modernity due to its pivotal role in the initiation of factory work, industrialization, and the possibilities of mass-marketing and consumption (Devries 1976; Goody 1982; Hansen 2000; Steiner 1985), cars can be considered the most enduring. Not only are cars the original "durable good," built to last, to be repaired, renewed, and eventually recycled, they may well represent the singular model or "metaphor for modernity" more generally (Thomas, Holden, and Claydon 1998, 1; Barthes 1972). The model for rationalized, industrial mass-production and assembly-line work—what economists refer to as Fordism—derives from the process of car manufacture. Cars at the same time speak to the Janus of modernity. Due to variation in makes, models, and use, cars convey the play of fashion, taste, and individual predilection equally characteristic of the modern age. Nearly as long as they have existed, cars have been stylized, incorporating and influencing the broader trends of the day. Accessorized to reflect personal needs and sensibilities, they embody and facilitate what Dilip Gaonkar (2003) identifies as the creative self-making of Baudelairian modernity.

Cars are also deeply representative of geopolitical location. Holden (1998) describes the way different car brands and design features convey distinct national values, a situation finding its roots in efforts throughout the twentieth century by states to establish national car industries as a sign of economic advancement and independence. In the making of modernity's distinctions in Africa, cars are foremost among the many commodities that force the confrontation of the industrial/nonindustrial divide. Despite the presence of automotive industry in South Africa and North Africa and the discussion of the possibility of motor-vehicle assembly in a number of African states (*Economist* 1999), automotive production is lower in Africa, particularly sub-Saharan Africa, than any other continent.[4] Thus, cars, in Ghana and most elsewhere on the continent always embody a modernity that is necessarily multiply and unevenly sited.

Attuned to these valences, Ghanaians notice cars and make much of the distinctions they represent. A friend explained to me, "Every Ghanaian who aspires to greatness is society aspires to own a car. Especially for the average Ghanaian who goes outside, his dream is to return with a car." Perhaps inspired by indigenous monarchical traditions of conspicuous consumption geared to the display of foreign wealth (Wilks 1993), Ghanaians abroad who send personal effects home almost always include cars or car parts—from dozens of tires, to motor engines and body parts, or entire vehicles—in their shipping containers. These exchanges not only enable personal aggrandizement of both the giver and the recipient but also incite "reciprocal moral duties" among those at home and abroad (Arhinful 2002, 154). If one cannot afford a new car, there are plenty of used ones in the offing as 80 percent of the cars coming into Ghana are secondhand. It is a highly profitable endeavor for European shipping firms to service the used car trade (Beuving 2004, 513; *Business Week* 2000). One informant close to the car business told me, "Some Ghanaians travel to Europe especially to bring cars down at the rate of 15–20 month and go into partnership with Europeans."[5] Arhinful asserts, "[O]ne can partly attribute the thriving secondhand car market in Ghana to the illustrious way migrants in The Netherlands and other European countries fulfill obligatory roles to relatives back home" (2002, 158).

Japan is equally the source of secondhand vehicles, a result of government policies and cultural norms encouraging residents to get rid of aging cars (Zaun and Singer 2004). It is also a common pastime of Ghanaians located in North America to supplement their incomes and status by partaking in the used-car trade, purchasing dozens of "accidented vehicles" at insurance company auctions and shipping them back to Ghana. Attesting to Africa's positioning at the crossroads of a myriad of global flows and a reminder of Ghana's shifting political and economic ties, the vehicles arriving in Ghana exhibit a range of makes and sources. A history captured in a 1970 advertisement for Moskvitch righthand drive cars offered by Volga Engineers, there are Yugoslav Ladas and East German Trabis, along with every imaginable Japanese make and model, Scandinavian brands and the usual host of American and Western European imports.

Considered damaged or "totaled" in the country of exportation, secondhand imports can be repaired by the army of high skilled and low-paid mechanics, fitters, body workers, and sprayers used to bringing back to life the detritus of the West.[6] In the capital, Accra, and other cities and towns, spare-part sellers, automotive repairs centers, and mechanics abound. Once repaired, secondhand cars are nearly equally potent markers of status as new goods, especially if they bear the mark of Benz, BMW, Audi, Citroen, or the rest. All car owners lavish care on their vehicles, giving them frequent washing and polishing and adorning the interiors with seat covers and decorations. While private vehicles may not be as graphically appointed as trucks and taxis sporting handpainted proverbs, slogans, and Christian, Islamic and indigenous iconography, they still display decals and insignia demonstrating religious persuasion, international connections, and ties to prestigious schools. Carefully cleaned and subtly adorned, the private vehicle ideally takes a form easily decipherable, with make, model, and owner affiliation clearly legible.

Acquired by civil servants, merchants, and prosperous farmers, as well as traditional leaders in the years leading up to independence (BBC 2006; Genoud 1969, 33), the position of the car as a marker of status and cosmopolitan consciousness has a long history in Ghana. Attesting to the scope of private car ownership, by the late 1950s there were Ford dealerships in five cities (where none exist now). On the advertising pages of the government-owned paper, the *Daily Graphic*, Mobil Oil could boast of "half a century of service to Ghana" and Texaco an "ultra-modern automated car-washing apparatus" at numerous locations around the capital. Cultivating forms of self-presentation borrowed from abroad, young men in Accra referred to themselves as Jaguars as did the popular Jaguar Jokers performance troupe, for whom the Jaguar marked the "quintessence of the modern imported urban dream of the fifties . . . to be fine, modern or of high class" (Collins 1994, 377). Capturing the enduring association of cars with rank and status, a well-respected academic recounted the importance of cars in making visible the social hierarchies of the University of Ghana in the 1960s and 1970s. The vice-chancellor, full professors, deans, and department chairs were known to drive, or be driven, in Mercedes-Benz 220s. Associate professors drove new Volvos of the GL140 range and senior lecturers typically owned Toyotas or Datsuns, also new. The lowest-ranking lecturers had to make due with a variety of secondhand models of no particular mark or distinction.

Not only did private citizens covet the car as the sign of wealth, status, and worldliness, in Ghana the state sought to possess the same vehicular modernity. In sharp contrast to Europe and North America where cars were initially a private possession falling outside the range of state regulation (Lavenir 2000, 130), in Africa the colonial government was the first

Figure 5.1 Mobil Oil advertisement from Ghana's *Daily Graphic* newspaper celebrating half a century of service to Ghana, 1957.

to use and bring large numbers of cars into the continent.[7] In the early decades of the twentieth century in the Gold Coast, colonial agents and administrators in the capital as well as outlying districts were often equipped with vehicles.[8] The colonial archive abounds with imagery of colonial officers and their African counterparts within or astride motorcars, an entanglement repeatedly and deliberately staged for the sake of posterity and public consumption. Recapitulating already established sumptuary codes, such an association of indigenous leadership, with the exclusive trappings of foreign power and superior mobility is evident, for instance, in the 1925 image of the Prince of Wales and the Prince of Larteh at Nsawam posed next to a new sedan (Hutchinson 2005, 324). Iliffe, a leading historian of Africa, has gone so far to suggest that the scope of transformation occurring during the colonial period can be traced through the motor car (1995). It was the vehicles of colonial officialdom and related colonial projects of road building and bridge construction that paved the way for cars in Ghanaian life and social imaginary.

As Ghanaian socialism took hold in the aftermath of independence, in the late 1950s and early 1960s the state reclaimed the vehicle as a marker of its modernizing capacity, purchasing and distributing cars to its many programs and backers. Evidence suggests, as early as 1954, for instance, that vehicles belonging to the state-owned Cocoa Purchasing Company were being used by members of the nationalist party (Blundo and Olivier de Sardan 2006, 49). With the fall of the Nkrumah in 1966 and rise of democratic and later militarist rule, the car remained a centerpiece of state power and patronage. Capturing this political moment, Kwesi Armah's celebrated novel, *The Beautyful Ones Are Not Yet Born* (1969), vividly conveys how, as the promises of the Nkrumah era crumbled, cars came to signify the abuses and attractions of state-based authority and, for the urban working class, the ever-elusive dream of material success.

In the 1980s Rawlings's Provisional National Defense Council (PNDC) government was nicknamed the "Pajero and Nissan Development Corporation." A friend in Customs explained how his interest in joining the service was piqued by a Mitsubishi Pajero that he saw an officer driving. In the 1990s Rawlings's National Democratic Congress (NDC) party is remembered for the many new pickups and campaign vehicles purchased and displayed around election time. In the 1992 elections, the government released a slew of Yugoslav Ladas, a strategy replicated and enhanced in subsequent contests. These distributions were not restricted to political patrons and very much included state agencies. Today the state continues to advertise itself through vehicular signs. Although it is now the employees of NGOs and international organizations who drive the newest and biggest vehicles, cars and trucks emblazoned with the logos of government departments, programs, and regions abound, many remnants of past regimes and initiatives. Just as the architecture of the Aflao border post described in chapter 3 conveys the enduring hold of the nation's political past, so too do these vehicles.

Customs and Cars: Vehicles of State-Making

In Ghana through most of the 1970s and into the early 1980s, cars were considered "personal effects" by the government and their private import (already made difficult by the shortage of foreign exchange [Pellow and Chazan 1986, 82]) was subject to only limited state oversight. But as neoliberal reform fell into place in the mid-1980s, and the rate and volume of car importation began to rise, there was an accompanying rise in Customs regulation. The intensification of state control of the car trade is boldly evident in the tariff and taxation schedules from this period. A glance at the duty schedules from 1986, 1994, and 1999/2000 shows the consistent and at times creeping grip of the state on car imports, contrary to the popular wisdom that market reforms inspire the free flow of commodities and the decline of state controls.

Drawing on Customs' longstanding history as a source of the upwards of 50 percent of government revenue, a situation with roots in the very earliest instantiations of colonial administration in the Gold Coast in 1839 (Anim-Asante 1988), the enlargement of Customs controls at this juncture is not entirely surprising, though it may appear to undercut the neoliberal tenet of government downsizing. Rather, the decline of government revenue streams in other areas affected by cutbacks and the growing dependence of the country on imports in the wake of protracted process of neoliberal reform in the closing decades of the twentieth century made Customs duties once again a particularly attractive source of wealth and power for the state. Indeed, revitalizing the relationship between the rise of revenue authorities and the strengthening of the state apparatus noted by Tilly (1985) for the early modern period, here we see

Table 5.1   Comparison of Customs duty and taxation rates in Ghana for passenger vehicles, 1986, 1994, 2000

Year	Size	Duty	Tax
1986	<1800cc*	—	—
	1800–2000cc	15%	10%
	>2500cc	30%	10%
1994	<1900cc	10%	—
	1900–2500cc	10%	15%
	>2500cc	25%	35%
2000	<1900cc	5%	12.5%
	1900–3000cc	10%	12.5%
	>3000cc	20%	12.5%

Source: Ghana Customs Excise and Preventive Service, 2000.
*cc = cubic centimeters

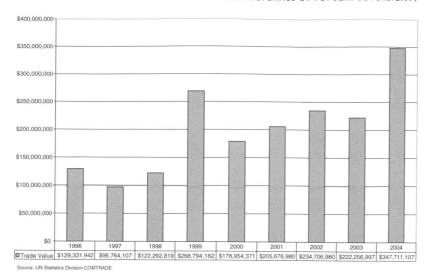

	1996	1997	1998	1999	2000	2001	2002	2003	2004
▣ Trade Value	$129,331,942	$96,764,107	$122,262,819	$268,794,162	$178,954,371	$205,676,980	$234,706,980	$222,256,997	$347,711,107

Source: UN Statistics Division-COMTRADE

Figure 5.2 Value of passenger vehicle imports to Ghana, 1996–2004.

the stirrings of a much wider neoliberal trend in which financial institutions, both public and private, claim increasing authority within and over the state apparatus (Chalfin 2006; Harvey 2005; LiPuma and Lee 2004).

In the early 1990s, after nearly two decades of deep economic decline and the virtual arrest of Ghana's once-promising trajectory as a middle-income nation, the country experienced a torrent of cultural and commercial modernization. Going hand in hand with a broader economic reopening associated with structural adjustment, Ghana found itself in the midst of its own sort of consumer *perestroika*. Suddenly there was access to CNN and Black Entertainment Television, the resumption of tourism and regular air travel, the opening of the market to all sorts of foreign-made goods, access to foreign exchange, and the movement of more and more Ghanaians overseas by dint of desire and opportunity as well as necessity (Manuh 2000). With this came a steady increase in car imports. Inspiring new roadbuilding projects that have transformed the city, by the early 1990s Accra's motorways were choked with traffic. Often acquired with the help of relatives abroad, the vehicles were both for private use and for hire. While the former reflected the renewal of bourgeoisie endowments and aspirations, the latter served as a key source of social mobility for a working class facing falling opportunities for state employment due to the privatizations and retrenchments that came with World Bank and International Monetary Fund conditionalities. Varied in both source and destination, in 1999 alone, more than 50,000 vehicles were imported into Ghana, followed by 35,000 in 2000 (*Public Agenda* 2001, 4).[9] Despite such occasional contractions, the importation of passenger vehicles has continued to rise throughout the decade, with notable surges in 1999 and 2004.[10]

The intersection of socioeconomic mobility and political-economic regulation with respect to cars finds a parallel in the sumptuary regimes of the early modern era. In the European setting governments restricted consumption of luxury items. Transcending the play of market forces and working through a combination of legal and moral prescriptions, early modern Europe sumptuary regimes protected social hierarchies through the involvement of state agents and institutions in the regulation of individual lifestyles. As in neoliberal Ghana, they targeted goods considered to a source social visibility and recognition (such as food, dress, and funeral and marriage arrangements) and focused their controls on members of the rising social classes—those persons "more" but not "most" endowed. Indicating yet another link among mobile property, sovereignty, and sumptuary rule, these legal orders were strongly protectionist in nature and typically tied to the emergence of discrete national economies and efforts to contain the entry of foreign goods (Hunt 1996, xii, 363).

Likewise, in Ghana at the close of the twentieth century, the boundaries of economic life were being rapidly renegotiated. At the turn of the millennium, a time when an established and new middle class aspired to car ownership due to falling prices, rising supply, and a renewed cosmopolitan outlook, the government asserted control over the terms of car access. Publicly justified through claims about defending of public safety and national interest, the state posed strict constraints over the type of vehicles imported and requirements of importation, with the onerous terms of Customs clearance further narrowing eligibility for car acquisition. In Ghana these restrictions did not work simply to police the boundary between elites and nonelites; they established the state as both the arbiter and subject of this divide. Because, many posts in the public service in Ghana, as elsewhere in Africa, typically come with "perks" such as cars (Blundo and Olivier de Sardan 2006, 95), government agents and agencies were endowed with the capacity to both allocate and accumulate vehicular wealth. With a double mandate exposing the tenuous standing of the ruling class in an era of transition, this project's legitimacy was to come under extensive public attack.

Figure 5.3 The object of desire. A brand-new Mercedes Benz at the port of Tema shipped to Ghana via cargo container.

Car Clearance: Sovereignty and the Paradoxes of Late Capitalist Property Regimes

In Ghana nowhere were the possibilities of car ownership and state quest to control them more evident than at the Car Park at Tema Harbor, overseen by Ghana's Customs Excise and Preventive Service. Tema, to be discussed at length in the next chapter, is Ghana's main seaport and the bulk of cars imports enter the country here. They are unloaded several hundred at a time from huge cargo ships, known as Roll-on, Roll-offs, or Ro-Ros, designed exclusively for the transshipment of motor vehicles (Beuving 2004, 235). While national law stipulates the terms of car importation—the type and age of vehicles that can enter into the country and duty rates and taxation regimes to which they are subject—it is Customs that carries out and enforces these mandates. Customs oversees the acres and acres of motor vehicles landed at the harbor and which remain there between the time of arrival and release. And it is Customs that has the authority to impose penalties upon and adjudicate challenges posed by those who contravene the government's legal directives.

Given the many meanings attached to cars within Ghana, at the harbor cars mark and mediate the interface between north and south, nation and transnation, socialism/militarism and neoliberalism, private property and public status, consumption and deindustrialization. The work and workers of Customs, in ways explicit and not, claim control of these transpositions in a contest both material and metaphorical to render the car a vehicle of a dually intimate and transcendent state. Here Customs is the state's interlocutor, at once amplifying and parasitic upon the multiple connotations of the motor vehicle. This capacity, as becomes clear below, would both bolster and undermine Custom's might.

At the harbor, through a prolonged process of clearance to which each vehicle is subject, Customs makes cars its own, turning them from private objects to the state's domain and back again. Once at the port, until a vehicle is cleared, it is separated from its legal owner and made the official property of the state. Sometimes clearance takes just a few days; in other cases, it may take weeks, months, or an eternity of years as vehicles fail to meet the requirements of importation or fall into a bureaucratic "black hole" brought about by a suspicious commercial history, doctored documentation, or simply their own allure. Whether the interval between a car's dis- and repossession is long or short, even after the legal restitution of private ownership has occurred, the imprint of the state lingers on in the body and the history of the vehicle. Representing a sovereignty that claims the priority of state dominion, the trace of the car—and the memory of its use as a platform for the playing out of a distinctive set of state capacities—likewise remain attached to the state.

In a betrayal of Ghana's socialist past, a break both recent and in many ways incomplete, the Customs Service asserts its oversight of car consumption and distribution largely through the symbolism of production. In such a setting, it is Customs officers—the workers of the state—who forge the ever-elusive tie between the specter of production and an

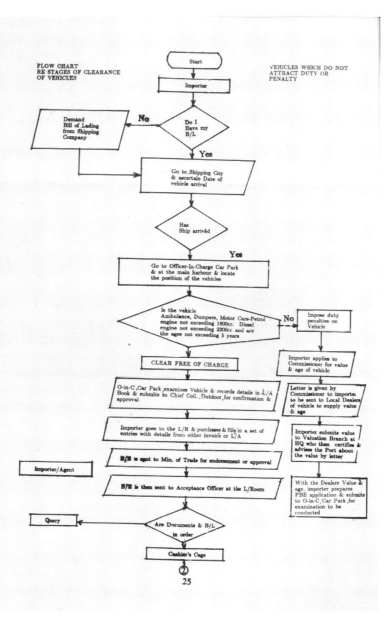

Figure 5.4 The bureaucratic labyrinth. Flow chart from 1986 Ghana Customs Guide outlining steps required for car clearance. Courtesy of Ghana Customs, Excise, and Preventive Service.

economy increasingly organized around the possibilities and limits of consumption (cf. Comaroff and Comaroff 2001, 9). A hybrid mode of commodity rule, the regulatory regimes employed by Customs betray and condense Ghana's multiplex political history at the same time they reveal the common foundations of socialism and industrial capitalism. Verdery's description of the rational of socialist governance is helpful in making sense of these tactics: "Power in this system is tied to social ownership of the means of production; enhancing the means of production so owned enhances the dominance of the political apparatus that controls them" (1991, 421). Equally relevant to the Ghanaian case, Verdery goes on to state: "[S]ocialism's central imperative is to increase the bureaucracy's capacity to allocate, [. . .] not necessarily the same as increasing the amounts to be allocated."

Demonstrating the play of this productivist logic, the rendering of cars as avatars of the state occurs through the dis- and reassembly of vehicles in the complex process of Customs clearance. Although by 2000 it had been reduced somewhat, in 1986 Customs clearance of a vehicle required forty separate steps. Simultaneously claimed and rejected, the distinctions of technological modernity embodied in the motor vehicle are a central trope of this transposition. Specifically, in the bureaucratic labyrinth that makes up the Customs controls, Customs officers recapitulate and rework cars' productive ontogeny by playing upon the schema of modern car manufacture. Giving state agents a hand in both production and allocation, this is a way in which the state carves out a relationship to the modern and transfigures it. Taussig's (1999) reading of state power through the lens of "defacement," a form of transgressive mimesis revealing the forbidden or submerged through its repetition, seems appropriate here. Deconstructing the source of the car's power only to reclaim it, this is a move at once affirming and parasitic, derogatory and enchanting.

Playing with these distinctions, the strategies of vehicular clearance are both self-aggrandizing and self-mocking. In the course of garnering revenue and commanding notice for the state, the many steps of clearance process can be regarded as a symbolic attempt by Customs to recreate an industrial past that even at the height of Ghana's socialist experiment the polity never had the means to realize. Due to the myriad conditionalities of multilateral-funded economic reform along with Ghana's inherently disadvantaged standing in the global economy, the possibility of either the private or public sector in Ghana realizing the ideals of industrial production is now ever more remote. Indeed, given their thorough-going reliance on forms of knowledge and expertise borrowed from the capitalist heartland, the very terms of Customs performances betray the impossibility of Ghana's economic autonomy. Perhaps triggered by the irrefutable force of change, here the practices of Customs clearance in relation to cars may be seen to reflect a nostalgic longing for a past that never was and a future that can never be. Deliberate in their pursuit by Customs officials, these moves are resented by a public contending with a different set of economic realities and fantasies.

Navigating Customs Bureaucratic Labyrinth

To understand the play of these intertwined logics—symbolic and material, political and economic, postsocial and neoliberal—we can look at the various steps of the clearance process which in 2000 and 2001 involved "booking," "examination," "valuation," "assessment," and "duty payment."

Prior to leaving the port, all vehicles—even brand-new ones direct from the factory—are to be examined by Customs officers. No matter what the importer or Bill of Lading states about the make or identification of the vehicle, Customs officers must compile an independent report of the car's physical and identifying features.[11] Not only must Customs officers report on the obvious attributes of the vehicle (type, make, mileage, color, two- or four-door, and the all-important cubic capacity), they are required to inspect the various components of the vehicle. Casting the totality in terms of its parts, this sort of conceptual disassembly is both a return of the vehicle to its essential elements and an assertion of the Ghanaian state's own capacity for determining the form of the whole. Examination officers look closely at components to verify the reported year of manufacture. As well, they climb under and into vehicles to ascertain the engine and chassis numbers.[12] Although such numbers are considered a vehicle's ultimate identifiers, there is the expectation that Customs officers look beyond the surface to determine if they have been tampered with, thus uncovering a history of production alternative to that claimed by the dealer or importer.

The process of car "valuation" by Customs officials at the harbor involves a similar recapitulation of a vehicle's productive history in order to both acknowledge and rework it. Valuation is central to the determination of duties, which are *ad valorem*, or value-based. For Customs, the establishment of a car's value by law begins with the determination of its cost when new, what is known in Ghana as Home Delivery Value (HDV). Tracing a car's value back to its original moment of production, asserts the state's claim on a vehicle's industrial heritage. At the same time, this convention demonstrates the state's mastery of high-modernist ideals of standardization and Customs officers' conversance with its evidentiary conventions (Riles 2006; Scott 1998; Torpey and Caplan 2001): namely, the production and decoding of documentation with the ubiquitous Customs Landing Account. The documentation entailed by car clearance, however, relies on a rather different knowledge base. Surprisingly reminiscent of Ghana's mercantilist past, it aligns the state and a decidedly corporate form of industrial capital in order to gain control over it.

Attuned to the nuances of the auto industry, officers at the car park's valuation-seat rely on copious documentary sources and details. On their desks are well-worn Blue Book guides and manufacturer, dealer, and distributor price books for nearly every make of car that enters the country, to which they refer for every car that is cleared. Standardized and widely used, these guides and the rates they receive from them have an international validity. Situating Customs knowledge and practice in a transnational space by means of a generic form, they connect Customs directly to automakers, transcending the values and relationships established by a given vehicle's owner or importer. Once the HDV of a car is established, it is subject to a series of standardized government-determined of depreciations, dependent upon on the vehicles age. In 2000 these ranged from 85 percent of HDV for vehicles between six months and one and a half years of age, to 50 percent of purchase price for vehicles between five and ten years old.

There are other clearance procedures through which Customs mimics and recasts the conventions of modern manufacture. Also related to the all-important process of valuation, many car importers, especially those bringing "accidented" vehicles into the county, seek "further depreciation" of the values initially determined by Customs. The idea here is that because of severe damage to the vehicles, the standard Customs value reflects neither the price paid nor the resale value, leading to unfair duty charges. Rather than documentary evidence, any application for "further depreciation" requires extensive inspection of the vehicle for missing and inoperable parts. It is then determined what percentage of the vehicle the lost and damaged parts represent and, with the approval of the Customs officer in charge of the harbor, the vehicle is revalued accordingly. Customs officers at the Car Park draw on these decisions to establish de facto standards of depreciation which they continually employ and refine. Here, Customs officers demonstrate their mastery of vehicle composition by developing their expertise with respect to cars' decomposition.

Of broad relevance in economic, cultural, and political life of less-industrialized locales, as the case of car clearance make clear, such a mastery of the modern through its absences opens up a space for its engagement and remaking barely imagined by those involved in the original processes of manufacture. Not just in the Car Park, all over the harbor, whenever goods are cleared, extensive consideration is given by Customs to their secondhand state. With Ghana, and Africa more generally, the receiving point of so much of the detritus of the "West," and increasingly the "East," from used clothes (Hansen 2000), to car parts, appliances, waste material, and industrial scraps, Customs officers are closely involved in the use and formulation of commensurate systems of grading and valuation. Indeed, if the modern is marked by the ongoing creation of a present (Gaonkar 2003), Customs handling of cars and other second hand goods crossing its borders, simultaneously recognizing decline and restoring value, fits firmly in this space. In the words of Gaonkar, this "license to play with form and reconfigure function according to the exigencies of the situation" is "one of the few privileges that accrues to the latecomer" on modernity's stage (21).

Sovereignty and State Seizure

These fiscal and symbolic disciplines are not the only ways cars come to be claimed by the state. The metaphoric recasting of cars as both products of the state and objects of its control operates side by side the very real possibility of confiscation. Customs has a long history of legally justified vehicle seizure. If a vehicle's documentation is not in order or is suspicious, clearance can be stopped or delayed. Likewise, any goods left at the port for more than sixty days without the payment of duty or demurrage can be confiscated by Customs. Adding to this mix, in 1998 a law banning the importation of overage vehicles, Parliamentary Enactment 552, was put in place, empowering Customs to confiscate and recycle (i.e., crush and scrap) all imported vehicles more than ten years old. Thus, by virtue of age alone, newly imported cars, whatever their condition or terms of importation, can be seized by the state. One newspaper claims that according to official records the government had confiscated 500 cars between 1998 and 2000.

Seizures are often irreversible. PNDC Law 330, the main Customs law, states in Article 93: "Any motor vehicle forfeited to the state under this law shall be disposed of by the commissioner in such a manner as the PNDC may direct" (Ghana Customs 1993). Once vehicles are seized, they are warehoused and Customs has the option to auction them if the owner fails to pay the penalties required for release. Ghanaian papers run public notices to owners of seized cars, announcing the date and location of

Figure 5.5 "Alarm Blow!" News article from the *Accra Mail* alleging Customs' role in the misallocation of vehicles. Courtesy of the *Accra Mail*.

their auction, along with information on the date of seizure, and make, model and chassis number of each car (*Daily Graphic* 2000b, 35). It is also the official prerogative of the Customs commissioner to allocate seized vehicles to state offices and functionaries. For example, a September 2000 article in the *Daily Graphic* reported on Customs impoundment of seventy vehicles. Four vehicles were auctioned, one re-exported, thirteen allocated to the Office of the President for special operations, and forty-six earmarked to the International Airport. Building on this tradition, even as late as the spring of 2001, the minister of local government called upon Customs to distribute confiscated cars to District Assemblies (Botwe 2001, 5). Allocation, a high-ranking Customs officer at the Car Park explained, was a type of selective auctioning. Cars would be given out to government offices and government employees at concessionary rates covering just the duty rate and a small "upliftment" rather than the market price of the vehicle. This after all, was about the government getting its due, not the sale of illegal or illegitimate goods.

As in the Chad Basin described by Roitman (2005, 98), in Ghana seizure was a forced mode of alienation, but whether undertaken by government officials, private individuals, or other regulatory agents, in its public announcement or enactment it was typically treated as a justifiable corrective to illegitimate or ill-gotten power. Sharing in this perspective, Customs made much of its powers of seizure, putting it to use and putting it forward in the public eye. In addition to being parked at the harbor, confiscated vehicles could be seen at select locations in downtown Accra. A sign of the state's mastery of foreign wealth and vivid evidence of its control of private property and private consumption, these vehicles were easy to spot in the parking lot of Customs headquarters, reserved for the most expensive makes and models where, a Customs public relations officer explained, they could be kept under close watch while cases are investigated (*Ghanaian Times* 2001a 9). On one afternoon in February 2001, I counted twenty vehicles crammed in the lot, mostly luxury vehicles. There was a sporty red Toyota coupe, BMWs, Audis, as well as SUVs (otherwise rare in Ghana because of their high cubic capacity and accompanying high duty rates), including a Jeep Grand Cherokee, two Land Cruisers, a Range Rover, Isuzu Trooper, and nearly a dozen Mercedes Benz sedans.

At the same time these vehicles were a clear testament to Customs' unbridled power, Customs presented these confiscations in moral terms and itself as moral overseer, articulating the same sort of moral justifications regarding the protection of individuals and society at large common to classic sumptuary regimes (Greenfield 1918, 86; Hunt 1996, 41). Playing up an idea of public good, whenever cars were distributed to state bodies, there would be a flurry of articles and announcements, as if suggesting that putting stolen or otherwise suspicious vehicles in the public domain would cleanse them of their moral taint. Seizures themselves were presented as a sort of moral rescue, attesting to the ability of Customs officers to see through the machinations of even the wiliest car smugglers. Comments like these were common: "a highly placed source at Customs HQ said . . . almost all the vehicles had had their chassis numbers tampered with and explained that the dealers have a very ingenious way of removing the old chassis and replacing them with new ones, which they weld onto the engines" (Donkor 2000, 32). Ostensibly contributing to the improvement of citizens' standard of living, the ten-year rule was presented as a way to protect the public from the influx of shoddy goods, never mind the advanced age of the cars already on the road.

All of this was posed as a necessary and reputable aspect of modern governance. Just as the power of the state to tax and regulate was renewed as liberalization proceeded, so too was the Customs mandate to seize private cars enlarged—along with its moral exhortation. Indeed, the renewal and legitimation of Customs vehicle seizures was tied to Ghana's status as a paragon of neoliberal virtue. By the end of the 1990s, after more than a decade of political and economic reform, Ghana was recognized worldwide as a stable democracy showing steady, if incremental, signs of economic growth. It had performed well as an international citizen, join-ing organizations like the WTO, and was an active and visible presence in the UN through its country man Kofi Annan and participation in a host of peacekeeping exercises. It had cozy relationship with world powers like the United States and the United Kingdom and was a signatory to many bilateral accords, a feat matched by few other African states.

One outcome of this was the active inclusion and participation of Ghana—through Customs—in a number of international and multilat-eral networks focused on stemming international crime: Interpol, CITES, the World Customs Organization, and numerous initiatives of the U.S. Customs Service (Chalfin 2003). As the spotlight on African participation in illicit trade and transit grew—including the laundering of stolen ve-hicles from Europe and North America—Ghana was enlisted in the fight against it (Akyeampong 2005; Duodu 2000, 1). Carrying out this charge, by the end of 1999 alone, over 100 vehicles suspected of being stolen were seized by Customs. Buffered from formal state sanction and free to act with impunity, here the case of Customs holds much in common with what Blundo and Olivier de Sardan (2006, 57, 72) identify as the tendency of large-scale aid interventions to create privileged bureaucratic enclaves increasingly separate from other state bodies.

Couched in the language of international crime-fighting, Customs' oversight of car circulation could now be posed as a symbol of moral responsibility, not just to the nation, but to the entire world. Justified through the political discourse of transparency and accountability, like the violent intrusions of the Custom commissioner described in the pre-vious chapter (West and Sanders 2003), this move was dually ideological and institutional. An odd convergence of older forms "state moralizing" (Ferguson 1993, 83) that came with ideologies of African socialism with the logics of neoliberalism, it legitimized anew what was already com-mon operating procedure by posing the rule of law as morally superior to the abuses of the market.

Popular Discourse and the Moralities Neoliberal Modernity

Despite the imprimatur of the international community, Customs' ve-hicle seizures emerged as source of heated public debate as Ghana's 2000 presidential and party elections drew near. Taken as a sign of corruption, patronage, and the squelching of individual rights, the issue of car seizure and reallocation remained a source of acrimony well after the election's close. Customs was once again tagged as a prime culprit in the commission of corrupt acts and a prime target of the new government's cleanup exercise. The third of three consecutive democratic elections, the 2000 race was a watershed event. Jerry Rawlings, after twenty years as head of state and two terms as president, was constitutionally barred from returning to power, guaranteeing regime change of a sort, whether a new player at the helm of the incumbent National Democratic Congress (NDC) or a whole new party in power. The result was victory for the New Patriotic Party (NPP), the longstanding opposition party, and its presidential candidate, John Kufuor.[13]

While the Central African road bandits interviewed by Roitman (2005, 98) explained their role in the seizure of both state and private property in terms of their aspirations for socioeconomic assimilation, a converse set of motives were in play in Ghana.[14] Here, state officials involved in questionable practices of car allocation were much more inspired by the quest to maintain sociopolitical distinction in times of radical political transition. As parties, players, and publics jockeyed for position, Customs' handling of cars was treated as an index of the character of the NDC government as a whole, defended by some and attacked by others. Caught in a contest for ideological supremacy taking place on the national stage through news articles and letters to the editor, radio talk shows and public conversations, cars became the object of a new sort of moral rendering and their disposition, the prime indicator of the moral failings and moral restoration of government more generally. Revolving around the ambiguous status of cars as both public and private property, this debate once again engaged the proper relationship between the morality of the state and the morality of the market. Recapitulating earlier anticorruption agendas also gaining force at moments of acute political transition—Nkrumah's disheartening fall in 1966 and Rawlings's stunning rise in 1979, among others (Jeffries 1989; Nugent 1995; Rathbone 1978)—in the leadup and aftermath of the 2000 elections, these concerns were articulated in distinctly neoliberal terms bound up with notions of wealth, individual achievement, and the inherent justness of the market.

Debates about the moral connotations of material wealth and accumulation are widespread in Ghana, as elsewhere (Martin 2002). At the heart of Pentecostal and Charismatic Christian worship in the early twenty-first century (Gifford 2004; Meyer 2004a), concerns about material gain, especially the acquisition of global markers of material success—a job, house, car, durable goods, and fashionable dress—are an essential element of sermon, prayer, and prophetic leadership in urban Ghana. While earlier rhetoric expressed a more protestant outlook in which commodities, especially imported goods, need to be cleansed of moral taint, this belief has been supplanted by a religiosity in which the deliberate cultivation and proud public display of material entitlement is the norm (Meyer 1999; Parry and Bloch 1989; Shipton 1989). A theology evident in the name of one of the largest and fastest churches of this creed, Winner's Chapel, material wealth is considered a sign of moral righteousness, not moral risk (Gifford 2004; van der Haak 2003). In Winner's and similar denominations, cars are a central symbol of spiritual attainment, as evidenced in the extravagant cars driven owned by church leaders and in the case of one prophetic church, "Victory Bible Church International," a logo graphically combining the insignia of Benz and Cadillac, with a "V" at the center (2006).[15]

In relation to these trends, the discourse regarding car ownership and the terms of state regulation and allocation is notable as much for its context as for its content. Rather than individuals using the exclusive forum of the church to cultivate their private eligibility for wealth through their personal relationship to the divine, individuals are using the public media of radio and print journalism to debate the eligibility of state bodies and agents for material gain. Here we have a public setting, a public conversation, and public target in which the collective is the arbiter of moral order. Articulated through a discourse focused on monetary value, individual work, and private property, these debates map the public sphere in distinctively neoliberal terms.

The public discourse surrounding cars in the press, like the portrayal of Pentecostalism in popular commercial video (Meyer 2004b) and televised church services also current in Ghana, involves the mass-mediation of a moral universe. In these debates, like others, the press promoted itself as a "moral 'watchdog' over the activities of the state" (Hasty 2005a, 108). If the instantaneously replicable and broadcast images of TV and the neo-real fantasy space of Ghanaian popular video (Dogbe 2003) derive from the technologies of the late- or postmodern moment, the print journalism central to the debates surrounding cars in Ghana represents both the endurance and versatility of an earlier invocation of modernity closely associated with the production of national imaginaries (Anderson 1991; Hasty 2005a, 2005b).

In this communicative mode, the contentions leveled against Customs and the state more generally regarding the handling of cars began to surface in the fall of 2000 when a spate of letters from private citizens and a corresponding set of investigatory articles and official responses from state agents and institutions were published in the Ghanaian papers. The letters, mostly, took the form of pleas to the Customs commissioner or other high-ranking state officials to return seized cars to rightful owners. In the letters, the removal of cars from the public domain and their return to private objects is presented as essential to the restoration of private personhood and the recapture of one's productive and reproductive efforts. These texts likewise equate the recognition of claims to property with accountability. This mixture of messages is evident in a letter of September 25, 2000, published ini the *Daily Graphic*, entitled "Where is car number GR 1466 J, CEPS?" which begins:

I am 45 years old and one time a civil servant. I strived seriously contributing money out of my labour and bought a Mercedes Benz car with registration number GR 1466 J from one Mr. Kwabena Ofori, a car dealer.

It subsequently turned out that the said car was seized by CEPS with the reason that duty on the car had not been paid.

I co-operated with the investigation of the CEPS officials and did not hesitate when they requested that I help in getting the car dealer arrested. The car dealer was subsequently arrested and sent to the Kotobabi Police Station from where he was handed over to the CEPS Head Office. Surprisingly, the Kwabena Ofori was set free without the duty being paid to the state, yet CEPS detained the car I duly bought with my hard earned money.

I am as a last resort appealing to the Office of the President through your medium to help me retrieve my money or car while Kwabena Ofori is made to pay the necessary duty to the state. What kind of society is this? How can someone be made to suffer like this for two whole years without justifiable course.

John Essandoh
PO Box 8301
Accra-North

A few weeks later, this controversy stirred again as another allegation of misappropriation by Customs made it to the press. In this case, two vehicles shipped by a Ghanaian resident in the United States were seized at Tema Harbor when the clearing agent attempted to remove them from the port without paying duty. The case was taken to court by Customs and the judge ruled in favor of the defense, asserting that the car owner did not conspire with the clearing agent to smuggle the car into the country. Although the complainant was willing to pay duties as ordered by the court, the Customs commissioner himself pursued a second court case against her; and when that was dropped, the car was still not made available. Painting Customs as legal wrongdoer and the source of personal harm impeding the realization of economic and social self-hood, the owner "pleaded with the CEPS boss to release her vehicles because she has been in the country for nine months, saying all her money was finished and she had left her three children in the United States" (Lartey 2000, 12).

When the election was over and the NPP, the longstanding opposition party, was determined victorious, the controversies already swirling around Customs and cars became the centerpiece of widespread public debate. Here, allegations of misrule, corruption, and decadence were collapsed, and the moral superiority of the new leadership was painted in the starkest terms. At the crux of these political *cum* moral deliberations was the issue of whether outgoing ministers of Parliament and ministers of state could retain the cars allocated to them while in office. A practice in place for years and considered "end of employment benefits," outgoing officials were typically allowed to purchase the vehicles used on the job at discount rates or take home cars they had purchased while in office at low cost through government concessions and loans, enabling them to maintain the distinctions of rank despite their resumption of civilian status.

Because a whole regime had fallen out of power, not just a few retirements or failed bids for re-election, and hundreds of persons were eager to secure the spoils of office before they were entirely out of reach, this became a controversy of epic proportion. Once it was revealed that cars has been hastily allocated by the outgoing administration at values far below the market rate by the outgoing president's chief of staff, Ato Dadzie, the matter came to a head (Allotey 2001, 6). Abetted by earlier scandals about cars and Customs, these claims gained new taint when it was alleged that a large number of the allocated vehicles had recently come from Customs itself (*Accra Mail* 2001a, 3; *Crusading Guide* 2001, 4; Plange 2001, 1). Whether stolen, under investigation, or pending restitution, they were already surrounded by suspicion and thus gave an added air of criminality to the allocation scandal. No longer simply a debate about end-of-service benefits, the state was graphically tagged as a purveyor of stolen and smuggled goods with total disregard for the common citizen or the market (Duodu 2001). Supporting such an indictment, one letter writer remarked (Adjei-Bediako 2001, 2):

If the action of . . . all those who bought those expensive vehicles from CEPS at those ridiculously low prices does not amount to stealing then what is it? Well, if it does not amount to stealing at least, it amounts to cheating and what is cheating? . . . [W]ith our newly won "freedom and justice" we can stand at the top of the roof and should that all those who bought vehicles from CEPS at those ridiculously low prices are nothing but THIEVES.

Much like a crime watch or police log, newspapers published lists several pages long containing row after row of names of hundreds of persons alleged to have received these vehicles, followed by descriptions of the vehicle type, chassis number, year of manufacture, and amount paid by the recipient (*Dispatch* 2001, 5; *Daily Graphic* 2001a, 9). In some of these accounts it was assumed that the vast discrepancy between the market price and discretionary values was obvious to all; in others the dollar and cedi amount with accompanying discussion of vehicle specifications were detailed. In an "outing" campaign reminiscent of the allegations made against friends and officials of the reigning regime when Rawlings first came to power in the late 1970s, the rosters revealed the names not only of government officials but also of private citizens who had been recipients (wittingly or not) of the state's now-suspect largesse.

Reflecting a sort of calculus or calculability of moral standing, in the lists of car recipients there was a tacit system of ranking at play in which the scope of wrongdoing could be gauged by the individual's position in government, the extent of the discount he/she received in purchasing the allocated vehicle, and the luxury value of the car. Government officials and party leaders who found themselves the recipients of four-wheel-drive SUVs, brand new Passats (a very fashionable car in Ghana at the time), expensive BMWs and Audis were singled out by the press (Coomson 2001, 1; A. A. Yeboah 2001, 8). For these individuals, the possession of the seized/resold vehicles was taken as sign of greed, duplicity, and illegal trafficking in state property. One MP, it was reported, after being sold an Audi seized by Customs, even after he was physically confronted by the owner in the parking lot of Parliament House, refused to give up the car, offering only to pay a feeble sum (*Chronicle* 2001, 1).

Capturing the attention and imagination of the public and pursued by members of the new government with the aid of the press, this was a political crusade in which transparency (by means of numbers, documents, and technical detail) was both the prime weapon. Along with the lists of car prices and recipients, a slew of official documents was made public by both the proponents and detractors of the outgoing administration. Through eyewitness accounts (of who was driving a car and where it was parked, for instance), surprise interrogations of suspects by journalists, and the collection of supposedly factual evidence (the original price of a vehicle, the exact moment a car disappeared from the Customs yard), the press continually sought to demonstrate its capacity to see through the claims of the past regime and thus discern a higher truth. Government records were combed for discrepancy and inaccuracy.

In the discrediting of the old regime as a source of danger and dishonesty, it is possible to discern the strains not only of a quasi-religious moralizing but also of the popular Pentecostal ideal of "making a complete breaking with the past" (Meyer 1998b). Whatever side one was on, the press made much of the personal risk and lawlessness that resulted from the misuse of power, property, and information by government agents. One article describing how the unauthorized disclosure of the name and address of car recipients by errant Customs officers to the original owners of the cars seized and sold by Customs, led to the "invasion of homes [. . .] and issuing out all manner of threats [. . .] rather than [the] petitioning of CEPS or going to court to challenge any wrongful action" (*Daily Guide* 2001, 1). Lifting the many veils of old power in this way, the new government and its adherents in the press were posed as seer and savior, protecting the public and rescuing the state from itself.

Rather than only looking at this debate in terms of the arguments of the opposing sides, it seems more helpful to consider their common themes. Despite the apparent differences, they reveal a convergent rhetoric centered on notions of the private subject and market value. Cultivating an ideal of the private self, one official, much like the earlier letters from car importers, defending his suspicious acquisition of a vehicle by referring to it as a "family heirloom" used by his wife for her business, which he intended to keep "in the family" (*Chronicle* 2001, 4). A detractor replied in similarly personal terms, mentioning the "Ghanaians abroad who work night and day in the cold to get money to buy such vehicles" (Adjei-Bediako 2001, 2). For every allegation made against specific individuals in the old regime, whether their power or status was great or small, there was frequently a rejoinder recounting their personal course of action or inaction absolving them of the charge (Amissah 2001; A. A. Yeboah 2001). In one case, a high-placed ambassador responded to accusation, that although the offer of an Audi V8 was indeed made, "I found the vehicle too grand for my modest personal purposes" (Amissah, 2001, 3).

Likewise, the notion of market value was invoked by those on both sides. As much as the question of allocation, the gravity of the whole car fiasco revolved around the price paid for vehicles (Allotey 2001, 6). On these grounds, there were suggestions that the outgoing chief of staff be prosecuted for "falsification of figures" and "acts to sabotage the economy of Ghana." after he had drastically reduced the values that were initially proffered by the official government valuer (Biney 2001, 1), eventually selling 1999 Passats for not much more than $1,000, a 1998 BMW for $3,500, a 1997 Benz for $2,500, and the like. At the same time, the resolution of the conflict rested on the very same terms. Eventually an agreement was brokered where officials would be charged for the cars on the basis of market value (Biney 2001, 1; Orhin 2001), to which both VAT and duty would be added. Any individuals who were unable to afford these prices were asked to return the vehicles or refrain from purchase. Seen to have the power to cleanse or somehow erase the history of questionable goods, for the new government the market was the restorer of moral order. Yet, caught in the same framing of material success as those they criticized, the press made no bones about emphasizing the reduced standing of officials who could not pay the adjusted real prices, running bold headlines reading, "Government Retrieves Cars: Ex-officials can't pay new prices . . . most of them have returned their cars" (Duodu and Bouna 2001, 1).

Conclusion

These discursive conventions can be read as a stirring of a popular sovereignty exhorting the new government to abandon an older populism poised on the idea of state as protector of the public from the predations of the market and embrace a newer one based on the idea of the state as the protector of private persons and property. In laying out the conceptual grounds of popular political debate and engagement, they suggest an extensive reframing of Ghanaian political terrain grounded in the classic tropes of neoliberalism—the individual subject and market price.

But in the Ghanaian case, these valuations give voice not to the sort of amoral techno-speak of neoliberalism described by Ferguson (1993, 1999) for Zambia in the early 1990s. Rather, reflecting Ghanaians' ongoing exposure and adaptation to nearly two decades of neoliberal rhetoric, it is a deeply contextualized and highly moral discourse in which notions of good and evil, the righteous and the fallen, truth and falsity, are central. Employing a popular political language that holds much in common with the tenets of Pentecostal worship (Gifford 2004; Meyer 2004a, 2004b) the religious undertones of discussions regarding the propriety of material accumulation is evident. With the substance of these disclosures and deliberations grounded in what are taken to be inalienable truths of the modern age (persons, price and property), here we see an example of what Pels (2003, 5, 35) describes as the quintessential "enchantment of modernity," doubly hinged on "representing the nation-state to its citizens [and] constituting subjectivity through commodification," further propelled by a moral discourse borrowed from the religious realm.

The public articulation of these ideals and their contribution to the process of sovereign transformation is worthy of note. With the "consuming self" the basis of political identity in neoliberal times (Comaroff and Comaroff 2001, 15), it is not an abstract moral-discursive register that popularizes these debates but the very palpability of their articulation via the car. Long captured in literature and an array of popular cultural forms and closely associated with state authority, both colonial and postcolonial, the car is a constant yet multilayered presence in Ghanaian public life at once invoking external fields of power and the reality of transnational mobility, more localized cultural meanings and aspirations and moral values, along with a distinct history of political struggle.[16] As a result, the car, though an object of personal property and individual gain, ironically stands as a prime vehicle of popular sovereignty and public alliance undermining claims to sovereign exception pursued by political elites. In this case Harvey's contention that the assimilation of "Neoliberalism required . . . the construction of a neoliberal market based populist culture of differentiated consumerism and individual libertarianism" is well proven. But in Ghana, the triumph of the market cannot be separated from a strongly moralizing collectivist politics. In a decisively populist recasting of sumptuary rule that avoids advocating "belt-tightening" or the immorality of conspicuous wealth, the discourse of cars provides the public a shared means to discipline state actors and institutions.

This version of popular sovereignty built on the alliance of consuming citizens (see Harvey 2005, 42), though articulated in moral terms transcending the state, does not seek to undermine institutionalized rule. Rather the intersecting allegations of the press and the public malign state-based practices of consumption and preferential allocation in order promote a distinctively neoliberal version of Lockean (1960) compact-based sovereignty in which the state stands as the protector of individual wealth and gain and upholder of a moral order. This is not a political *cum* moral economy that disputes the sovereign authority of the modern state, but one that affirms it, and one in which mobile property—as much territory—is central.

Though not advocating the disappearance of the state, this sort of popular political discourse surrounding the sovereignty of commerce and consumption does however involve the critique of specific state institutions, notably Customs. In the same way that cars, as symbol of individual status and state authority, hold a charged position in negotiating the boundaries of rule, Customs emerges as a state institution caught in the cross-hairs of neoliberal reform and thus a focal point for the expression of wider paradoxes and contradictions of late-modern state-making. On the one hand, while precipitating the decline of state enterprises overall, the explosive growth of trade and a huge dependence on foreign markets and imports coming with neoliberal reform, along with the expansion of international regulatory regimes, gives Customs a much broadened arena in which to assert itself. In the resultant administrative gap, Customs is both burdened and emboldened.

Representing the contradictions of the late-neoliberal project, this outcome of neoliberal intensification sits uncomfortably with another. After two decades of economic adjustment, neoliberalism's exhortations to "get the state out of the market" is much more than an abstraction emanating from the chambers of multilateral lenders. Thoroughly assimilated by Ghanaians in a range of economic positions though debunked by state institutions and actors still holding on to the conventions of Ghana's socialist/militarist/mercantilist past, it is a mindset Customs cannot escape. Within Ghana, the marginalization of consumers already hugely disadvantaged in the world market due to high cost of transport and lack of clout in bi- and multilateral trade pacts is only intensified by the exactions of Customs applied to nearly every item consumed. For the significant proportion of Ghanaians who seek financial gain abroad as domestic employment opportunities have shrunk—many of whom participate in the car market as consumers, merchants, or financiers and are highly familiar with neoliberal rhetoric—state-imposed trade barriers are perceived as a particularly egregious relic of a bygone era. (As will be explored in chapter 7 on Ghana's international airport, the political targeting of the many expatriated Ghanaians upon whose wealth, support, and return the new regime depends [Manuh 2000], is by no means exclusive to car importation.)

For the Customs Service, the interplay of public resentment and official re-endowment has precipitated a rather audacious retrenchment. Bordering on the retrograde, Customs duties and bureaucratic requirements and intrusions with respect to cars intensified as did vehicle seizures. Played out through an idiom of production, these protocols—in surprising ways neomercantile in nature—reference older aspirations for socialist-styled state industrialization at the same time they are fundamentally dependent on a detailed understanding of multinational commerce and capital. But betraying a power more performative than permanent, these procedures pave the way for misappropriation and illegal allocation, rendering Customs even more vulnerable to attack and allegation.

The modalities of this critique are as significant as the institutional target. The discrediting of Customs and the outgoing regime more generally hinges on ideals of transparency. Closely intertwined with notions and practices of calculation and calculability, also a decisive feature of neoliberal rule (Mitchell 2002), they are key to the simulation of a sense of public witness or reckoning. Operating within this rubric, it is the supposedly factual revelations of the press—whether journalists or the corresponding public—that make evident the duplicity and malfeasance of political actors. Through such conventions, corruption and transparency emerge as paired discourses, and corruption, although tagged to private or somehow concealed acts, is strategically manufactured as a political category in the public sphere (Hasty 2005a). Joined up with the internal allegations of misrule described in chapter 4, here it is used by the public against the state as a primary idiom of sovereign might and its limits.

Emerging at a particular historical moment framed by the electoral transition of 2000 and 2001 and the double decades of structural adjustment, these optics maintain an enduring presence in the Ghanaian press and public sphere. Throughout 2004, leading up to the presidential and parliamentary election and in its aftermath in 2005, public discussions of political corruption and entitlement continued to dwell on the allocation and ownership of cars by public officials, spilling over from the press to websites and on-line chat groups (*Ghana News Agency* 2004). A measure of moral, political, and economic order moving from one regime to another, car value and consumption remain a key diagnostic of the failings of the state in Ghana as well as a motor of public monitoring of sovereign power.

Once again indicating the critical place of select bureaucratic realms in the unfolding of neoliberalism's political-economic rubric, the case of Customs and cars signals the displacement of democratic participation and election-based political transition into the arena of the market and its popular cultural representation. Here, Customs political promotion marked by its increased autonomy and international standing sits uncomfortably with the new forms of socioeconomic and sociocultural mobility afforded to the broader public by the neoliberal turn. As in the instances of reform sketched out in the chapters on Aflao, the restructuring of Ghana Customs via the debates about car circulation and consumption are shaped by the twists and turns of Ghana's recent history. When diverse strands of the neoliberal discourse and regulatory rubrics are woven together, the result is a mix of popular representation, moral rhetoric, and sovereign rule focused on the alignment of national subjects with the global markets as a way to discipline—but not advocate the disappearance of—the state. Indeed, confronting the neoliberal in fully social terms, in this popular exhortation of state sovereignty, the moral and the material share a common political register.

SIX

Technologies of Sovereignty: The Politics and Phenomenology of Privatized Rule on the Maritime Frontier

Introduction: Tema Harbor and the Frontiers of Economic Governance

In Ghana the expanded circulation of the commercial machinery of neoliberal modernity—and the ensuing renegotiation of the very terms of state sovereignty—is by no means restricted to car imports. Twenty-first-century Ghana is deeply dependent on overseas trading partners for basic manufactures and staple foods in addition to raw materials, manufacturing equipment, and an array of high-tech and luxury consumer items. A trend bucking Nkrumah's socialist-styled quest for agricultural self-sufficiency and import-substitution industrialization in the immediate postcolonial period, and the subsequent period of economic stagnation and trade decline in the 1970s and 1980s brought about by drought and the global debt crisis (Pellow and Chazan 1986), these commercial flows center on the country's main port of Tema. Located on the Atlantic Coast just twenty miles east of Accra, Tema is the country's most active and profitable commercial frontier. Attuned to the entanglement of neoliberal reform and sovereignty, this chapter takes the operations of the Customs Service at Tema Harbor as its centerpiece.

Since national independence in the mid-1950s, Tema has been transformed from a fishing harbor and fledgling industrial site to an international trade-hub accommodating global shipping lines and cargo carriers serving the entire West African coast and subregion (Chalfin 2009). Millions of tons of maritime cargo move through the port each year (see table 6.1). While the harbor's warehouse section is pervaded by the scent of cocoa beans (Ghana's main agricultural export) ready to be loaded into the holds of ships bound for Europe and eventually North America, the harbor's quays, roadways, and yards are choked with cranes, lorries, and articulator trucks loading imports of all kinds. There are consumer staples: bag upon bag of bread flour, sugar, and rice piled by the thousand for immediate evacuation to Ghana's urban centers and rural hinterlands. Ships dock en route to and from Europe, increasingly, Asia, and less often,

Table 6.1 Port of Tema cargo traffic, 2000–2006 (in thousand tonnes)

	2000	2001	2002	2003	2004	2005	2006
Imports							
Total	5,308	5,379	6,020	6,553	7,264	7,959	6,561
Liquid bulk	2,064	2,096	2,079	1,963	2,608	2,417	1,266
Dry bulk	1,576	1,289	1,258	1,139	1,202	1,052	1,120
General cargo	257	311	233	323	530	737	556
Bagged cargo	493	724	1,024	1,112	737	1,069	627
Containerized	916	958	1,425	1,997	2,185	2,683	2,990
Exports							
Total	910	931	819	536	844	1,290	1,117
Liquid bulk	291	335	248	215	356	385	152
Dry bulk	37	34	38	52	64	51	44
General cargo	162	157	159	45	59	108	122
Bagged cargo	60	53	28	42	37	40	95
Containerized	350	334	344	480	660	704	703
Total cargo	6,218	6,310	6,839	7,389	8,108	9,250	7,678

Source: Ghana Ports and Harbours Authority, World Trade Organization 2008.

Figure 6.1 Panoramic view of the updated port complex from the Ghana Ports and Harbors Authority main office, 2008. Ships, cranes, container yards, and the ports industrial zone are visible.

the Americas. With ships bearing the names of the world's major shipping lines like Maersk and Delmas, or vessels of uncertain provenance, flying the usual "flags of convenience" (Liberia, Panama, and the like) along with Ghana's tricolor "Black Star," the berths and breakwaters of the harbor witness a steady stream of maritime traffic (Chalfin 2009).[1]

Double- and triple-stacked cargo containers fill the port premises. When I began my research in 2000, Tema handled roughly 300,000 container loads annually.[2] In the face of tremendous growth, by 2006 there were over 400,000 container loads entering the ports, with projected rates for 2008 reaching the half-million container mark.[3] Unpacked, there is no end to what they may reveal: machinery, industrial inputs, construction materials, tinned and packaged foodstuffs, textiles, shoes, clothing, housewares, pharmaceuticals, and secondhand goods of every and any ilk: recycled paper, gas cookers, TVs, VCRs, computer monitors, and used apparel of all sorts. A substantial percentage of containers are devoted to personal effects sent home by Ghanaians residents either living abroad or returning. Filled with the contents of entire households, from cars to appliances, snack foods and baby toys to bathroom

Table 6.2 Ghana imports and exports, 2000–2006 (US$ million and percent)

	2000	2001	2002	2003	2004	2005	2006
Total Imports (US$ million)	2,894.9	3,171.4	3,048.8	3,211.5	3,766.2	9,021.7	5,320.0
Origin of Imports (%)							
Americas	11.5	11.9	11.4	12.3	12.0	11.6	11.8
Europe	45.8	42.6	39.1	38.0	39.5	42.0	38.1
CIS[a]	0.7	0.7	0.5	0.6	0.7	1.0	1.0
Africa	22.3	24.6	29.6	25.2	20.7	15.8	19.5
Middle East	2.9	3.6	2.0	1.9	2.3	2.5	2.6
Other	1.6	1.9	1.1	0.5	0.0	0.0	0.1
Structure of Imports (%)							
Total primary products	*39.2*	*46.0*	*41.0*	*38.2*	*30.7*	*24.0*	*29.0*
Food	12.3	17.6	18.0	16.1	13.5	12.5	13.3
Manufactures	*58.1*	*52.8*	*58.0*	*59.1*	*68.1*	*74.5*	*69.4*
Machinery	29.9	26.4	28.2	29.3	34.5	35.2	33.9
Textiles	2.2	2.3	2.0	1.8	1.7	1.9	1.9
Clothing	0.4	0.3	0.4	0.8	0.4	0.4	0.6
Other consumer goods	4.7	3.8	4.4	2.9	8.6	8.8	8.5
Total Exports (US$ million)	1,611.1	1,715.6	1,799.2	2,328.5	2,450.2	5,596.1	3,682.6
Destination of Exports (%)							
Americas	8.9	7.5	8.1	3.3	3.8	33.9	3.8
Europe	72.9	72.6	63.0	79.4	67.1	32.9	43.6
CIS	0.8	0.9	0.9	0.9	0.1	0.4	0.0
Africa	10.7	11.6	21.5	10.1	22.9	22.8	40.8
Middle East	1.1	1.1	1.2	0.5	0.7	0.7	1.0
Asia	5.2	6.2	5.1	5.4	5.1	9.3	9.6
Other	0.4	0.1	0.2	0.4	0.2	0.0	1.2

Table 6.2 (*continued*)

	2000	2001	2002	2003	2004	2005	2006
Structure of Exports (%)							
Total primary products	*52.3*	*52.6*	*47.5*	*54.6*	*49.9*	*63.7*	*46.4*
Cocoa beans	15.4	15.1	15.3	29.0	24.6	14.2	29.8
Mining	16.6	17.6	10.8	2.5	2.1	6.5	2.6
Manufactures	*6.5*	*7.3*	*11.0*	*6.5*	*23.2*	*19.7*	*20.8*
Textiles	0.8	0.5	0.4	0.4	0.1	0.1	6.3
Other consumer goods	2.3	2.9	3.6	1.8	0.8	0.7	6.6
Other	*41.3*	*40.1*	*41.5*	*38.9*	*27.0*	*16.7*	*32.8*
Gold	36.5	35.9	34.6	35.6	23.9	15.5	30.7

ᵃCommonwealth of Independent States
Source: WTO Secretariat estimates, based on data provided by the Ghanaian authorities. World Trade Organization 2008.

fixtures, some items will be used to build or refurbish second homes, others will be sold or distributed to family and friends or "dashed" to Customs officials.

The rise in commercial traffic passing through Tema's port is strongly associated with the neoliberal turn both in Ghana and worldwide. The growth of multinational firms and ease of operating across borders coming with the drop in trade and manufacturing barriers has both intensified and accelerated global commerce (Robinson 2004). More goods are now available from more places, allowing for vast variation in price and quality to meet the purchasing power of all the world's consumers. Likewise, the growth and integration of the shipping and logistics industry, facilitated by the combination of economic financialization and corporate deregulation (Palan 2003), have eased the burden of transoceanic and intercontinental trade.

Amidst these general trends, the specific escalation of trade in Ghana is a direct outcome of the obligations of external market engagement mandated by the country's international financial partners. Making the country more and more import-dependent, the suspension of nearly all state-based industrial pursuits has been a staunch conditionality of World

Figure 6.2 Customs officers inspect personal effects imported from abroad at Tema's container yard.

Bank and International Monetary Fund structural adjustment lending since the 1980s. Likewise the injunction to open markets brought about by WTO membership has led to the displacement of locally cultivated agricultural produce (including foodstuffs) in Ghanaian markets and households by externally grown and processed goods (Ghana 2001).[4] The popularization of cosmopolitanism outlooks and consumption habits, long pursued by Ghana's elites and aspiring middle class (as the case of cars in chapter 5 attests), also fuels the desire for foreign-made wares. Symptomatic of declines in government employment brought about by neoliberal austerity, these changes go hand in hand with the increasing transnationalization of the Ghanaian labor market. A dynamic generating growing access to hard currency by way of remittances, it concomitantly underwrites the purchasing and trade of imports along with the movement of persons and consumption practices across borders. Tax incentives offered to foreign firms willing to invest in Tema's harbor-side industrial "free zones" and export processing enclaves in the name of market-based growth so dear to the proponents of the neoliberal Washington Consensus further augment the scale and variety of maritime trade in Ghana (Williamson 1993).

In light of Ghana's avowal of the neoliberal turn, not only has the scope of trade at Tema shifted with the millennium's turn, so too has the governance of trade: that is, the way the movement of goods through the harbor is understood, overseen, and regulated by the authorities of the state, Customs included. This chapter then, rather than focusing solely on the commodities circulating across Tema's maritime frontier, uses the lens of Customs to explicitly consider the conditions under which they circulate and the subsequent implications for state sovereignty. Notably, the chapter hones in on two cutting-edge Customs technologies at work at Tema that put Ghana on the forefront of twenty-first-century commercial governance as a direct result of neoliberal economic restructuring. These technologies include a giant x-ray cargo-scanner and a countrywide electronic data network, both funded and managed by multinational firms.

Customs Regimes, Multinational Rule, and High-Tech Governance at Tema Harbor

The new technologies of commercial governance at work at the harbor are closely aligned with the outsourcing of Customs operations and the expanding breadth of multilateral Customs directives touched on in previous chapters. Tema, most of all, is the centerpiece for the rollout of the privatization of Customs operations in Ghana, tried here first and at a much larger scale than anywhere else in the country. Indeed, at Tema the employment of private "management contracts" for multiple aspects of Customs operations far eclipses the scope of Customs privatization nearly anywhere else on the continent and puts Tema port at the forefront of Customs reform worldwide.

Fully dependent on high-tech digital and electronic media, these developments involve the input of multinational trade logistics firms.[5] They include the formulation and hiring of a multinational conglomerate to implement in full an all-important WTO Agreement on Customs Valuation, tested on a much smaller scale and without full access to Ghana's commercial partners at other border stations. In addition to process of valuation, at Tema Harbor the crucial job of Customs inspection (i.e., the physical examination of goods) is also in the hands of a multinational inspections firm that owns and oversees the operation of a massive gamma-ray containerized cargo scanner. And finally Tema is the central to the development and operationalization of a countrywide electronic data exchange (EDI) network linking Customs to all its stakeholders in the public and private sector via a computerized interface.

While features of all of these projects are neither entirely new nor unique, Ghana's case is remarkable in its grand scale and the deliberate interlocking of various modalities of rule under the rubric of a thoroughly privatized economic development agenda. Most notably, this development marks the outsourcing of essential government functions. This sort of arrangement is not to be confused with the sale of state-owned enterprises such as factories to international commercial interests, or the privatization of those services that are necessary to the logistical operations of state, such as recordkeeping or garbage collection. Rather, it involves the transfer and transformation of those state capacities that are fundamental to the very existence of the state as a sovereign entity commanding the legitimate use of force, centralized administration, rulemaking, and exclusive territorial control. In this way, the privatized restructuring of Customs operations is in many ways akin to the increasingly common practice of states' contracting private security services through firms such as Executive Outcomes (Reno 1998).[6]

The case of Tema is particularly significant in the way the widespread multinationalization of Customs operations simultaneously compromises and shores up state power, with the one masking the other. This is a situation where the state is abrogating its exclusive territorial control—to a foreign body, no less—in order to strengthen its capacity to regulate and oversee that territory and build national legitimacy from without as well as within. As in other instances of globalization (as when central banks implement externally devised regulations regarding capital markets [Sassen 1996, 42]) or when trade ministries institute the commercial policies of other states, such as the United States Container Security Initiative (U.S. Customs 2003; Chalfin 2007), this may be considered a separation of state's rulemaking and rule-enforcing capacities.[7] Yet, unlike those other arrangements, here the state is not solely relegated to an enforcement role, surrendering its rulemaking authority to others. Instead, the state continues to make many of the rules, ceding aspects of enforcement to others. But as we shall see, the modalities of enforcement, dependent on new forms of knowledge and expertise, bear their own governmental logics not entirely in sync with pre-existing means or ends. What's more, as described in detail below, the combination of the changing materiality and mechanics of trade paired with new technologies of governance retools the very ontology and epistemes of rule: not only who governs and how they govern but what in fact is governed and what governance is deemed to be. In this way, the technopolitics of Customs privatization reorient the very premises of state power.

Surveillance and Spectacle

At Tema these dynamics are boldly evident in the case of Customs inspection. The inspection of goods like the collection of revenue (as already intimated in previous chapters) lies at the heart of Customs work worldwide. Knowing what an object "is" as a material form is integral to its classification and the application of the appropriate Customs regime, whether outright prohibition, entry restrictions, or tariff requirements. Since the 1970s Ghana had in place a dual inspection regime for overseas imports: one off-shore (at the port of embarkation) and one on-site (at the port of entry). The latter was the sole and prime purview of Ghana Customs. The former, known as Pre-Shipment Inspection or PSI, was in the hand of private concerns, namely, a specialized group of Europe-based trade logistics and security firms, with French Bureau Veritas, Swiss-based SGS, and Swiss COTECNA the leaders in the field involved.[8] In place for nearly fifty countries, mostly in developing countries in Asia, Africa, and South America, the PSI system was initially devised to reduce trade malpractice, enforce international standards of compliance, and shift the burden of proof onto exporters rather than importers.

In 2000 Ghana overturned a Pre-Shipment Inspection system to institute a process of Destination Inspection (DI) through an agreement brokered by the Ministry of Trade.[9] Destination Inspection concentrates the performance of inspections—including the operations of private firms—within Ghanaian territory. The rise of DI responds to the growth of overseas trade and consumer demand, the increasing ease of corporate consolidation and subsidization across national frontiers, and the popularization of digitially mediated communication—all features of the neoliberal turn (Robinson 2004). Ghana's Program of Destination Inspection was made the purview of a Swiss-based multinational, COTECNA, a leading PSI companies (COTECNA 2002a) involved in Customs work globally. Although the implementation of DI was just starting to materialize at the millennium's turn, COTECNA was already involved in Customs administration in fourteen different countries in Africa and South

America (COTECNA 2002b, 2002c).[10] Its Japanese partner, OMIC International, operates in fourteen Asian nations and the COTECNA-OMIC partnership is just one among a host of firms performing similar work for governments around the world.

Among the most dramatic signs of the new DI regime was the construction of a giant x-ray scanner at Tema Harbor.[11] Purchased by COTECNA for several million dollars from Heimann, a German firm, the scanner was a showpiece of the DI system. It was officially run by COTECNA's domestic subsidiary, Gateway Services Limited (GSL) with the hands-on assistance of Heimann's on-site maintenance team. After the government of Ghana opened up the contract for DI to competitive bidding in 1999, COTECNA was awarded the sole right to serve as an agent for the state in this regard. COTECNA's capture of the contract was explained by the company's chair to be a result of their offer to undertake inspection through a joint-shareholding arrangement taking the form of GSL. A hybrid corporate entity representing the ease of cross-border management and capital flows in Ghana's outward-oriented business climate, GSL is a largely privately owned multinational consortium in which COTECNA holds a 70 percent share, the Ghana Customs Service holds 10 percent, the Ports and Harbors Authority 5 percent, and a difficult-to-identify group of Ghana-based private businesses the remaining 15 percent.[12]

Through a specialized x-ray technology, the massive scanning device under COTECNA ownership, GSL management, Ghana Customs operation, and Heimann maintenance is designed to produce detailed images of the contents of fully loaded cargo containers. Bypassing the time-consuming process of physically examining goods, a job requiring the prolonged investment of time and energy by Customs officers (as already evidenced at Aflao and in the case of cars), with this new surveillance technology in place, trucks can simply drive through the scanning site, wait less than a quarter of an hour for their cargo to be scanned and the scan read, and exit the port.

Putting Ghana "on the map," so to speak, by providing a highly desired and accredited service unavailable elsewhere in the entire West African subregion, the scanner contributed to Ghana's global repositioning. The only one of its kind in Africa and one of less than a dozen worldwide at the time of inauguration in 2000, the scanner established Ghana as a new global stopping place. A testament to this fact, after merely six months in operation, governmental delegations from around the world had made their way to Tema to inspect the scanner (*Accra Mail* 2001b). In another telling sign of the country's new international profile, Ghana's scanner

Figure 6.3 Advertisement for the Heimann Cargo Scanner featuring "Port of Accra" (actually Tema), Ghana.

was showcased in Heimann's promotion of its "relocatable" technology in an image found on the company's Web site.

On the face of it, the transition from one inspection regime to another (PSI to DI) appeared smooth enough. When I attended the inauguration of the scanner in December 2000, I found myself part of an elaborate commissioning ceremony. Celebrating the power of both the Ghanaian government and the private consortia behind the scanner, the commissioning contained all the trappings of a classic rite of political incorporation in ultimate Ghanaian style (Geertz 1983; Shipley 2003). In addition to speeches and opening and closing prayers, there was perambulation. Guests were invited to witness the first truck to drive through the scanning device, walk through the scanning unit en masse, read the commemorative plaque (soon to be a radioactive holy grail), and afterwards partake in lavish refreshment. Dignitaries of all stripes attended the by-invitation-only event. There were high-ranking officials from the ministries of Trade and Finance, the Customs Service, and the Ports and Harbors Authority. GSL and COTECNA executives were also there, along with members of the Ga traditional and Tema's municipal authorities, representatives of international shipping lines, Ghana's Shippers Council, journalists, and diplomats. Ghana's outgoing Head of State, Jerry John (J. J.) Rawlings, was slated to lead the program as guest of honor.

Against the backdrop of cargo containers, guests to the scanning site were welcomed by the police department's marching band and regaled by "professional libation pourers" from the Ga House of Chiefs who were invited to consecrate the scanning site. Representing an autochthonous force as well as a spiritual authority, their presence signaled the local recognition of the scanner and its emplacement within the landscape of the surrounding Ga District.[13] This was accompanied by a spatial reorientation of the port itself, routing traffic to the new official exit point besides the scanner and a way from a long-used central gate on the other side of the harbor.[14]

The commissioning rites also effected a second and perhaps more important process of incorporation. Symbolically melding the state and the inspection firm by making visible what was already contractual, the ceremony dramatized the national government's reclamation of Customs operations through the proxy of the private company. Between the speeches of the Port Director and Minister for Trade, the chairman of COTECNA, having traveled to Ghana from Switzerland for the express purpose of attending the scanner's commissioning, shared his remarks on the new inspection system. A telling sign of the extension of power from the state to multinational capital, the significance of the COTECNA chair's presence was all the more pronounced by the President's failure to show—caught up as he was in the fury of last-minute campaigning for the impending election. Indeed, it was the COTECNA chairman who was given the honor of walking under the shelter of umbrella—typically reserved for highest-ranking officials, in the fashion of the neo-traditional Akan *durbar*, now the model for most state ceremonial (see Shipley 2003).

This spectacle and the new sort of international alliance it sought to embody was equally significant for what it did not allow to be seen or heard. Other than the Minister of Trade's reference to Customs' "image problem," conspicuously absent from the ceremony was the representation of the Customs Service. Certainly, the commissioner of Customs was in attendance, as was his public relations officer, the official Customs photographer, and a few other officers. But despite the fact that the scanner was being used for Customs work and Customs was a major shareholder in GSL, no one from the Customs Service—not even the commissioner—was invited to make any formal remarks. Drawing attention to processes of localization on the one hand and multinationalization on the other, the ceremony seamlessly glossed the simmering rift between the rank and file of the Customs bureaucracy and high-ranking officials within the national government foreshadowed in the center/periphery strains visible at Aflao.

Technologies of Surveillance: Old and New

For all the wishes and lapses gaining symbolic expression in the course of the scanner's inauguration, the ceremonial surrounding this event nevertheless put in motion a much more dramatic set of realignments whose political scope and dynamics could not be so easily orchestrated or contained.

The shift in inspection processes brought about by the new Customs regime laid bare the inherent tensions of Customs work. As discussed in chapters 4 and 5, these tensions are not just between the national and the global, but between sovereign rulers and petty bureaucrats within the nation, and regard the very substance of state power. Taking the scanner as their object, the contests and collaborations among these various parties in Ghana center on the visibility of power: both how power itself is made visible (or not) and how power makes visible knowledge about persons and things. If we compare the inspection techniques practiced by Customs prior to the installation of the scanner with the operations of the scanner itself, it becomes apparent that the two ways of "seeing" exemplified by each were bound up with particular forms of authority.

In Ghana, prior to the arrival of the scanner a good deal of customs work at Tema, like Aflao and car clearance, involved the physical examination of goods. This was so despite the required use of PSI companies by importers. Taking place off-shore and carried out by private actors with virtually no connection to the Ghanaian scene, PSI was routinely dismissed by Customs officers as an empty and specious credentialization necessitating rather than obviating Customs' checks on-site. At Tema Harbor, this required unpacking all cargo shipments. A spectacle of sorts, Customs examination was carried out in the presence of Ghana Ports and Harbor Authority's locksmith and security force, the importer's clearing agent, and often the importer, with the help of any number of casual laborers. After unpacking the container (what Customs officers refer to as "unstuffing"), a team of Customs officers count the boxes and parcels in a shipment, opening a selection of them to verify their contents, quite often taking or requesting a sample. A laborious process, it is typically performed out of doors in the harbor's container yard or else in a huge shed. A form of knowledge based on "sensual proximity" (Foucault 1979, 216), it provides Customs officers and those who witness and work with them a direct experience of the goods coming into the country. With a convention of 100 percent examination, this meant in PSI days Ghana's Customs officers came into contact with every ream of paper, second-hand bike and TV, bale of used clothes, bag of flour, and more, imported into the country. Here, objects were given a public and material presence and state power, personified.

The DI x-ray scanner, in contrast, operates according to a very different logic. Where physical examination is palpable and public, scanning is much more private and removed. It provides a form of knowledge based on enclosure rather than exposure. With scanning, a cargo container is loaded onto a truck and driven through the x-ray apparatus. An image operator in an adjoining office is the sole individual to view the contents via a computerized image. While the physical inspection may take several hours, the scanner provides nearly instantaneous knowledge. Despite the overwhelming presence and unmistakable force of the scanning technology, from the perspective of Customs officers the source of its power is nevertheless diffuse and difficult to locate due to its remote and depersonalized character. At the same time, the scope of the knowledge produced by the scanner, given the application of x-ray technology that automatically distinguishes the material composition and internal arrangement of the goods in each container scanned, is considered deeper and more intensive.

Once installed at Tema port, the scanner did not replace physical examination entirely, but it did overwhelm it. Uniform consignments of cargo, making up the bulk of imports, were sent to the scanner rather than the container yard for examination. When physical examination was used, it was reserved for personal effects and mixed consignments favored by small-scale merchants. Other than that, in the new inspection regime, physical examination was reduced to an occasional form of surveillance called upon in response to computer generated request for random inspection or at the request of scanner personnel—further distancing Customs officers from control over it.

Visions and Revisions of State Power

Signaling a debate about and a recognition of the changing character of state control at border (and thus, state sovereignty), the singular investment of Customs officers and GSL representatives in these distinct forms of inspection and the systems of power allied with them were evident in the competing views of the scanner they put forth. Here, Customs officers' contentions were as much (if not more) concerned with the *means* of Customs inspection undertaken by private operators as the structural conditions of privatization: that is, the modalities of rule as much as the source of rule.

On the most fundamental level, the debates and disagreements between Customs and GSL centered on what the scanner could in fact visualize. According to GSL's general manager, the scanner's vision was total. He asserted that the "scanner could monitor on-screen every item in a container without necessarily opening it" (*The Independent* 2001). Press releases stressed the scanner's ability to discern not only the different materials in a cargo load, but also the exact quantities—and sometimes weights—of even the smallest and most unusually shaped goods. As reported in a front-page story in Ghana's leading newspaper, according to GSL:

[T]he importer declared that his container was carrying 12,000 dozens cartons of toothbrush, when the container was scanned, it was detected that it held three times more than declared; 36,000 dozens. In another instance, the importer's declaration said he was bringing in 400 cartons each containing 10 water heaters . . . instead of the 10 water heaters in each carton, there were no less than 100. In another example, the importer declared that he was bringing 4800 cartons of paint thinner, each containing 4 tins. The scanner, however, detected 6420 cartons, 15 toys, 100 kilograms of used clothes and 700 cartons of masking tape. (*Daily Graphic* 2001b)

Significantly, GSL presented these revelations in terms of the thousands of dollars in "savings" they provided for Ghana and Ghanaians. By pointing to "savings" rather than the actual "earnings" the scanner's discovery of taxable goods made possible, GSL deflected attention away from the substantial gains the company itself made from the new inspection regime, at the tune of 1 percent of value of all cargo cleared.

Customs officers did not hesitate to question the legitimacy and legality of GSL's mandate (*Evening News* 2001a, 2001b). Included in their critique was the widespread complaint that the new inspection regime had been foisted upon them suddenly from above, with little warning or explanation. Customs officers' grievances about the scanner were as much directed against GSL itself as against the top-ranking government ministers, including Customs official overseers in the Ministry of Finance and its unofficial guardians in the Ministry of Trade who struck up the deal with COTECNA in the first place.

Directly challenging GSL's self-presentation, Customs officers considered the images produced by the scanner both partial and insignificant to the true work of their agency. One officer commented, "The type of scanner we have isn't appropriate. It is only an image scanner. It doesn't give quantity, enclosure, description, or quality of cargo. Therefore, the information essential for customs valuation is not available." Echoing his colleague, another argued that the scanner's inability to discern the true nature of the items being brought into Ghana allowed "shoddy goods to be brought into the country" and "caused the loss of state revenue." With remarks such as these, Customs officers sought to reestablish the necessity of older practices of physical examination and the priority of revenue generation over trade facilitation within Customs' governing mission.

Embedded in the discussion of what the scanner could and could not see was a concern with who exactly fell within the scanner's optic. GSL's revelation of "all" the scanner could see was posed against a public image of Customs officers as corrupt, habitually obscuring the truth and hiding their gains and operations. Engaging a similar register of moral rhetoric (as noted in the discussion of cars in chapter 5), GSL in the meantime sought to endow the scanner with a "moral vision" and presented its imaging capacities as a means to uncover the misdoings of both importers and customs officers, thereby actualizing a wider project of social reform. In one newspaper, a source from GSL was quoted: "dishonest importers were learning quickly that the super modern X-Ray scanner would pick up mis-declarations very easily. Honest importers are now able to enjoy the much greater facilitation of trade which destination inspection brings" (*Ghanaian Times* 2001b). Employing the same sort of moralizing rhetoric embedded in a widespread neoliberal tendency to pose "transparency" as a prerequisite of political and economic development, also echoing the value-laden discourse articulated around car consumption discussed previously, from this perspective the spoils of globalization could be won only by those who policed themselves.

Not only traders and importers but also the Customs Service found itself subject to this sort surveillance. GSL touted the benefits of DI by explaining how well it worked to "curtail the discretionary powers of some customs officers" (K. O. Yeboah 2001). This targeting did not escape members of the Customs Service. Voicing a wider concern regarding the overwhelming power of the scanner, one Customs official remarked, "GSL [employees] have protective vests; Customs do not. The X-rays of mobile scanner reach the road and the larger one is more powerful, yet there are no safety measures in place." Although an obvious comment on workplace hazards, this remark equally reflected Customs officers' sense that the power of both GSL and the scanner were uncontained and misdirected. In posing an actual physical threat, the scanner stood for a more abstract and encompassing revelatory power, in the face of which Customs officers had few defenses.

Negotiating Alternative Sovereignties

Eminently concerned with the terms of movement across the border and within national space, the competing perspectives about the scanner voiced by Customs officers and GSL indexed and enforced a transposition of sovereignty. Both strengthening and undermining the supremacy of the state, even as Tema's maritime frontier remained a site for the expression of the state economic and territorial control, this sovereignty had a different genesis and a different configuration than in the past. Facilitated by and reinforcing the consolidation of state power, the new inspection agreement fostered an image of a strong and all-knowing state. Not only could this entity harness the penetrating vision of a cutting-edge technology, this was a state that could make and break rules and contracts, a state that could summon international entities to serve its interests, a state that could attract resources away from other states. But given the veiled kinship with foreign capital and expertise on which it depends, such an aura of sovereign renewal—geopolitical, territorial, and technological—comes at the cost of less exclusive control. As a result, the assertion of state authority via the DI system belies a process of contestation, not consensus. We see the fragmentation of sovereign power rather than its constitution from a singular source.

Rendering the sovereign (taken here to mean the ultimate reaches of state authority) more remote and more powerful, this shift, oddly enough, drew new force from the uncertainties unleashed by the construction and utilization of the scanner. Of the state but no longer exclusively controlled or constituted by it, much like the fragmentation of Customs centralized authority described in chapter 4, the exact configuration of the scanner's sponsorship (private or public, national or multinational) was not well understood by Customs officers or the public. Equally, the uncertainty about the scanner's vision—how it was produced and deciphered, and what exactly it saw—made the scanner's power harder to locate and therefore more potent.

From the Margins of Bureaucracy to the Bureaucracy of the Margins

All of this made Customs officers at Tema in their own eyes less an autonomous source of state authority than a subject of both distant and intimate scrutiny as their control over physical examination was officially reduced to an adjunct of the scanning process. There were, however, other shifts in Customs operations—also brought about by neoliberally inspired initiatives—that provided new possibilities and new spaces for the participation of Customs officers and incited other sorts of political *cum* sovereign realignments with regard to the governing of trade at Tema.

Most important was the posting of a select corps of Customs officers to the headquarters of GSL. Located in a multistory office building in the suburbs of Accra, GSL headquarters represents a new style Customs control center, mixing high-tech communication with a range of command functions. During my research the office was led by an expatriate management team from the fringes of Northern and Southern Europe (Scotland and Greece, to be precise) and staffed primarily by Ghanaian data entry technicians, much like the workers in Ghana's other fledging off-shore service centers. In between stood a corps of carefully selected mid- and senior-level Customs officers whose expertise was essential to the functioning of the entire office. Although Customs made up only 15 percent of GSL's 200-plus employees, their key role in assessing duties and monitoring the inspection process based on hard-won professional experience gave them an importance to GSL operations far greater than their actual numbers suggest (GSL 2000). Though paid by GSL these individuals were still officially considered Customs officials, understood to be on temporary assignment to the private firm. They were expected to work in tandem with the private employees of COTECNA's dozens of corporate affiliates around the world via electronic communication networks.

The positioning of Customs officers within GSL went hand in hand with the adoption of a new mode of Customs valuation to which the specialized skills of Customs officers were crucial. Mandated by the WTO as a condition of membership, this was the new system of "transaction valuation." As explained in earlier chapters, classification and valuation are the *sine qua non* of Customs work. Before duties can be applied to goods coming into a country, Customs officers have to know what they are—that is, how to classify them—as well as their worth or value, since different types of goods attract different duties and duties are computed on the basis of value. The first task of classification is resolved through the use of harmonized commodity codes established by the Brussels Declaration.[15] For the determination of value, Ghana for many years used a system known as "Commissioner's Value." In this case, the commissioner of Customs established a list of values to be applied to goods coming into the country.[16] With the WTO system of "transaction valuation," Commissioner's Values were nullified; every commodity coming into Ghana was instead to be valued based on the price paid by the importer, replacing a state-controlled valuation system with a market-based determination. The outsourcing of Customs operations to private multinationals for the purposes of transaction valuation, though occurring early in Ghana, was soon adopted by other states in the neighborhood. Following GSL's suit, SGS took control of valuation in Senegal, Bureau Veritas in Benin, and GSL's corporate parent COTECNA in Niger (Blundo and Olivier de Sardan 2006, 101).

Requiring application on a much larger scale at Tema than the piecemeal approach taken at Aflao, the new determination of value required a substantial reorientation of Customs procedures. Joining the multinationalization of inspection, the new system relied on the peculiar outsourcing arrangement embodied by GSL. Occurring in a whole new context and under a new command structure, the execution of transaction valuation also brought the heavy hand of a new operational logic.

If visibility—whether through manual inspection or mediated by the scanner—was the defining logic of classification, documentation as a mode of truth production lay at the heart of the new valuation system.[17] This procedural shift and the complications surrounding it centered on the generation and interpretation of new sorts of documentary evidence, both paper-based and digitized. Transaction valuation requires a rather different sort of documentation than the old Landing Account discussed in chapter 4. Where the Landing Account served as a viable record in its own right configured largely from the immediate observations of Customs officers, the system in place at GSL was mired in the work of cross-checking. Tracing every good and transaction to its source and requiring the production and gathering of copious records from importers and exporters at all ends of the supply chain, this was a retrospective and evidence-based form of value creation embodying the more general trend toward audit culture characteristic of neoliberal governance at capitalism's core as well as periphery (Gledhill 2004, 340; see also Strathern 2000).

Tied to a wider project of standardizing processes of commercial governance worldwide, the documentation process required by the WTO system of transaction valuation actively inserted the material flows circulating between manufacturing and consuming zones in a common rubric of governance, much like the IMF auditing routines linking donor and debtor nations described by Richard Harper (2000) for the pseudonymous Acadia (a country bearing a striking resemblance to Ghana). But rather than linking only financial elites across state boundaries as in the IMF case, the WTO system required the ongoing exchange of information between mid- and low-level trade specialists (technocrats of a sort) working for the state but situated outside of it. What's more, through their interactions with manufacturers, middlemen, and import/export entrepreneurs, these bureaucratic proxies enrolled a broader public in a common vantage point that brought the retrospective sensibility of audit for the purposes of governance (as opposed to more conventional uses in inventory or forecasting, for instance) to the fore.

The documentary evidence gathered through the WTO valuation system was to be compiled by Customs and GSL/COTECNA to form a "transaction price database" containing records of hundreds of thousands of transactions in "real time" (GSL 2000, v). The computerized bank of documentary evidence would be used by both Customs officers and COTECNA partners around the world to assess the validity of the information presented by importers to GSL in Ghana. Ideally, for each transaction presented by an importer, the database would provide comparable data on all other transactions made by that same importer, as well as information on all other transactions of the same and similar goods, and all transactions by the same exporter and manufacturer. In this way, the database would allow GSL and COTECNA to assess the credibility of the figures provided by businesspeople, all the while entraining them to engage in accurate reportage. As with the scanner, physical examination could be avoided, costs cut, and commerce accelerated.

In practice the use of the price database was far from straightforward. Rather than providing definitive assessments, GSL representatives and their COTECNA affiliates used the database alongside an array of secondary "valuation methods" authorized by the WTO. Just as the GSL structure unhinged Customs officers from Customs service, and in effect from a discrete national state, the valuation system effectively unhinged a commodity's assessed value from its actual transaction. The WTO for example lays out a series of valuation methods to be used in sequence.

The first method is simply "agree with importers declared value." If unacceptable, the next method to be used is "importers own previous transaction value." If all else fails, "nontransactional evidence" may be used. As a result, "transaction value," departing from any definitive notion of value or proof of worth, came to be determined by interactions among GSL and COTECNA officers about value in both specific and general terms, but always to a degree displaced from the goods at hand and their "actual" transaction. For Customs purposes, the determination of value became located not so much in the process of authentication (whether of goods or documents), but in the practices of verification.

Seeking to make sense of the uncertainties of verification, Customs officers stationed at GSL and employees of COTECNA partners around the world were constantly engaged in discussions about the nature and locus of value. Played out over and over again in the most mundane of interchanges, these communiqués nevertheless took on epistemological proportion, pertaining to the nature of knowledge. This is evident in a series of emails showed to me by a Customs officer at GSL between him and an employee of a COTECNA affiliate in Miami about whether list prices could be accepted as transaction values. In the words of the Customs officer, "list prices are prices indexes; they give a range and are therefore not transaction specific." According to WTO valuation standards, pricing should be based on transaction. In an email, he wrote: "I'm not saying that listed prices are unhelpful, what I am saying is that they are not transaction prices to the country of importation. It is important to allow for some sensitivity to importers problems."[18] The Miami affiliate, in response, argued that "list prices are computed from captured transactions." Moreover, according to him, "It may not be possible for us to have actual transactions on real values unless we come across good exporters and importers who honestly go against the normal way of trade in developing countries and bestow us with the real and actual transactional invoices."[19] The Customs officer readily admitted the impossibility of capturing actual transactions in the face of what he described to me as "increasing commoditization worldwide, where markets were characterized by extreme volatility, advance contracts, and futures speculation." Yet the Customs Officer, employing a logic that derived its authority and credibility from a sense of place, sought a determination of value that captured at least to some degree, in his words, "the specific conditions faced by the Ghanaian importer."

Paradoxically, at the same time GSL's international partners found security in the virtuality of the market and dismissed the possibility and relevance of locating "actual" transactions, they still relied on their

Ghanaian partners to provide them with documentary "truths." This too attributed greater capacity and insight to a place-specific sensibility. Indeed, the GSL office was made the depository of all documentary material required by the DI regime. An example of the way documents and their social interlocutors induce particular forms of agency (Riles 2006, 21), not only were the Customs officers at GSL supposed to collect this documentation, it was their responsibility to verify it—an expectation that imputed a higher power of discernment to those GSL representatives who were considered "locally" situated compared to those only virtually positioned within COTECNA's global network. Because of this, the inspection of the actual documentary evidence became the crux of Customs work at GSL.

Reliance on documentary evidence proved highly problematic. Arifari (2006, 213) notes a similar struggle over documentation at work in the COTECNA-led valuation in Niger: "Nigerien traders and customs officers positively despise Cotecna [as there is] no declaration processes without the Cotecna paper." Going hand in hand with the increasing call for documents and the renewed effort to check their credibility through the database was the presentation and production of false documents. As one officer put it, "fraudulent documents are big gray area. The framers of WTO did not consider problem of genuine documents and honest declaration." This was followed a few months later by the public pronouncement from a Customs officer that "it is an open secret that between 90–95% of all invoices presented by traders are either fake or fictitious, resulting in GSL issuing low values without challenge from Customs" (*Daily Guide* 2001). No doubt this was a project in which Customs officers played a hand. Even during working hours at GSL it was not usual for an officer to take a "break" to meet with a clearing agent to help organize documents. Officers frequently received telephone calls from importers and agents asking for advice. So much was this a problem that cellphones were banned in the workplace and from time to time both non-Customs GSL employees and Customs officers were fired from their posts.[20]

These actions reveal much about the complexities and contradictions of Customs officers' own repositioning at GSL. Within GSL Customs officers, as "private employees" of a sort, were removed from the usual authority structure of the Customs Service and little subject to state oversight. Now operating within a global network, from the point of view of Customs officers the ultimate authority of the Ghanaian state appeared not so absolute, or at least open to negotiation. And value itself, according to official and venerable sources of COTECNA and the WTO, was supremely flexible. Indeed, officers easily equated what they called "the more fluid world of trade" that they experienced at GSL with what they described as a "shared working environment where everyone is open to one another." With value and authority in such flux, colluding with traders seems not a departure from but a replication of the mores of the market and the workplace. At the same time, by contravening the official mandates of GSL, Customs officers may well have been reasserting their separate status and autonomous authority as state agents. As my Customs officer friends at GSL did not hesitate to remind me time and again, "Loyalty to mother Ghana should be the core consideration of work at GSL."

Conclusion

What bearing does this all have on the character of Ghanaian sovereignty? How do the microtactics of inspection and valuation help to constitute the state's ultimate control over movement in and through national territory and the very notion of the nation as a singular and governable space? An analytical frame implied but not well explored by Ong (1999, 2006) may be helpful here. As mentioned in chapter 2, Ong speaks of a system of "graduated sovereignty" (1999, 215) emerging in Southeast Asia where different spaces and categories of citizen are subject to different constellations of state power, depending on their significance to the global economy.[21] Taking a step back from the type of outcomes Ong describes to hone in on their enablement, the Ghanaian case draws attention to how the variegated sovereignties of the state and its agents come into being.

What I am arguing is that with regard to Customs operations, Destination Inspection and the WTO guidelines, more than simply altering the manifestation of state sovereignty, reform the very capacity of the state to express itself as such. Within the new Customs regime we see shifts in the *source* of sovereign power from national to multinational resources, from the nearly exclusive purview of nation-based bureaucrats to the combined purview of government ministers, foreign executives, technicians and a corps of uprooted bureaucratic actors operating within a multinational realm. With regard to both inspection and valuation, there is an attendant shift in the *logics* and *mechanics* of sovereignty as well, from sensory, experiential and language based (as seen in the system of physical examination and the traditional Landing Account), to retrospective and evidenced-based modes mediated by digital technologies.

Quite significantly, despite the "denationalized" (Sassen 1996, 2000) character of these shifts (and pointing to the distinction between "denationalization" and "destatization" [Jessop 1999]), taken together they work to amplify the impression of the state's sovereign might. Despite the tradeoff for the Customs officers involved, the externalized endowments of the DI system shore up rather than undermine domestic sovereignty, both in terms of state capacity and the very perception of the state as the ultimate source of authority. What's more, the operation of the scanner as a generic mode of border control, rising above the personalized and embodied power of individual Customs officers to screen all that passed with a consistent and uncompromising lens, contributed to Ghana's growing international recognition as an exemplary form, boosting its sovereignty in the international realm. Once again boosting the status of Customs as a "privileged functional enclave" of state authority (cf. Blundo and Olivier de Sardan 2006, 72) as we saw at Aflao, here officers sacrificed their personal power to contribute to the greater might of the state forged from a range of international and infrastructural resources at the maritime frontier.

But before reading the terms of Ghana's sovereign refashioning from the vantage point of the Tema maritime frontier alone, just as in the case of the Aflao land frontier, it is worthwhile to heed Andreas's insight, expressed in his book *Border Games* (2000) on the U.S.-Mexico border, that the power of the border is fundamentally performative. For Andreas, the dramatization and escalation of power in the border zone, despite its ideological force, is always a subterfuge of sorts, distracting attention from equally profound but less easily resolved political processes and concerns occurring elsewhere in the state apparatus.

At the same time we see the purview of rank-and-file Customs officers compromised and Ghana's official sovereignty enhanced (via better border surveillance, more centralized administration, and increased international acceptability), the implementation of WTO transaction valuation gives new form to Ghana's sovereignty in another way. Within the offices of GSL, the virtual spaces of computer correspondence and networking, and the muffled notes of cellphone conversations, there seems to be a highly select sort of "bureaucratic sovereignty" emerging. Namely, the official and unofficial opportunities available at GSL put a select group of Customs officers at the boundary between the nation-state, multinational corporation, and global economy, endowing them with an unprecedented authority. Working at once for the government of Ghana and a private firm and representing Ghana and a multinational network, these officers sought to meld WTO norms of circulation with their own notions of location in the reckoning of value, restoring a sense of place to exchange in a manner that specifically invoked an ideal of national territory. Likewise, in their rendering of documents, Ghanaian Customs officers claimed a space for themselves in a form of invisible trade unanticipated by WTO or Ghana's ministers of state.

This sort of bureaucratic influence, including the images of place on which it is founded, was equally constituted by the corporate structure of the GSL/COTECNA alliance. The GSL/COTECNA valorization of place should not be considered an innocent reclamation of an older logic of localization or a promotion of some sort of Ghanaian self-determination. Rather, GSL's reliance on Ghanaian document management may well be considered an extension of the logic of multinationalization, justifying the "in-sourcing" to Customs officers of the very jobs the state officially "outsourced" to COTECNA. Similar to the "commercialization of sovereignty" described by Ronan Palan (2003) in his discussion of off-shore tax havens and financial zones, this then may be the production and preservation of a sort of place-based authority—call it sovereignty, if you like—as a form of value functional to capital and the state.

As in the case of the "off-shore" state enclaves discussed by Palan (2003), it is not immediately clear where this sovereignty lies in territorial terms given the fact that its means are nonisomorphic with its ends. Although these mechanisms of rule invoke the control of both territory and mobility as the basis of authority, these claims are unabashedly enabled by the transnational environment and instituted by a small corps of mid-level bureaucrats who operate at the periphery of the state hierarchy. The long-term implications of these dynamics are difficult to predict. Nevertheless, in the mix of contemporary Customs reforms we can begin to identify an emerging modality of "transnational governance" (to borrow a phrase from Ferguson and Gupta [2002, 996]), which occupies and reproduces the old spaces of the state as a cover for new initiatives within the state and outside of it, and where each thrives on the borrowed authority of the other.

Postscript: Derivative Sovereignty, National Branding and Electronic States

After completing my field research in Ghana, I continued to research Custom trends in Ghana and more broadly. I found myself paying close attention to the workings of the World Customs Organization, the main body involved in coordinating and overseeing Customs operations worldwide. In the fall of 2003 I traveled to South Africa to attend a World Customs Organization regional forum focusing on information technology. At this forum I became aware of another flux in Custom functions brought about by the pressures and possibilities of neoliberal reform in which Ghana was once again at the fore. With significant implications for the character of sovereignty in Ghana and more broadly, in this latest mode of sovereign restructuring Ghana's Customs was enmeshed in series of exchanges not just with multinational state service providers but with a set of equally entrepreneurial microstates. Together they authored and put into play a strikingly innovative modality of national economic governance uniquely transferable between states.

In this example the means of making sovereignty emerges as a fungible entity whose value is realized in the course of exchange. This is not a form of sovereignty that is purchased from or shared with a private firm but a more laterally inspired transformation deliberately produced by a state for the transfer to other states for profit. Exemplifying a dynamic that can be described as "national branding," in this transaction the sovereignty product bears the mark of its state of origin. In the same move, the state of origin in the course of transferring a component of its own sovereignty takes on a multinational corporate form.

The emergence of this order is closely tied to the WCO's Information and Communication technology campaign laid out in the 1999 Revised WCO Kyoto Convention. Known as the Electronic Data Initiative, it has formed a central part of the WCO agenda over the past decade and covers a range of information technology concerns. Obviating face-to-face interactions with Customs officers and visits to the Customs offices, the most significant and widespread development is the push to automate Customs clearance via the on-line submission of all Customs entries by importers, shippers, clearing agents, and other relevant parties relevant to the supply chain. This move goes hand in hand with a much wider campaign to adopt electronic surveillance technologies such as scanning for cargo inspection (as tried early on in Ghana) along with the provision of e-learning modules and virtual seminars by the WCO for officers within member administrations.

The breadth of the WCO Electronic Data campaign was apparent at the October 2003 "IT for Customs in Africa" conference in Johannesburg. Over a hundred high-ranking Customs and government officials from across Africa, including the acting commissioner of Ghana Customs, were present. Despite Africa's presumed position on the downside of the so-called digital divide, from the attendees' comments and displays it was evident that information and communication technology programs and parlance had made its way into Customs work and other areas of governance on the continent. Participants were lectured on South Africa's comprehensive e-government initiative designed to provide an electronic interface for all state services, from the attainment of birth certificates to employment benefits and job information. They also heard from the chair of NEPAD (New Partnership for African Development) e-Africa Commission, about the promises of e-commerce and the fading away of borders and barriers in the digital economy. Even in the absence of the capacity to fully implement and coordinate these initiatives, the facility with which they were discussed by participants suggested that these norms had at least achieved a global reach as a framework for speaking about and practicing governance.

Embedded in the Electronic Data Initiative is the development of new forms of Customs work, not simply new ways of carrying it out. Closely tied to the imperatives of security mentioned above, much of this involves possibilities borne out of high-tech: new modes of scanning, monitoring and tracking based on x-rays, electronic sensors, satellite relays, digital coding, and more.[22] Less noted, yet going hand in hand with the development of sophisticated surveillance tool, is the expansion and refinement of much more mundane databasing capabilities.[23] Generating new possibilities of knowledge manipulation grounded in the logics of "actuarialism," these developments underwrite a qualitative shift in the way state power operates and is experienced within Customs regimes.

The story of such sovereign transubstantiation begins in Singapore, a country known as a hotbed of authoritarianism capitalism. It centers on the operations of a business by the name of CrimsonLogic: the offspring of Singapore Network Services, a corporate entity in which the Singapore Trade and Development Board, a government body, owns a majority stake and the Port of Singapore and Singapore Telecom hold the remaining shares (World Bank 1998).[24] Singapore Network Services (SNS) was formed in 1988 as part of the Singapore government's "master plan" to build the "country's position as an international trading hub" (*Channel Business* 2002). At this time, SNS spearheaded an e-governance initiative seeking to develop an electronic interface for the provision of government services spanning the legal realm, customs and taxation as well as education. Two products resulted, one, eJudiciary for electronic litigation, and TradeNet, of particular importance to customs. TradeNet, CrimsonLogic/SNS claims in its promotional material, was "the world's first nationwide electronic trade declaration and clearance system" and one which the company both "conceptualized and developed."

These accomplishments are certainly technically impressive. What is more significant is the direction in which they were taken. In a matter of years the decision was made for SNS go international, establishing offices around the world and selling its products and services, including those relating to Customs, such as TradeNet. This decision was accompanied by a move to develop SNS into a corporate brand—what we know now as CrimsonLogic—and to pursue, in the company director's own words, a "fully global branding strategy" (*Business Times Singapore* 2002). True to this global creed, CrimsonLogic's literature makes little mention of state roots.

CrimsonLogic has met with notable success with respect to Customs services marketing its product line. Canada Customs and Revenue Agency uses CrimsonLogic's on-line Customs entry software (Hunter 2003; *Purchasing B2B* 2003). The Panama Canal Authority has a contract with CrimsonLogic to set up the infrastructure for all maritime security and transit operations (*Business Times Singapore* 2004a). CrimsonLogic has even set up a Web portal that gives Singapore firms a direct link to U.S. Customs (*Business Time Singapore* 2004b). Reiterating its success as a global purveyor of sovereignty services, of late CrimsonLogic is building a new Customs network for the Saudis, with a "five year $20million plan to reproduce all the features of Singapore's existing Tradenet system" (*Business Times Singapore* 2004c).

Indicating yet another shift in the form and formation of sovereignty service, Crimson Logic found a customer for its TradeNet program in the Mauritius Customs and Excise Service. Mauritius, like Singapore, is a highly entrepreneurial state. A tiny island nation with an economy once reliant on sugar-cane production, Mauritius over the past few decades has positioned itself as a crossroads of African and Asian economies and a lucrative "off-shore" investment site. Often referred to by development experts as the Mauritius miracle, the country is a leader in value-added light industry and service provision, from the textile production and garment assembly to data entry.[25] Employing these entrepreneurial capacities to the customs industry and government more generally, Mauritius used its claims to Crimson Logics TradeNet product to dual ends.[26] Not only did Mauritius employ TradeNet within its own customs administration, in 2000 Mauritius Customs entered into a contract with Société Générale de Surveillance, the Swiss-based inspection company, to development e-customs portal for the government of Ghana with whom SGS is contracted to develop a new product known as GCNET.[27]

As a manifestation of a global sovereignty industry, these arrangements are remarkable. What we have here is the making of sovereignty— specifically, sovereignty services wrapped into the e-customs product—

into a commodity: fungible, alienable, and eminently transactable. To fully appreciate the implications, it is worthwhile to look closely at the dynamics of transaction. From the government of Singapore to the government of Ghana, we have a fourfold exchange, accruing value at each turn. The sovereignty product, much like a kula valuable (Malinowski 1922), carries its own history of transaction and spawns value as it circulates. While the packaging of sovereignty as a form of intellectual property contributes to the production of generic or modular capacities, in these transactions the state itself is a highly unstable form. In an sophisticated system of sovereign commercialization (cf. Palan 2003) this string of exchanges are made possible by the morphing or shape-shifting of the source of sovereignty from country to company, from nation-state to multinational corporation. In this model of national branding, the nation-state becomes known internationally in its corporate rather than political incarnation. At the same time, in its dissemination, it replicates its own course of emergence, engaging states who themselves become "branded" as they engage other states.

SEVEN

Affective Sovereignty: Airport Anthropology and the Shifting Contours of Citizenship

Kotoka International Airport, which came into existence on small-scale in the pre-war years as a military aerodrome, is now the largest civil airport in Ghana. Since 1946, when the Royal Air Force pulled out and the port was turned to civil use, it has become increasingly associated with international civil aviation and air transport activity in Ghana. The idea of civil aviation in the Gold Coast was conceived on 22nd October 1918 when the first two letters concerning aerial transportation in the colony were received by the Governor from the Vickers Aviation Ltd. This was followed by the first landing of the first powered aircraft by Captain R. S. Rattray, Provincial Commissioner and famous Anthropologist. A few visits to the country by some other aircrafts such as the 3 Royal Airforce Planes in 1930 led to regular air mail service established between the UK and the Gold Coast by Imperial Airways which later became the British Overseas Airways Corporation. This could be referred to as the birth of civil aviation in Ghana.
—GHANA DEPARTMENT OF CIVIL AVIATION, 1969

Introduction: Airports and Affect

Focusing on the encounters between Ghanaian Customs officers and travelers at Ghana's Kotoka International Airport (popularly known as KIA), this chapter examines how the sovereignty of the Ghanaian state—its capacity to make rules, identify citizens and subjects, and command compliance—

is produced in the context of the transnational movement of persons, things, and policies.

At Ghana's international airport, the fiction of the supremacy of sovereignty's rational-legal face is boldly evident. Although the airport presents itself as a space of rote formality, of regulation and compliance, in Ghana and elsewhere it is lived as a space of emotion and embodiment in extremis. Airports the world over are spaces of physical distance and physical encounter (Augé 1995, 87), emotional loss and emotional reunion, fatigue and exuberance, and always, force, manifested in the mass of the aircraft, the jolt of takeoff and touchdown, the burden of luggage, the spaces of containment, cordoning off, gates, security wands, examinations, x-ray machines, and the bodies and gazes of plainclothes and uniformed agents. Further complicating expectations of a singular or formally codified political order, airports such as KIA are also spaces where the disjunctures of global modernity are brought to the fore (Appadurai 1996a). A multiplicity of national and supranational agendas and transnational circuits collide and coincide, forcing self-examination, dissension, and the contemplation of new forms of social order among state agents and state subjects alike.

Customs officers, among all the state authorities present at Ghana's airport, have the most sustained contact with travelers and their wares. Indicating the centrality of affect and imagination to sovereign reckoning, the encounters between Customs officers and international travelers at KIA reveal the play of force and sentiment, domestic authority and extranational power, social contract and individual conviction: what Caroline Humphrey calls the saturation of sovereignty with "ways of life" (2004, 435). Not only must travelers contend with the specter of a never fully knowable governmental authority in the context of air travel and transit but Customs officers also must confront and negotiate the repositioning of self and state as they try out new capacities and cope with the loss of older entitlements within the space of KIA. Indeed, in the transient sociality of airport encounter—a sociality both attenuated and intensified—one can identify a reciprocal recasting of state subject and state agent, of citizen and sovereign. This is neither an equalization nor a swapping of identity but a momentary reflection enabling the sensing of other subjective states even as differentials in authority and entitlements are asserted and affirmed.

Moving beyond an examination of the administrative tactics through which the state rules (Foucault 1979, 1991), this perspective entreats one to consider how the aura of sovereign ultimacy is sustained and

Figure 7.1 Aviation and the national imaginary. Postage stamps issued in 1970 to commemorate KIA's expansion. Courtesy Ghana Postal Company, Philately Division.

internalized by those actors considered to be its source and its object, how state agents configure, replicate, and renew the ability to rule and how they come to be known and felt as a source of rule over others. In short, from this vantage point, the "sovereign," as subject, symbol, and sentiment, as well as a system of sanction, becomes opens to investigation. Begoña Aretxaga, drawing on the insights of Philip Abrams (1988), speaks eloquently of the relevance of such a perspective:

Repositioning the question of the state in relation to the meaning of sovereignty [is] particularly crucial . . . at this moment of globalization. . . . The question of subjectivity emerges as critical in a variety of ways. On the one hand, there are the subjective dynamics that link people to states . . . on the other hand is what one could call the subjectivity of state being. How does it become a social subject in everyday life? This is to ask about bodily excitations and sensualities, powerful identifications, and unconscious desires of state officials; about performances and public representations of statehood; and about discourses, narratives and fantasies generated around the idea of the state. The state cannot exist without this subjective component. (2003, 395)

Yael Navaro-Yashin, in her research in Turkey (2002, 15), likewise takes seriously the political implications of such reflections and associations. Embedded in streams of consciousness, they are an inherent feature of public life for both the agents and subjects of the state, no matter how fleeting or submerged their enunciation. Similarly, in Ghana the encounters between travelers and Customs officials are as much about relationships of power (i.e., who has more and who has less) as they are about the power of relationships to conjure new experiences and potentials of personhood. At KIA, as in Turkish political life, these struggles over position, to borrow Antonio Gramsci's term (1971), dually engage modes of being and modes of resource control, modes of expression and of repression. Michael Herzfeld (1997, 2005) uses a similar concept of a relational self to explore the convergence of values that occurs between state officials and ordinary citizens in negotiations over rights and resources—a process he labels "cultural intimacy." These works lead one to recognize that the traveler, as well as the Customs officer, occupies a spectrum of subject positions and a spectrum of agencies. A reality heightened in the context of prolonged but ever-acute neoliberal transition in Ghana, this multiplicity of selves lends contingency and possibility to their encounters. Despite the apparent tension between subject and sovereign, their interactions, exemplifying what Herzfeld calls "the tangled skeins of complicity" (2005, 372) between rulers and ruled, provide a mutually enlivening and legitimizing force. Indeed, the sovereign and the citizen-civilian may exist within the same individual as Customs officers simultaneously engage in the constitution of themselves as persons of worth and personages of power.

Informed by these insights, the analysis of the intertwining of political sociality and political economy at KIA presented in this chapter is driven by the contention that state sovereignty must be endowed with meaning to be known, turn on experiences of self to be felt, and in some way be socially transactable to matter. Ever-present features of sovereign rule, these dynamics rise to the surface in the face of the multiple disjunctures of neoliberal reform.

African Aviation as a Hidden Neoliberal Frontier

Ghana's position at the forefront of neoliberal reform in Africa (Rothchild 1991; World Bank 1994a, 2003) profoundly impacts KIA. The country's entire aviation sector has been subject to a decade-long overhaul, putting the airport at the center of the country's economic-development agenda. Over the course of the 1990s, the government of Ghana with the backing of international donors and financiers devised a plan to establish KIA as a hub for international commerce, investment, and travel for the whole of the West African subregion (Solignac-Lecomte 2002, 8; see also the 1999 comprehensive development framework from Ghana's Ministry of Roads and Transport). The plan, known as the Vision 2020 Gateway Initiative, was funded by an array of innovative international economic partnerships and encompassed the rebuilding of the physical structure of the airport, the reorganization of airport services, and the implementation of a host of new aviation policies.[1]

With aviation a hidden frontier of liberalization on a world scale, the recrafting of Ghana's airspace went hand in hand with a wider effort to bring the African continent into the fold of global standards.[2] Spearheaded by the International Civil Aviation Organization, or ICAO (Economic Commission for Africa 2001), in Ghana the result was the "Liberalized Skies" policy adopted in 1997.[3] Like the establishment of export-processing and tax-free zones in the Tema area, with which it was paired, liberalization of the airways was seen as a way to attract investors and facilitate trade (Solignac-Lecomte 2002, 8; UN Office for the Coordination of Humanitarian Affairs 2000). Because only four other African states—Egypt, Ethiopia, Morocco, and South Africa—were able or willing to abide by the ICAO accord, these protocols situated Ghana within an elite sphere of global circulation, endowing Ghanaian airspace with a sort of value added, bringing greater traffic, resources, and recognition (Knipe 2000; Pedersen 2001).[4] In turn, over the course of the 1990s, Ghana's aviation sector experienced spectacular development, seeing more passengers, more routes, and more carriers, and creating accessibility not available in most other African nations (Boachie 2003).[5] Between 1995 and 2000 alone, passenger throughput and aircraft movement grew more than 50 percent, and aircraft movement increased to close to 10,000 flights, up from 6,500 (Pederson 2001, 57).

As is evident in these developments, in Ghana as elsewhere, airports and aviation are held to be central to the attainment of global modernity, both following and overtaking the pathway of the car. Like global cities (Sassen 1998, 2001), satellite relays, and digital communication networks (Appadurai 1996a), airports are fundamental to participation in the global service economy, though their presence (even in Africa, as the opening quote attests) long precedes these other developments. Facilitating the mobility of persons, information, and objects, the aviation sector sustains the spread of capital and the possibilities of time-space compression. Marc Augé identifies airports as archetypical "non-place[s] of supermodernity" (1995, 86), locations of similitude where national distinctions blur in favor of an anonymous internationalism. Taking the airplane as a point of reference, airports are crafted as spaces apart, with no particular or fixed locations and with interchangeable décors and layouts geared to a common functionality of transit. A case in point, the London-based Azhar Architechture firm, well known for its design of total environments incorporating work, living, and transit space, was responsible for KIA design (Azhar Architecture 2005).

To this, Ghana is no exception. Cultivating an order in which the

Figure 7.2 Airport as neoliberal frontier. New airport exterior, completed in 2001, designed by Azhar Architecture.

currents of neoliberalism—of commerce, economic extroversion, foreign financing, and the quest for seamless global integration—are on full display, the updated KIA now boasts new passenger and cargo terminals capable of accommodating wide-bodied jets (Intertec 2003). It has a new check-in area, an expanded departure area, and an upgraded arrival hall. With high-powered air conditioning 24/7, bright lighting, sleek marble interiors, and signage incorporating the requisite yellow and black international symbols, the stylistics of the KIA renovation conform to widely shared models of airport architecture and amenity. Except for a gift shop selling carvings, tie-dyed outfits, and Ghana-made chocolate bars and a decorative exterior wall reminiscent of the patterning of Ghana's famous Kente cloth, there are only the barest suggestions of the airport's Ghanaian location.[6] In contrast to the internationalist state architecture of the postcolonial period, whether the monumental Nkrumahist structures of the capital (Hess 2000) or the later copycat projects of Acheampong at outposts like Aflao, the latest renovation of KIA reflects a rather different mission. If the former sought to put Ghana on economic and aesthetic par with other nation-states, the airport's redesign is much more about the transcendence of national space and the overall smoothing of circulation.

Although moving Ghana from the global periphery toward the non-place of global position, lying beneath the stylistic manifestations of supermodernity preoccupying both Augé (1995) and the architects of airport rehabilitation, the reordering of Ghanaian aviation is enmeshed in a complex political economy in which nation and state are ever-present. Providing a stage for the renewal and redrawing of the parameters of Ghanaian sovereignty, the redevelopment of KIA namely engenders myriad struggles over regulations, resources, and recognition both within Ghana and without, and in which Customs plays a central role. To whit, building on their longstanding role as "effective sovereign" (Weber 1995), Customs officers working Ghana's revamped aerial frontier are ensconced in a process of administrative promotion. As at other frontiers, they are endowed with new capacities for the sanction and oversight of cross-border traffic along with access to international networks and recognition. At the same time, these endowments alter the means available to Customs to set and enforce the terms of inclusion and exclusion in the nation-state. The result is the compromise and, in many cases, the suspension of the very criteria through which Customs officials act and are recognized as purveyors of national order. Of note, however, this is less a clash between state authorities and global forces than the play of the multiplex determinations of sovereign statehood in neoliberal times: political and economic; national, supranational, and transnational; and social and cultural.

What's more, extending the claims put forth in preceding chapters, the interplay of these regulatory rubrics in the making of late-modern sovereignty is as much moral, emotional, and ideational in character as it is bureaucratic. Specifically, findings from KIA challenge the idea that the rise of trans- and supranational engagements and the concomitant expansion of bureaucratic administration are necessarily anomic, widening the divide between the subjects and agents of rule (pace Agamben 1998; Durkheim 1964; Weber 1968). Rather, the encounters and interactions between travelers and Customs officers at the airport suggest that the retooling of sovereign authority in contexts of neoliberal reform rests on the production of new sorts of intimacies—whether social identifications, fantasies, emotions, or notions of self. Affirming the call for a fully cultural approach to the state sensitive to the realm of desire and the psyche (Aretxaga 2003; Linke 2006; Navaro-Yashin 2002), here it is evident that the systems and symbols of authority that constitute sovereign statehood are as much structures of feeling as they are structures of force:

congeries of affect as much as of action. Indeed, in states such as Ghana, given the confluence of multiple and fluid regulatory registers occurring in official spaces of mobility as a result of neoliberalism's unbridled advance, affective exchange emerges as a primary means of expressing and experiencing sovereign authority.

The disregard of these concerns in current discussions of neoliberal sovereignty appears to be tied to the tendency to operate on a plane that can be described as "experience far," privileging the relative (discussions of more or less) over the substantive and putting contractualism (i.e., policy and structure) before emotion and experience (Ong 2006; Sassen 2006). All of this divorces the sovereign from the subject, denying the play of self and sentiment in the production of power. Yet even the earliest theorists of sovereignty acknowledged its fundamental duality: as constructed from above and below, exceptional and popular, suspended and embedded, deriving from law and living in a collective will (Merriam 1900). Nevertheless, this remains a strain only faintly acknowledged in discussions of sovereignty (see Aretxaga 2003; Biersteker and Weber 1996; Humphrey 2004).

Transnational Mobility and Airport Ethnography

My appreciation of this vantage point emerged over the course of ethnographic research I conducted at KIA over a span of three months in the spring of 2001. My research assistants and I spent several evenings a week at the Arrival Hall awaiting the landing and deplaning of flights from Europe and the United States, as well as elsewhere in Africa. We watched and listened to processes of passenger clearance: the character and conventions of declaration, interview, and interrogation; baggage examination; and duty computation and collection. We also noted the material manifestations of global travel: the boxes, parcels, suitcases, and product samples accompanying travelers; travelers' dress and comportment; and the documents and currencies they carried and displayed. We paid close attention to the sociality of airport life: the tenor of the relationships between travelers and Customs officers as well as among varied ranks of airport personnel.

Despite our receipt of official permission to conduct research, granted in the spirit of "transparency" by the commissioner of Customs and Customs overseers in the Ministry of Finance, much remained inaccessible to or deliberately hidden from us. Although issues of secrecy color almost any fieldwork endeavor, at KIA this condition was compounded by the climate of suspicion in which Customs officers across the country operated and the distinct status of the airport as a security installation. Although my research assistants and I were free to visit the airport during off-hours and were often welcomed by Customs officers, the conduct of research was far more difficult once flights arrived. To gain permission to enter the Arrival Hall during these times, I was asked to present my program and credentials to the head of airport security, who then authorized our procurement of the official Ghana Civil Aviation Authority ID tags requested on our behalf by the chief of KIA Customs, which allowed us access to particular areas of the airport for a limited time. Even with the requisite identification, security guards were reluctant to let us enter the airport premises.

By dint of personality or political disposition, some Customs officers were, nevertheless, at ease in our presence, happy to reveal and reflect on the travails of their position, and in some cases share in its spoils (including the tips they received from travelers). Whether out of suspicion or the sheer intensity of passenger clearance, others were much less comfortable with our curiosity about their work routines. In response, we positioned ourselves in out-of-the-way corners, setting ourselves up in predictable spots so as not to take anyone by surprise, and engaging in informal discussion groups during lulls and breaks in traffic. Yet, in the hurried course of the work and hundreds of hours of observation, a great deal was revealed or at least adumbrated.

Research at the airport brought into view nearly every global flow making its way to and through Ghana. A remarkable contrast to the 1980s, when air traffic trickled, by 2000 the airport was served by over a dozen passenger airlines, from Europe, the former Soviet Union, the Middle East, and Africa: Alitalia, British Airways, KLM Royal Dutch Airlines, Lufthansa, Swissair, Aeroflot, Egypt Airlines, Middle East Airlines, Ethiopian Airlines, South African Airways, Air Afrique, and Ghana Airways. On the transcontinental front, KIA saw multiple daily runs to and from Europe and two or three flights per week to the United States and Asia. Ghana Airways, along with the occasional Nigerian carrier, served the West African coastal route, and the Ethiopian and South African airlines each maintained several flights per week serving the rest of the continent.

The new conditions of Ghanaian aviation intertwine with a diverse social field. The largest portion of passenger traffic at KIA is made up of Ghanaian and other West African nationals or former nationals caught in the vortex of transmigration, tourism, and ex- and repatriation. With over 10 percent of the population estimated to live abroad (Manuh 2000), the airport is the primary point of transit for hundreds of thousands of Ghanaians who work or seek work in Europe, North America, or the Arabian Gulf region.[7] Although Ghana is touted as a model student of neoliberal reform, the country's supposed economic revival has stimulated and is fully dependent on an economics of exodus. After two decades of shrinking state support and the promotion of international trade at the expense of self-sustaining production (Aryeetey and Tarp 2000), a substantial percentage of the Ghana populace is compelled to seek resources outside of the country (Fine and Boateng 2000; Van Dijk 2003), illustrating what has become a pan-African dynamic (Kane 2002; Koser 2003; MacGaffey and Bazanguissa-Ganga 2000).

The airport is also a regular site of departure and return for a Ghanaian and Levantine business class moving between Ghana and commercial destinations in London, Dubai, Thailand, Milan, and neighboring West African states on weekly or monthly shopping trips (Darkwah 2002). As is evident in earlier conventions of Commonwealth Citizenship (Carter 1958; Kelly 2004) and other longstanding vectors of transmigration within the continent, these trajectories are not entirely new (Kopytoff 1987; Swindell 1995). Yet the ongoing imbalance of trade and resource extraction has come to necessitate the expansion and augmentation of older patterns and pathways, some, like the clandestine flows of the drug, gold, gem, and currency cartels, moving in unanticipated and unofficial directions (Simone 2001). Alongside both these well-trod and hidden trajectories of travel is an array of subsidiary circuits. Ghana hosts growing numbers of heritage tourists who enter the country by way of KIA (Bruner 1996; Hasty 2003). They are joined by adventurerers and eco-tourists, students from abroad, researchers, missionaries, investors, diplomats, and development workers.

Although the multiplex circuitry of trade, travel, and transmigration render the airport a place of global ecumene, the operation and display of state power at KIA is extraordinarily dense. This is not a forgotten strain of state regulation, soon to be nullified by the tide of global circulation. In Ghana the completion of airport renovation in 2001 coincided with the intensification of state controls. The airport, to begin with, represents a frontier like any other (Donnan and Wilson 1999; Kratochwil 1986; Prescott 1987). Comparable to the numerous border stations guarding land and maritime boundaries, it is a space where state power is concentrated and the movement of persons and goods assiduously monitored. In addition to the Customs Service, KIA is occupied by personnel from Ghana's Immigration Service, Ministry of Agriculture, Ministry of Health, Bureau of National Investigation, Police Service, and Army. The edges of the airport are flanked by a military training school and the Burma Camp army barracks. Although no armed soldiers are present in the public areas of the airport, military personnel oversee the airport and movement is highly regulated, requiring ID badges, escorts, and permission slips for those not in possession of an air ticket, as my research team and I readily learned.

The airport is truly a citadel, and whoever controls it controls the city and, potentially, the entire state apparatus.[8] The airport is considered a prime target of coup makers following in the footsteps of those who plotted the putsch to unseat the airport's namesake, General Kotoka, in which he was murdered. Well aware of this history, Ghana's outgoing head of state, Jerry Rawlings, continued to put military men in the airport's high-ranking posts, even after winning successive democratic elections. Operating with a similar concern, in the wake of the 2000 election, the new government quickly replaced top security officials at KIA and called for a review of security procedures.[9]

Effective Sovereignty and the Recasting of Customs

With personnel stationed at the departure gates and Arrival Hall in the passenger terminal, on the tarmac, and at the air cargo facility, interactions between Customs and travelers are intensely personal. From the opening of suitcases, parcels, and wallets to the exchange of words, documents, and wealth (in modes official and not), Customs officers are endowed with the authority to scrutinize and make demands on— including the right to detain—every person and object that crosses the airport threshold. At the Arrival Hall, after disembarking from the aircraft, getting one's passport stamped by the Immigration Service, and collecting one's baggage, all travelers must pass through the Customs area. Here, Customs officers inspect travelers' luggage and documents. In addition to paying duties on items of commercial value, travelers are interviewed by Customs officers about their identities and itineraries. They are also required to make official declarations to Customs officers about their business in Ghana, their plans for departure, the cash and other valuables they may be holding, and whether they have any unaccompanied baggage or cargo.

In the aftermath of Ghana's historic 2000 elections, which ushered in a new regime after twenty years of rule dominated by a single party and leader (Gyimah-Boadi 2001), Customs officers at KIA find themselves caught in the throes of a complex repositioning emerging out of the shifting interface of state power, transnational connection, and supranational supervision at work at the airport. Forced to contend with new obligations and capacities as well as a new context of operation, officers at KIA have to somehow make workable the changing terms of their authority and that of the Ghanaian state more generally. Some of these shifts are circumstantial, tied to the logistics of airport renovation and the rapidly rising tide of passenger and cargo traffic. Others are more pointed in their implications. The Vision 2020 Gateway Initiative, for one, made the airport the center of attraction for new, primarily foreign, investment, broadening Customs' mandate and its significance both nationally and internationally. Customs officers are expected to accommodate new types of commodities and commercial regimes, like those serving Ghana's fledging export-processing and nontraditional export sectors and tax-free zones (Ghana 1999). Following the government's intent to make the airport a gateway not just for goods but also for investors, there is pressure on Customs from the Ministry of Trade to reorient the organization's mentality from surveillance and defense to reception and to shift Customs' functional focus from control to facilitation.

In keeping with this agenda, Customs officers have little choice but to adopt a host of new protocols. Like the emulation of international style and the crafting of interchangeable layouts and décor in the remodeling of the airport, this is a critical element of synchronizing Customs operations with wider transnational trends. As a leading edge of Ghana's embrace of global bureaucratic rationalities, Customs is responsible for implementing the accords of an array of supra- and international organizations, ranging from the ICAO and the WCO to the WTO, World Health Organization (WHO), and Interpol. Ghana is equally a partner in numerous bilateral Customs and trade agreements. Whether to increase speed or predictability—what Customs specialists refer to as "harmonization"—these policies are all about imposing a common blueprint of neoliberal modernity on Customs' work. This is not a world without borders but a world in which all borders operate according to uniform terms that make mobility their priority.

At the same time that these shifts foster the enlargement of Customs' mandate and heighten Customs' profile internationally, Customs' power and position are under threat domestically. Most problematic for officers at KIA is the process of political diminution confronting the Customs Service as a whole that was incited by the monumental feat of democratic regime change initiated in the 1992 and 1996 elections and finally realized in 2000. In the face of efforts by the new government to wrest power from entrenched and, often, corrupt bureaucracies and relocate it in within what is considered to be the legitimate center of government—that is, the electoral order—officers at all levels and locations of the Customs Service, from low-ranking officers to the Customs commissioner, find themselves under intense scrutiny and sometimes criminal investigation, as we have already seen in the case of the Aflao frontier and car allocation. Although Customs officers may have been engaged in corrupt practices (as reported in the 2001 corruption report by the Center for Democracy and Development), their activities did not change as much as the climate around them.[10]

Because of the place they already held in public consciousness, Customs officers at KIA and elsewhere were made scapegoats for the ills of the outgoing administration. Fueled by a neoliberal rhetoric of transparency championed by the World Bank and Transparency International (West and Sanders 2003), the allegations against Customs officials and their attendant repercussions were particularly vicious. The commanding Customs officer at the airport, with over a decade of experience at his post, was transferred and demoted as soon as the new government came to power. Dozens of other officers at KIA were accused of allowing close associates of the outgoing administration to take unauthorized leave of the country, allowing them to avoid investigation and protect illicit assets. As a result, the entire Customs staff at the airport was threatened with mass transfer. A sign of a more general climate of bureaucratic improvisation—of a political sociality successively unhinged—working conditions at KIA were highly unpredictable in terms of where staff inspect and store goods, interview passengers, or simply place their desks, tariff and duty schedules, and phones.

Embodying Sovereignty: Red and Green, Black and White

Indicative of the dual dynamics of empowerment and uncertainty, at KIA's Arrival Hall the most forceful engagements between travelers and Customs officers revolve around efforts to bring the conventions of passenger clearance in line with international standards. International protocols are very much perceived by Customs officers to demonstrate their membership in a supranational order and to legitimate the intensification of state scrutiny. Despite the assimilation of Customs officers into this higher order of rule, the disciplinary tactics officers employ in their encounters with travelers are premised not on alienation but on the very capacity for identification.

To become familiar with globally sanctioned procedures, Customs officers at all levels of the service commonly participated in international initiatives. Nearly every high-ranking officer at KIA has traveled outside of Ghana to attend international seminars. When I first met the commanding Customs officer of the Arrival Hall, he had just returned to Ghana from a two-week course at the International Customs School in Malaysia sponsored by the WCO and the ICAO, with funding from the government of Canada. Customs officers from other countries, including a whole contingent from the United States and United Kingdom, came to Ghana at least once a year to run seminars, distribute reference material, and train trainers in intense bursts of educational effort.[11]

On a rhetorical level, at least, international agendas are taken to heart. By the middle of 2000, the KIA Arrival Hall was reorganized into two different channels for passenger clearance: one Red, for passengers with goods to declare, and one Green, for those without. A "Risk Management System" was put into place based on the tenets of "security," "facilitation," and, most of all, "selectivity," the new term for "profiling," according to U.S. Customs agents. The status of Customs officers as middle figures, at once allied with travelers yet doubly authorized, first by the state and next by the international community, to rule over them, is most apparent in regard to selectivity.

In theory, selectivity was to be systematically applied by Customs to different flights and different sorts of travelers. Risk criteria were based primarily on drug smuggling, at the time of fieldwork the basis of Ghana's significance to international Customs agencies. Ethiopian Airlines and South African Airways flights were ranked high risk because of their possible link to drug-smuggling routes, whereas the Swissair flight was considered low risk because of the high cost of tickets and low likelihood that it would be the flight of choice for illegal couriers. Passports of passengers on flights arriving in Ghana from other parts of Africa were checked for stamps from countries like Burma and Thailand, well known for their drug supplies, and dozens of drug smugglers were apprehended annually by Customs officers at the airport (*Ghanaian Chronicle* 2002).

Beyond this focus on smuggling, the way selectivity was put into practice had little to do with the professed standards of the U.S. Customs Service or WCO, the leading forces in international Customs training. It was no secret that the Red and Green channels were used to enforce a divide between Ghanaian and non-Ghanaian travelers and, more generally, between Africans and non-Africans, a distinction described by Customs officers as one between "black" and "white." Customs officers of both junior and senior ranks time and time again echoed the words of

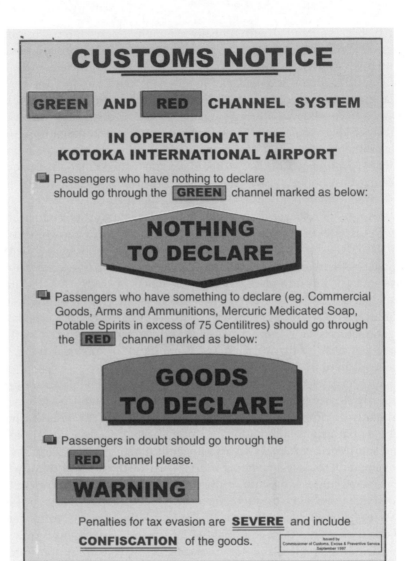

Figure 7.3 Red and Green, black and white. Customs notice posted at KIA. Courtesy of Ghana Customs, Excise and Preventive Service.

their boss: "The integrity of the Ghanaian should not be relied on. Out of ten blacks only three will tell the truth about themselves and vice versa for the white traders that we already know, we only narrow them down and the principle of selectivity comes in here." Or as another officer put it, "The Red channel is for the blacks. We let the whites through; the blacks—the 'Africans'—won't tell the truth. The whites will even tell you one or two gifts are commercial, but the blacks. . . . Indigenous African-Americans are okay, but any African, Nigerian, etc, [no]."

This sort of profiling on the part of the state agents, built on notions of an embodied morality, conform to what Herzfeld identifies as the state's tendency to rule through tropes of cultural intimacy that use "the language of kin, family and the body to lend immediacy to its pronouncements" (1997, 1). Here, Customs officers' use of racial attributes to signal criminal character masks the shifting ground of their authority brought about by the call of a new master at home and abroad. Invoking an "us" and "we" of common stock—the officer who knows what Africans are like because he or she is one of them by dint of shared history and kinship— these terminological ploys counter the actuality of instability with the aura of allegiance. In staking out a supracategory of "African," Customs officers endeavor to broaden the scope of their rule through a rhetoric of identification and inclusiveness. Transcending more transient nominations based on residence or political affiliation, these assignments counter the republican model of citizenship, or *jus soli*, with a broadly rendered notion of citizenship as a community of descent based on the principle of *jus sanguinis*. Reversing a more typical scenario, in which subjects new or marginal to the state seek out resources and recognition through the claiming of "effective citizenship" through normative rather than formal legal means (Sassen 2002, 13), here the sovereign seeks to claim citizen-subjects through the imposition of informal yet systematic terms of discipline and belonging, both emotionally and morally charged.[12]

Contravening the legal definition of citizen, even those travelers holding foreign passports but bearing a Ghanaian name or demonstrating proficiency in Ghanaian languages are accorded the privilege of being treated "as a Ghanaian" by Customs officers. These sentiments result in a clear-cut separation of Ghanaian nationals and other Africans from other visitors—whether African American, Afro-European, Asian, or Euro-American. Ghanaians are well aware of the extra scrutiny to which they are subject at the airport. As one journalist wrote in his weekly column, "Come to Ghana and what I have learnt is that foreigners get better treatment than Ghanaians. . . . These foreigners are just like the nationals but their foreignness gives them an advantage nobody, and no Ghanaian

Figure 7.4 The frictions and frustrations of "super-modernity." Travelers and baggage queue for Customs check before exiting the KIA Arrival Hall.

enjoys abroad even if he is a VIP or somebody in his own Ghana. This discrimination must be cut out" (Blay-Amihere 2001). Ghanaian travelers complained that if they were to be scrutinized, so too should other travelers. Time and again, Customs officers heard the refrain, "These people should be searched, just as you are searching us. You should see how they treat us when we are at their place."

A dynamic suggesting that the importance of border control to the Ghanaian state hinges on the discipline of its own citizenry, such an egregious exercise of state power by Customs officers is not directed at so-called aliens but primarily those targets considered to be nationals. Playing on the very distinctions between foreigner and national, stranger and autochthon, to be recognized as an insider of note within Ghana's gatekeeping regime, one must move outside the boundaries of the state.

A form of "deep-play" (Geertz 1973) testing the limits of rule, these strategies hinge on Customs officers' double-edged identification with travelers, at once asserting experiential parity with them and instituting social divisions among them. Shot through with desire and disdain, such encounters are as much affect-charged as they are legal and material in grounds and outcome.

The extent of Customs' investment in a de facto policy of free movement for so-called foreigners became evident one night when the Arrival Hall was packed with hundreds of pilgrims who had just returned on chartered flights from Mecca. Their arrival caused huge delays in passenger clearance, and there seemed no end to the persons or merchandise crowding the Arrival Hall. The thick crowd congregated outside the exit doors to welcome their kin back from the hajj added to the crush, making it all but impossible to leave the hall. Taking the matter into his own hands, the Customs officer in charge for the evening commandeered an otherwise locked door to create a new point of egress. He made it clear, however, that this separate and expedited exit, which bypassed Customs examination, was for foreign travelers only. The remaining Ghanaian travelers, pilgrims and nonpilgrims alike, were detained in long lines, and they and their luggage were subject to careful inspection.

These dynamics offer a telling reconsideration of the relationship between sovereignty and citizenship conventionally understood through an

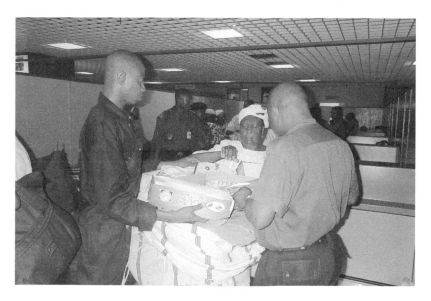

Figure 7.5 Merchant pilgrims. Clearing goods at the airport upon return from the Hajj.

Aristotelian notion of "encompassment," in which citizens are contained within states that set the standards of behavior and belonging (Painter and Philo 1995, 110). Reversing this formulation, in locations marked by geographic and political transience, such as the airport, the conditions of citizen-civilian existence are no longer exclusively framed by the state. Rather, a mobile citizenry shapes the character and capacities of state actors and institutions. Under these conditions, the gatekeeping operations of the state come to center not so much on the discipline of aliens or the categorization of outsiders but on persons considered natives.[13]

Customs and Classification: Discursive Sovereignty and Self-Determination

Again interweaving tactics of alienation and affiliation, legal judgment, and personal justification, the Red and Green channel system and selectivity principle are put to further effect. Although most Ghanaians, and other Africans for that matter, are corralled through the Red channel, they do not as a group experience the authority of Customs officers in identical ways. But the differential treatment meted out by Customs officers, contrary to what one might expect given Customs' fundamental concern with the collection of duties, does not correspond to the commercial goods carried by the traveler. Rather, officers' application of Customs law depends as much on the attributes of the traveler as on the things with which they travel—commercial and noncommercial items alike. Here, a very distinctive form of "profiling," to use the term actually preferred by Customs officers, is put into effect.

Much of this profiling centers on the determination of each traveler's profession. After greeting a passenger and asking him or her to open bags, Customs officers invariably follow up with the question, "What work do you do?" This coincides with a glance at the passenger's passport, which in Ghana includes on the frontispiece a line specifying the passport holder's profession just below the entry for name, address, and date and place of birth. The effort to determine profession is repeated through the examination of the passenger's landing card (form C-70). Containing a bold line asking for statement of profession, this document had recently been reissued by the Customs Service at the time of fieldwork, and all airlines were required to distribute copies to passengers while on board. When I inquired about the landing cards, I was told that, given the nature of both the Ghanaian and global economies, a person's profession could change at any time, making it important to obtain a current record not always captured in the passport entry.

Although ostensibly fixated on verifying passengers' reported professions, Customs officers, in actual fact, make little effort to discern whether or not passengers' material endowments are truly professional in nature. This is so despite the explicit directive of Customs Law PNDC 330 that "tools of one's trade" can be brought into the country duty-free. Much more so than determining whether passengers carry objects necessary to their work, Customs officers appear to be interested in the wide array of personal items—from wardrobe to type of suitcase and gift items—a traveler brings into the country. Drawing on the shared symbolic knowledge of state subjects and agents (Herzfeld 1997, 29), these encounters invoke an intimacy related to historically specific constructions of socially significant personhood. In twenty-first-century urban Ghana, this is a personhood thoroughly bound up with class. Somewhat tied to profession but not entirely explained by it, this class-derived identity has everything to do with habits of consumption (cf. Bourdieu 1984; Meyer 1998a). Time and again, my research assistants and I heard officers explain the correlation between a person's work and his or her material entitlement. We were told, "You can't treat all passengers the same. The question of discretion comes up all the time . . . [take a] lawyer, medical officer [who] . . . goes out of the country once in two years, buys three pairs of shoes and twelve shirts. You don't treat him/her the same as someone who travels once a month and has a boutique." Another officer reiterated, "If a man who lists his occupation as the executive director of a company has a suitcase full of twelve three-piece suits, he is likely to get away without paying duty on them. On the other hand, a woman or man listing her or his occupation as a farmer who has these same items in her or his suitcase will be asked to pay tax on them."

To understand the place of class and classification in the making of sovereign rule, one needs to consider the strong connections among Customs, consumption, and political standing. In the minds of many Ghanaians both within and outside of the service, Customs work is an express lane to modern affluence. Although nearly all Ghanaians aspire to similar sorts and signs of upward mobility, in contrast to other occupations, work in Customs is considered a direct means to this end, which is attained in the very course of employment through gifts, payoffs, and preferential access to commercial goods and opportunities. For Customs officers, the achievement of these aspirations is not about wealth alone but visibly conveys a capacity for a distinct sort of self-determination integral to the type of self-made sovereign supremacy discussed by Enlightenment scholars like Jean Bodin (1992). This is not so much about standing above the law but about cultivating an authority that is self-endowed and, therefore, prior to it. The potential for material gain in Customs is closely tied to where one is posted and KIA is one of three Customs stations, along with Tema Harbor and Aflao on the Togo-Ghana frontier, known as the "Golden Triangle." A sign of one's success and connections within the Customs Service, in line with this logic of "privilegism" (Blundo and Olivier de Sardan 2006, 95), officers at the airport see themselves as having a special purchase on entitlements of and to rule.

As the possibility and necessity of international air travel for Ghanaians from all walks of life intensified in the wake of neoliberal restructuring, the premises of Customs officers' assumed right to rule were called into question. Compared with Customs officers, the travelers the officers inspect and interrogate at the airport have followed a very different spatial and economic itinerary that is providing lucrative returns, whereas Customs officers' own material aspirations remain unsatisfied. Customs officers pride themselves on their educational credentials, yet many in the growing ranks of economic migrants have little education and have climbed the socioeconomic ladder through unskilled work. They are garnering substantial material gains, sending cars and high-priced consumer items back to Ghana and building houses for themselves and their families, whereas Customs officers back home struggle with a devalued cedi, low official salaries, a rising cost of living, and a tarnished reputation.

Customs officers are explicit about their dislike for travelers, who they feel are beneficiaries of undeserved gains. Referring to a large number of young men from central Ghana who find their way to Germany and are popularly referred to as "burghers," one Customs officer remarked, "Asanti burghers in their mid-30s who got a visa out of the country by a stroke of luck think of themselves as being better than everybody else."[14] Another confided, "Ghanaians who have gone abroad think they are superior to the Customs officials, meanwhile, they do menial jobs when they travel abroad." The disdain of Customs officers for Ghanaian travelers is often reciprocated. It was not uncommon to hear travelers haranguing the officers who inspect them: "Search it, put your hands inside and search it. You don't know how to do your job." One woman responded to the request to be searched by asking, "Do you want me to throw my panties on the floor?" to which the Customs officer replied, "Stupid idiot." Powerless to directly combat the abuse, yet conveying the sentiment that she was no longer fully under the purview of the

Ghanaian state, the woman then remarked, "If we were outside, I would have worked you over real good. Unleash this kind of behavior on someone else." In such exchanges, Customs officers' sense of their moral and material entitlement to rule, along with its acknowledgment by others, is under blunt attack.

Sparked by the drama of these encounters and the objects and emotions conveyed, impressions linger long after passengers leave the Arrival Hall. In exchanges among Customs officers, sentiments not only of insecurity but also of renewal can be heard. Conversations consistently touch on themes of wealth and mobility. Demonstrating Customs officers' knowledge and longing more than personal reality, when we asked about their economic aspirations, they were quick to mention their interest in traveling abroad: "to send my wife to Dubai to purchase goods for her shop, to work in London to raise money for a new car, or taking a fantasy vacation to a Caribbean island." Officers suggested that treating passengers well at the airport could lead to the opportunity to leave Ghana, as, I was told, had happened to a former Customs colleague, who was invited to the United States by a traveler and is now a U.S. citizen. In a bout of verbal play, a group of officers joked that they were "trillionaires" with the capacity to hand out BMWs and fly my research assistant—by helicopter—anywhere in the world she wanted to visit. Turning fantasy into reality, one of the senior officers at the airport Arrival Hall proudly confided that, when he was voted the top Customs officer at KIA in 2000, he received a free ticket to the United Kingdom on British Airways and spent a month in London.

No doubt these verbal jousts have a competitive, compensatory edge. But what sort of sovereignty is at stake in these exegetical interludes? If one takes seriously this mode of "fabulation" (Stewart 1996), one can see how these commentaries enable Customs officers to project themselves into a realm of agency and endowment built on the catalog of ideas and objects gleaned from transnational travelers. No less powerful for its phantasmagoric form, this discursive space mediates the contradictions of political and economic transposition and brings to the surface the emotional and discursive terrain of sovereignty in the face of shifting material conditions and relations. These narratives reflect the very sort of structures of feeling and feelings of structure of concern to Marxist culture theorists such as Raymond Williams, in which, as George Marcus and Michael Fischer observe, "dominant and emergent trends in global systems of political economy are complexly registered in language, emotions and imagination" (1986, 78). Interlacing the material world and the world of desire and taking mobility as their root metaphor, these flights of fantasy exemplify the type of imaginative work identified by Arjun Appadurai (1996, 31) as characteristic of transnational experience. Extending Appadurai's insights, these exegetical interludes demonstrate the centrality of the transnational imaginary not only to those who cross borders but also to those who occupy and enforce them. More than simply a commentary on conditions of dislocation, these expressive conventions provide a means to alter and arrest them.

High-Tech Elites and Supranational Endowment

Other realms of transnational trade and travel provide Customs officers with a more direct path to empowerment and status elevation. In the spring of 2000 Ghana, along with a host of other developing countries, was put on notice to carry out a series of decrees emanating from the WTO as a condition of continued membership (WCO 2002b). These dictates centered on the WTO Agreement on Customs Valuation and required Customs officers to use a new and radically different procedure for determining value, the very basis of Customs duties. As explained in earlier chapters, rather than officers using a list of fixed and standard values generated by the Customs Service itself, as they did in the past, the new guidelines required an approach to value based on "market" determination. Known as "Transaction Value," this is "the total payment made or to be made by the buyer to or for the benefit of the seller for the imported goods. It includes all payments made as a condition of sale of the imported goods by the buyer to the seller or by the buyer to a third party to satisfy an obligation of the seller. In most cases, this will be the invoice price" (WTO 2003a). Vividly illustrated in the preceding discussion of GSL, the WTO also stipulated that Transaction Values be verified by cross-checking the received value against those obtaining in similar transactions, a process requiring communication with sellers and manufacturers by means of electronic networks and computerized databases (WTO 2003b).

Handed down from on high, the WTO valuation agreement may well be considered a sign of what Sassen (1996) calls "denationalization," in which the state answers the call of other masters. The WTO directives, like the principles of selectivity and risk management, equally operate as a means of state empowerment, giving Customs a supranational legitimacy and endowing Customs officers with new grounds and techniques for rule, enmeshing them in the social fabric of the nation at the same time as they reposition them globally. These adjustments are not entirely in conformity with the WTO's vision or intention, but in a different way at the airport than GSL and Tema. Despite the commercial ease and acceleration promised by the WTO, putting the Customs Valuation Agreement to work at KIA was beset by numerous challenges. Importers rarely present credible documentation because they typically purchase goods in low volumes, off the books, or secondhand. Although Customs headquarters and the offices at Tema Harbor were undergoing preliminary computerization at the time of fieldwork, it had yet to hit the airport.

These gaps and ambiguities become glaringly apparent as Customs officers grapple with new commercial trends, among them, the growing trade in high-tech consumer items. The airport is becoming a major conduit for the movement into Ghana of cell phones, computers, and computer parts and accessories, such as scanners, printers, PC cards, and more. Customs officers face the perennial problem of determining whether these goods are being imported for commercial use or if they are personal items. Although officers encounter this consideration in the clearance of other commodities, because of the high value of high-tech items, quantity—the usual arbiter of the personal-commercial divide—is a poor indicator of economic intent. In a situation giving rise to new sorts of trading roles and new sorts of individuals entering into trade, high-tech electronics, even if imported in low volume, can be the source of substantial profit. The problem is compounded by an even more basic challenge of correctly identifying and classifying the goods at hand. Many items are so new or so specialized that Customs officers have little knowledge of their function, leaving them ill equipped to assess the items' value in a manner in keeping with WTO protocol or to determine their proper duty rate.

Because the old standardized Customs values did not even mention the new sorts of imports and the Transaction Value system could hardly be applied to the small-scale importer in a manner envisioned by the WTO, Customs officers at the airport were left to their own devices. In the face of this reality, they generated a database of values specific to the Arrival Hall. Not exactly what the framers at the WTO had in mind, the database was gleaned from an unusual sort of public culture. Effecting a sort of bureaucratic mimesis, it included the few credible invoices officers could find and a whole array of promotional material—catalogs from discount electronics distributors in the United Kingdom, brochures from the Dell computer company, flyers and advertisements from international newspapers, and even an Amazon.com brochure I gave them.[15]

All of this information was compiled in a handwritten reference volume consisting of a packet of long lists, photocopies of invoices, and attached pieces of paper that was copied and recopied and stored in the desk drawers of the senior officers charged with assessing value. To maintain this unofficial but consistently referenced data bank, officers were constantly engaged in informal market research. One of my research assistants noticed a Customs official intently reading the information on a box containing a scanner. I heard another ask a traveler, "What are IO cards? Are they like smart cards?" Working hard to ascertain not just what these products were but also their worth, several senior-ranking Customs officers charged with the assessment of duties cultivated alliances with specific importers they saw as reputable leaders in the computer business and relied on them to provide both product information and values.

The documentary bricolage compiled by officers at KIA constituted a parallel symbolic form to the social poetics worked out through jokes, secrets, and body language as described by Herzfeld. Combining formalism with irony (Herzfeld 1997, 15), this assemblage both parodied the promise of the electronic database and took its place. A uniquely Ghanaian version of WTO protocol, it contained values gleaned from personal experience and the physical artifacts of transaction, rather than from anonymous and electronic data envisioned by the WTO Agreement on Customs Valuation. But in contrast to cultural formulaics discussed by Herzfeld (35), which ultimately reinforce state hierarchy, in Customs officers' making and utilization of their database, the terms of authority are less clear-cut. Although the database references the WTO's overarching authority and conveys Customs officers' command of the new form of bureaucratic knowledge, as an approximate and somewhat parodic form it equally references the autonomous interaction of Customs officers and travelers from which it was actually created.[16] Accomplishing another inversion of power and position, the database similarly avails otherwise unorthodox high-tech traders of the documentary authority of the state while it connects Customs officers to a category of commodity and realm of transaction that extends beyond their territory and control. Although Customs officers demonstrate their ultimate authority in the assessment of value, their dependence on private-sector entrepreneurs makes for a new sort of elite alliance.

Rising to the WTO standard yet set apart from it, the pacts and adjustments made by Customs officers and travelers in the creation of the ersatz database mark a claim to a distinctively Ghanaian sovereignty. Like the Asian capitalist networks described by Ong (1999), this is an authority not restricted to state agents but shared by ruling elites who operate within the state and outside it and who situate themselves within Ghanaian territory and a wider global commercial circuitry. Although more practical than official, gaining force from a complex cultural imaginary, this is a sovereignty that is national and transnational without being fully subordinate to the supranational even as it partakes of and gleans recognition from its norms.[17]

Undeclared Baggage: State Discipline and Sovereign Restoration

Travelers passing through KIA are not merely targets or objects of control on which state agents draw in the public and private fashioning of their authority. Exemplifying classic republican ideals in which sovereignty depends on the authorization of "the people" (Philpott 2003), Ghana's mobile citizenry are keepers of the state in their own right, actively involved in establishing and policing the parameters of rule. Conveying what might be considered a Hobbesian submission to sovereign oversight (see Hobbes 1968), such policing is not always about curbing state power but also involves its reinstatement. At KIA, this dynamic can be discerned in the negotiations surrounding the filing of a Passengers Unaccompanied Baggage Declaration, or PUBD. Most Ghanaians returning home, whether for a short visit or a longer stay, send unaccompanied baggage by airfreight or as containerized cargo in addition to checked passenger baggage. Although they might include commercial goods explicitly destined for market, more often travelers ship goods they intend to distribute to friends and family or invest in their own property in Ghana. In addition to personal items such as clothing, these goods include building supplies, household fixtures, electricity generators, agricultural implements, and even automotive parts.

When the yearly budget was released in early 2001—the first year of the newly elected New Patriotic Party (NPP) government—it included a provision (Section 7 of 1996 Act 512 Amended) requiring a 1 percent processing fee on personal effects coming into the country in addition to a host of other special taxes, all of which Customs was obligated to collect. At the same time that the new fees signaled at least a superficial commitment to the tariff reductions demanded by the WTO free-trade agenda, they provided an alternative source of revenue to the state from the influx of new and used goods that are a hallmark of the neoliberal era. Further instituting a market-based economic logic in line with WTO standards, the new ruling on personal effects also required the PUBD to include a description of each item along with a declared market value from which the aforementioned processing fee was calculated.

Explicitly distinguished from a tax, the fee cast a wide net and was applied to a range of goods and transactions, even those determined tax exempt by Customs statutes, from goods imported by churches and religious bodies to gifts and educational materials. The new provision marked a departure from earlier procedures, which only required a general description of contents and approximation of their combined value from travelers declaring personal effects; the goods were then allowed into the country duty-free. For several months after the new policy was announced, travelers remained unaware of the new fee. Sharing in the tendency to peg self-worth to material wealth, they inflated the value of their unaccompanied baggage when interviewed by Customs officials, much as they had done in the past. Conscious of the judgments of fellow passengers queued behind them and the possibility of flaunting the value of their cargo to friends and relatives who might accompany them to pick up the items, travelers commonly reported shipments and parcels containing tens of thousands of dollars worth of goods.

Deliberations around the new policy created a frustrating situation for travelers and Customs officers alike. When travelers finally collected their unaccompanied baggage from the harbor or airfreight office, they were shocked to find a new payment in store. Likewise, Customs officers clearing the goods were expected to make time-consuming calculations requiring the detailed valuation of all items—from weighing used clothes to researching the market value of used appliances—all to apply the 1 percent fee. Customs officers at the Arrival Hall consequently found themselves besieged by travelers requesting adjustments to the values originally declared on the PUBD many weeks after their original date of arrival.

Seeking to stave off the growing onslaught of petitions and voicing their newfound sense of parity with the traveling class, Customs officers manning the Arrival Hall's PUBD desk decided to inform travelers of the new fee and ask them if they wanted to reassess the declared values of their goods. Giving voice to the anticorruption rhetoric increasingly central to neoliberal ideology both at home and abroad (Hasty 2005b), numerous travelers reacted with suspicion to this "customer-friendly" application of the law, bringing complaints to higher levels of the Customs administration, much to Customs line officers' surprise. Adding to the general discrediting of the Customs Service already in the air, so vocal and vehement were these charges that several officers at the Arrival Hall were subsequently transferred or demoted.

It is not difficult to attribute travelers' response to Customs officers to their overarching disdain for the state's mounting intrusions. But these confrontations may also be read to reveal another level of signification, rent with the ambivalences of "attachment and disavowal," characteristic of citizens' attitudes toward the overarching specter of state authority, more generally (Aretxaga 2003, 399). Specifically, Ghanaian travelers' resistance to Customs officers' attempts at empathy might be interpreted to signify an almost nostalgic longing among transnational citizenry for a style of rule in which state authority is distinguished from the public (Herzfeld 1997, 111). Although vicarious, Customs officers' sense of identification with travelers is nevertheless central to their efforts to renew their authority in the face of shifting economic and political conditions.

Blundo and Olivier de Sardan (2006, 110) remind us that many "African citizens have a Western model in mind when assessing the functioning of the 'real state'" in Africa. It is unclear whether travelers, in challenging Customs officers' entreaties, were deliberately articulating a language of transparency driven home in the European or North American states where they resided or, alternatively, if they were seeking to impose claims on their state of origin to redress their often temporary and always tenuous standing as Africans abroad. What does seem apparent, however, is that the transnationals involved in these encounters sought to instate a boundary between Customs officers and themselves, no matter how similar their origins, aspirations, worldviews, or consumption habits. It is possible to speculate that, for these travelers, the state was a domain apart; although it could be approached, negotiated with, reformed, and maligned, it was not to be assimilated, at least not on its own terms. At once expressing disdain and desire for state authority, evident here is a societal struggle to police the terms and agents of rule, even if to reinstate them in more proper form. These interactions and accompanying imaginaries, hence, represent a domain in which the tenuous yet ever-powerful boundary between state and society is objectified (cf. Mitchell 1991).

Conclusion

In this chapter, I train my lens on Ghana's KIA and Customs personnel to argue that air travel and the manifold policies and infrastructures that enable it represent a hidden frontier of neoliberal reform. Ethnographic observations at KIA suggest that the proliferation of supranational regulatory rubrics and transnational flows within the airport do not undermine state authority. Rather, they provide a means for state officials to intensify their scrutiny of mobile subjects in ways both highly technocratic and deeply personalized. Through the extraction, imposition, and assimilation of various forms of intimate knowledge, Customs officers simultaneously gain mastery over and identify with a traveling citizenry.

Such adjustments and repositionings, far from existing as purely contractual relations between rulers and ruled, are shot through with desire and the prerogatives of self-making. Moving beyond the *communitas* of the "cultural intimacy" of bureaucratic encounters identified by Herzfeld (1997, 2005), these interchanges not only rely on the affirmation of a common culture but their articulation also serves to recalibrate political distinctions much more than to mediate difference. The dynamics in play at Ghana's airport thus provide a striking illustration of the always exploitative potential of the "fantasy" life at the foundation of state authority captured by Aretxaga, who asserts that "rational technologies of control [are necessarily] animated by a substrate of fantasy scenes" (2003, 402–3). Indeed, from a comparative vantage point, one can argue that the political force of the state's imaginative terrain is most pronounced in conditions of flux, whether in Ghana or the context of political and cultural upheaval described by Navaro-Yashin (2002) in her examination of Turkish public life. Although in a different context than the mass spectacles showcased by Navaro-Yashin, a similar form of affective production can be found at Ghana's international airport, a domain committed to the heavy hand of bureaucratic procedure and intense dyadic engagements between state agents and subjects, rather than collective ceremonial.

The case of Customs at KIA, moreover, suggests the importance of moving beyond the examination of bureaucratic intimacy in terms of the semiotics of isolated interactions (pace Herzfeld 1997, 2005) to the way these "close encounters" configure and are configured by the wider institutional and historic context. Namely, the material *cum* sentimental transpositions occurring in the course of Customs clearance magnify as much as rework the wider disjunctures of neoliberal reform. Specifically, in the rendering of sovereignty at the airport, it is transnational actors— namely, Ghanaians by birth or citizenship who have invested themselves in the circuitry of international trade and travel—who present the greatest challenge to the substance and distribution of state authority and are the targets of state intervention. A twist on conceptions of popular sovereignty in which the populace authorizes the right to sovereign rule (Locke 1960) and on classic conceptions of citizenship in which states set standards of behavior and belonging (Painter and Philo 1995), Customs officials manipulate the markers of popular identity and experience to manage a stratum of citizens-subjects who are increasingly geographically and socioeconomically mobile.

As evidenced in the exchanges between Customs officers and high-tech importers, such adaptations alter the basis of rule as well as the boundaries of the ruling class. Visible in Customs officers' compilation of a simulated database at once instantiating and mocking the authority of the WTO valuation regime, state agents garner the means to rework supranational conventions and interventions as they see fit. Bridging the personal and the official, the stuff of commerce and the stuff of regulation, the domestic and the imported, this example demonstrates that the components of sovereign imaginaries—from dreams of wealth and travel to computer hardware and data-management systems—have a broad currency by no means exclusive to national governance.

Another lesson learned about neoliberal statehood from the case of Ghana's Customs authorities and international airport is the limitation of studying state-making exclusively in terms of the conventional realms of politics. In Ghana, for instance, there is tremendous attention focused on electoral reform, democratic consolidation, and executive power by policymakers and scholarly analysts alike. This exclusive focus on formal arenas and codes of participation and representation may be misplaced. Although I do not suggest that the electoral realm in Ghana is only a mask or diversion deflecting attention from the real stage of power, as do Nina Glick Schiller and Georges Fouron with respect to Haiti, I emphasize the need to look closely at the interplay of what they term the "apparent state" (Glick Schiller and Fouron 1999, 210) and parallel productions of political order—what might be called the "effective state"—within the bureaucratic arenas of Customs and border management, among others. Namely, it is ostensibly marginal political domains—the airport, borders, and Customs officials, along with expatriated citizens and travelers—that emerge as crucial sites for the transformation and constitution of political authority. This is not because the airport represents a site of the open-ended, deracinated supermodernity of global flows, as Augé (1995) would have it, but because the airport concentrates an assemblage of distinct and not always compatible forces of reform, each of which claims the state in different ways. Among them are various international regulatory fields of the WCO, WTO, U.S. Customs, the World Bank, and the ICAO. The airport also concentrates the flows and aspirations of a population whose members are rendered increasingly mobile by the attractions and attenuations of market-based government and whose entry and exit are intensively policed by authorities in the North Atlantic states where they work and reside. Redesigned and reimagined, the airport is, likewise, a site of contestation and collaboration between a plethora of state overseers from the private sector, including architecture and construction firms, investors, and development banks.

Revealing the aerial frontier to be a critical space of political and economic endowment in global neoliberalism, Ghana is not alone in its overhaul of airport facilities, engagement of international regulatory rubrics, or the intensification of air travel among nationals and non-nationals alike. Neither is Ghana unique among developing and transitioning countries in its heavy reliance on Customs revenue and the ongoing expansion of Customs responsibilities. Indeed, in Ghana and elsewhere, the conjoined revamping of airport infrastructure and Customs conventions reveals the creation of zones of denationalized rule (Sassen 1996) paired with a dynamic of state inscription in which the state's managerial role is put on full display. Like the growing autonomy of national financial bodies with regard to the flow of currencies, capital, and debt (LiPuma and Lee 2004), here the technocratic control of the mobility of persons and commodities via Customs authorities comes to stand as a necessary (if minimal) criterion of stateness in neoliberal times.

In this context, compared to the zones of exclusion described by Giorgio Agamben (1998), in which the suspension of law serves as the sovereign's modus operandi, one finds a rather different process of depoliticization at work, fostering a much more diffuse and dynamic reconfiguration of sovereignty. Although Customs officers at the airport find themselves reendowed by the rise of international rubrics, with little national or official recourse to their formulation, they nevertheless stand outside of these regulatory domains. Once again similar to that of the petty sovereigns described by Judith Butler (2004), here as at other political frontiers, Customs officers' power lies not in the capacity to shape or suspend the "law" but in their discretionary imposition of technicalities of rule already considered "paralegal" in the sense of being both trivial and matter of fact.[18] Transnational travelers, in turn, find themselves objects of intensive regulation. Their mobility is contingent on the attenuation of their full participation in national politics, but the same mobility provides them a purchase on the very international norms that have come to infiltrate the governing practices of their state of origin, enabling them to challenge and augment the new terms of rule.

Attesting to the critical importance of the return to "the subject" in studies of political economy called for two decades ago by Marcus and Fischer (1986), for the diverse categories of persons who work and move through the airport, the ambiguities and possibilities of neoliberal conjuncture are engaged by way of the social and affective realm. Similar to the haunting emotional worlds of unauthorized migrants described by Susan Coutin (2005), in spaces of transit and transition such as KIA, beset by incompatibilities and ever-shifting agendas, subjective states—narratives, identifications, moral judgments, fantasies, and fears—offer an unparalleled archive of the multiplex registers of sovereign authority and transformation for state agents and subjects alike.

Working the Border: Neoliberal Sovereignty in Comparative Perspective

Theorizing from the Periphery: Ghana Customs as Model of and Model for the Fiscal-Bureaucratic Sovereign

Devoted to the study of sovereignty in the context of the neoliberal turn, this book engages a series of analytical projects. At the book's empirical core is an account of the implementation of an array of neoliberal political and economic reforms in Ghana explored from the vantage point of the country's Customs authority. But as much as it uncovers the nuances of Ghanaian sovereignty, the foregoing account is never about Ghana alone. The investigation of Ghana Customs' operations over time and across national and international space demonstrates that colonial and postcolonial state-building projects are always embedded in wider schemas of political ordering. Whether self-consciously imperial or couched in the neutral language of multilateralism, the bureaucratic contours of the Ghanaian polity are both shaped by these wider fields of intervention and delimit their possibilities.

To put it succinctly, Ghana's Customs administration, at its founding in the nineteenth century and its return to the political-economic fore in the early twenty-first, is most

Figure C.1 Customs' expansive mandate. A Customs officer provides security at the polls during the 2000 presidential elections. Photo by Daniel A. Smith. Courtesy of photographer.

of all, to borrow Clifford Geertz's (1973) heuristic, both a "model of and model for" the ascendance of fiscally based expressions of state sovereignty. The book uses the case of Customs in Ghana to speak to the social and political implications of the rise of fiscal-bureaucratic realms as primary arenas of national governance in the late-modern moment and considers how this nexus is not only functional to neoliberal state and economic formations but also historically possible.

A reality largely hidden behind a strongly technocratic self-representation and therefore receiving little explicit recognition by scholars and policymakers, there is indeed evidence to suggest that Ghana Customs represents a paradigmatic case of early twenty-first-century governmental restructuring. Illustrative of as well as informing a worldwide trend toward the intensification of fiscally based governmental administration, the expansion and promotion of state fiscal capacities is neither unique to Ghana nor to the realm of Customs administration. Across the more and less developed world, the closing decades of the twentieth century and the opening years of the twenty-first have been marked by the rising clout of select sectors of the state expressly concerned with regulation and revenue: from ministries of finance and trade, to central banks and a range of fiscal authorities (Sassen 2006). Closely linked to the emergence and broadcasting of the neoliberal paradigm, we can see this early on in the United States with the monetarist economic shocks orchestrated by Federal Reserve Chair Paul Volcker and the parallel retooling of financial architecture in the United Kingdom allowing for an increasingly permissive banking structure in conjunction with fiscal belt-tightening on the part of the state occurring in the late 1970s and early 1980s (Harvey 2005, 23, 56).

Not only do similar examples rapidly come to the fore elsewhere in the highly industrialized states of the "first world," in the ensuing decades this trend is further evidenced by the formidable role played by financial ministries and central banks of the world's growing cast of debtor nations, no doubt intertwined with the rising clout of international financial institutions.[1] Whether in traditional "developing" states or new "transitioning" ones, state bodies instrumental to negotiating the terms of loans, credit, and the attendant financial conditionalities surrounding exchange and interest rates and debt rescheduling have gained substantial authority and increasing autonomy, often divorced from the pressures and preferences of other sectors of the state apparatus (LiPuma and Lee 2004). If the 2008 spearheading of the bailout of the U.S. financial industry by Secretary of Treasury Henry Paulson in league with Federal Reserve chairman Ben Bernanke and similar moves among their European counterparts is not proof enough of the ascendance of this logic of rule, earlier examples abound from all corners of the world. By the 1990s this phenomenon was taking shape in states as diverse as Mexico (Babb 2001), Brazil, India (Fox 2000), Ecuador (Sawyer 2004), Hungary (Phillips et al. 2005) and Egypt (Mitchell 2002), all allied by their early responsiveness to neoliberal pressures (Simmons and Elkins 2004).[2]

Demonstrating the rise of this orientation among African states, Ghana included, evidence from Paris Club negotiations regarding private debt relief further exemplify the authority and insulation of national financial officers and their expanding portfolio (Callaghy 2009). In Ghana, this process has not gone unnoticed. Pointing to its near inevitability in the Ghanaian setting, in a March 2007 speech commemorating the fiftieth anniversary of Ghanaian independence, legal scholar H. Kwasi Prempeh sketched the plight of the "neoliberal sovereign." According to Prempeh (2007), not only is Ghana's Minister of Finance considered the most important officer in the executive branch, eclipsing ministries attending to pressing domestic concerns, but the President himself is doing the Finance Ministry's bidding: devoting his time to raising funds from foreign sources and managing relationships with donors and creditors.

Despite the broad thrust of these trends, the remaking of the state form at this historical juncture, as the close reading of neoliberalism's unfolding in the case of Ghana makes evident, is not a simple pattern of the export of pretested models from the global north to the global south—from advanced capitalism's core to its periphery. Rather it is built on a complex geography of exchange and experimentation.[3] The specific case of Customs reforms in this way affirms as well as complicates Harvey's claim:

The uneven geographical development of neoliberalism, its frequently partial and lopsided application from one state to another, testifies to the tentativeness of neoliberal solutions and the complex ways in which political forces, historical traditions, and existing institutional arrangements all shaped why and how the process of neoliberalization actually occurred. (Harvey 2005, 13)

Namely, as opposed to a situation of nearly unbridled contingency—a nearly endless number of "actually existing neoliberalisms" suggested by Harvey, the example of Customs revitalization reveals conditions of *systematic* and *shared variation* in which peripheral states such as Ghana by dint of necessity as well as historically honed state capacities are the source of considerable innovation and the activation of political-economic strategies later applied elsewhere. Not only are "crisis"-prone polities of the developing world prime sites for the trying out and refinement of untried neoliberal solutions, whether homegrown or externally imposed or a combination thereof.[4] As the Ghanaian instance suggests, those states with a record of international cooperation are availed of prolonged investment in policy implementation, even if the outcomes are not always in conformity with official goals. On the "supply side," one reason is that multilateral institutions in the quest for credibility find it imperative to showcase their own models, whatever their imperfections. On the "demand side," governments and citizens of many less-developed states profess a strong need for international assistance, ranging from direct financial aid and infrastructural investment, to models of administration and social development. Indeed, the ruling regimes of "successful" developing states such as Ghana are increasingly savvy and aggressive about courting assistance, whether or not truly necessary or appropriate, or socially desirable.[5]

Notable in the case of Ghana's precocious embrace of the broad battery of fiscal and regulatory forms surrounding Customs administration, the historical legacies of particular states also endow them with distinctive features that are particularly attractive to new political economic agendas. In Ghana, the long-established fiscal-administrative apparatus of Customs enduring from the dawning of the colonial period (and likely, earlier indigenous conventions of taxation and tribute) presents a nearly ready-made space for intervention. A living legacy of an older paradigm of infrastructural power (Mann 1986, 2008), it is nevertheless largely consonant with the new paradigm of fiscally based government and much more immediately amenable to immediate reform than the states of the old capitalist-industrial core. Here we find a ready illustration of Sassen's (2006, 403) observation that "emergent global assemblages coexist with vast stretches of older historical formations constitutive of the modern nation-state. . . . [C]apabilities significant to the older order can be critical to the formation of the new order, albeit subject to insertion into new organizing logic that may alter the valence of these capabilities."

Additionally accounting for Ghana's position at the cutting-edge of global Customs reform, compared to more developed polities, the "small" states of the developing world, reduced in budget, size and capacity (and only sometimes territory), serve as pliable "controls" of a sort. Akin to the clinical medical trials practiced on the bodies of their citizenry (Nyugen 2005), also common to late neoliberalism, they are both open to experimentation and productive of observable results that can be copied and analyzed in the service of further reform. A clear case in point, the bulk of the Customs modernization initiatives in place in Ghana were implemented prior to their adoption elsewhere, from the scanner, to the electronic data interface, DI system, and private management contracts. Not only does the Ghanaian experience figure into the design of Customs technologies and protocols for use within other states, Ghanaian personnel play a leading role in training and advising their regional counterparts. The very fact that the Ghanaian case is showcased among just a handful of other developing states in numerous World Bank publications on Customs modernization attests to Ghana's place as a model for governmental reform (De Wulf and Sokol 2004a, 2004b).[6]

Reflecting a distinctive late-modern and late-capitalist context, what we see here are features of the state becoming available for "selective disaggregation," much like the commercialization of sovereign prerogatives showcased in Palan's (2003) work on tax havens and other off-shore financial systems common across the world's micro-states. Cultivating the partible potentials of national sovereignty, technological change has made features of the sovereign state, similar to the late modern body, increasingly abstractable and mobile (Collier and Lakoff 2005, 34). Though most strikingly apparent in Ghana with the formulation and commercialization of "sovereignty services" via new systems of electronic government and national branding, this logic applies to the whole of the phenomenon of neoliberal Customs reform, extrapolating a single feature of the state to restructure the whole.

Mapping out a frontier of political reform similar to and distinct from other modalities of fiscally based governance, the twenty-first-century resurgence of Customs regimes in Ghana provides an example of the profound political entailments of the expansion of the state's fiscal bureaucratic apparatus. In particular, the investment in Customs reforms in the late-modern era signals the revitalization but also a reworking of the sort of multistranded political expediency noted by Tilly (1985) in the case of tax collection as a sovereign prerogative in early modern Europe. In the historical setting the generation of revenue involved harnessing claims to territory along with popular fealty, the amassing of codified knowledge of the public realm, and the formulation of an enduring link between the populace and the state agents.

Likewise, in twenty-first-century Ghana Customs authorities serve a wide array of functions. Not only is Customs responsible for the collection of substantial revenue, unlike the arcane echelons of other arenas of financial administration, Customs personnel span the quintessential street level bureaucrat (Lipsky 1983) to the highest levels of state authority (as evidenced, for instance, in Customs executives' position on the board of the Ministry of Finance and involvement in international negotiations). Controlling the circulation of persons and things through the extraction of rents and the sanctions of force, Customs wields tremendously broad governing powers.

Again, in contrast to other financial arms of the state, here we see not a restricted expert-epistemic community but a bureaucratic corps who is a conduit for the communication of technocratic knowledge forms and in direct and quotidian relations with society at large. Bringing to life a distinctive sort of infrastructural power based not on abstract control at a distance but a visible and immediate co-presence with the governed, in an era of state-streamlining Customs provides a highly effective modality for broadcasting changing logics of governance, financial and otherwise.

Equally important, Customs expansive presence and long-established mission make it an attractive institution for the accretion of new governing powers. In Ghana, as we have seen, Customs has long been a vector of multipurpose government, with its ranks carrying out the responsibilities of allied government agencies, from the Immigration Service and the Bank of Ghana, to the ministries of Health and Agriculture, to the Armed

Services. Indeed, in the neoliberal era dedicated to the rolling-back of state investments and operations in order to facilitate global flows, Customs surfaces as the perfect mechanism for the realization of a neoliberal vision of *government minimus*, consolidating a broad regulatory reach within a single state apparatus.

Exemplifying a mode of state revitalization distinctive of the neoliberal trend toward the "governmentalization of the state," this is a dynamic originating in the technocratic ideal of efficient economic administration in order to create favorable conditions for private exchange and accumulation (Riles 2006). In the case of Customs processes in Ghana, this mode of governing extends beyond Customs' established revenue functions to infuse Customs' growing policing functions regarding the general public as well as internal processes of administration. Neoliberal Customs reform hence at once represents the promotion of the *fiscal sovereign* as well as the promotion of a *fiscally styled modality of sovereignty* where the configuring of rule for other purposes is modeled on the principles and practices of fiscal governance.

The Political Paradoxes of Customs' Late-Modern Revival

The implications of these developments for the constitution of state sovereignty—the conception, ordering, and exercise of state power and its distribution among the state, society, and the supranational—are profound. And while some of these outcomes are predictable, conforming to preconceived aims, most fall into the category of unintended or unacknowledged but nevertheless largely systematic and systemic effects (cf. Ferguson 1994).

On a macropolitical front, Ghana Customs is emerging as a key arbiter of the nation's international legal sovereignty. Customs executives represent the Ghanaian nation-state in a variety of international institutions, from the World Bank and the World Trade Organization, to the World Customs Organization and International Civic Aviation Organization. In these forums Customs officials demonstrate Ghana's conformity with the basic benchmarks of statehood. Largely autonomous from other governing authorities, here they play an instrumental role in agreeing to the domestic application of variety of international instruments. These instruments encompass international trade as well as other critical features of international relations such as security, international crime, and the collection and relay of information about those who cross and trade across the nation's borders.

Exemplifying the absorption—a sort of ascendance—of Customs into an arena of global standards-making, Customs executives act as bearers of sovereignty. They call the shots nationally and do so with the added authorization of external political agencies. The tradeoff, not surprising in an international system, is that they are expected to conform to the expectations of other states. As I have observed at World Customs Organization meetings, sometimes this requires submitting to the expectations of global powerbrokers such as the United States and the European Union. At others, African Customs executives are beholden to the aggregate interests of southern coalitions (Chalfin 2006). Given their large numbers, however, the coordinated efforts of African representatives alone can sway policy and are often courted by their more powerful peers (WCO 2005b).

Paralleling the terms of Customs' privatized management contracts, here we see a select group of Customs officials (many of whom have moved up the ranks from positions as line-officers) mediating the state's relationship with the supranational realm. As a result, these agents gain purchase on a new sorts of authority in the national realm, enhancing their authority over state subjects and in relation to other state actors. Contra Sassen's (1996, 2002) earlier predictions that international accommodation precipitates denationalization, in both cases we see the externalization of sovereign authority strengthening rather than compromising Customs domestic sovereignty. A inversion of Tilly's (1985) reading of the place of fiscal authority in early modern state formation where domestic fiscal control boosted a fledging state's international might, in the late-modern moment we observe state participation in the production of shared standards of fiscal regulation as instrumental to gaining international clout and in turn, bolstering authority at home.

Taking a cue from recent anthropological discussions of bio-availability (Cohen 2005; Nyugen 2005), the result is a situation that may be labeled "sovereign availability" where the state out of sheer financial habit and necessity is retooled for a price according to terms that expressly benefit of external players, whether international financial institutions, regulatory authorities or multinational capital. But unlike the biological example where the consequences are typically grave (Scheper-Hughes 2005) with Customs we witness a process of sovereign renewal. Here, the resuscitation of a single organ of the state deftly engages the pressures and expectations of supranational bodies to claim oversight of the national polity and populace. Much like what Palan (2003, 61–62) describes as the "paradox of offshore," with the outsourcing of state functions appearing to undermine sovereignty but ultimately reaffirming it, these arrangements cannot be cleanly understood in terms of the state's rise or fall and, "must be seen within the context of the continuing process of state formation."

Following this logic, to fully comprehend the dynamics of neoliberal state formation in Ghana, it is critical to identify not just the presence of absence of state authority but to track the structural underpinning of state power in neoliberal times and the possibilities that follow from those structural conditions. Illustrating Sassen's (2006, 325) more recent observation that in the era of neoliberal globalization "the national is not necessarily eliminated but some of its components are given new meanings by new organizing logics," in the Ghanaian case, we witness a distinctive dis- and rearticulation of the state apparatus. Sharing a vague resemblance with the imperial Customs regimes of the colonial era, national Customs authorities are being absorbed into the supranational arena as the very basis of their authority but nevertheless retain a primary investment in the reproduction of the nation-state. These conditions do not alter the ends of sovereign rule as much as they change the mechanisms of sovereignty's production. Indeed, it is in the process of sovereign production that the politics of neoliberal reform are most insidious, masked on the one hand by their technical character and on the other by their strongly ideological cast. As a result, the conditions of political accountability and participation depart significantly from their official representation.

Good Governance and the Techno-Politics of Democratization

The hidden political entailments of Customs' sovereign ascendance in neoliberal times are especially apparent in the workings of the "good governance" agenda that has emerged as the central plank of the second generation of neoliberal reforms in which Ghana is deeply enmeshed. Contradicting their professed aims of increasing accountability and promoting democratic values, a clear example of what Sawyer (2004, 91) in her study of neoliberal reform in Ecuador calls "neoliberal ironies," this program has fanned the flames of authoritarianism and closed off opportunities for participatory governance. Indeed, although construed as a corrective to the "anti-politics" (Ferguson 1991) of earlier rounds of neoliberal intervention, in them we see the resuscitation of pre-existing inequities and systems of domination. These well-publicized initiatives stand in sharp contrast to the expansion of Customs' bureaucratic might by decree and arcane international agreement. Echoing Gledhill's (2004) notice of the persistent might of neoliberalism's political backstage, the retooling of Customs' massive administrative edifice thus stands as a shadowy—yet insistent—partner to the battery of electoral benchmarks celebrated by the public, the press and the donor community and typically considered emblematic of Ghana's twenty-first-century neoliberal political face.

At the Aflao frontier, as discussed in chapter 4, the authoritarian potentials of the good governance platform are realized through the Customs commissioner's unbridled quest for accountability, efficiency, and transparency—neoliberalism's technopolitical triumvirate. Carried out by means of surprise visits, verbal discipline, the authorization of numerous task forces and the threat of interdiction and dismissal, here we see the "terror of transparency" at work, combining older forms of personalized rule with newer techniques of discipline and surveillance. By the same token, the neoliberal bid to evaluate political problems like corruption as exceedingly onerous provides the opportunity for state agents to claim excessive and emergency powers. In this case, the antidemocratic fallout of neoliberal reform does not simply represent the fanning of nationalist flames or entrenched interests but is an inherent underside of the programmatics of a global platform of governmental self-discipline.[7]

What's more, like the protocols of transparent governance, the parsing of Customs operations across a diverse class of agencies creates a sort of neoliberal heterarchy without a clear distribution of control and command functions. Confounding systematic access and participation, the movement of Customs functions out of the public domain and into private industry justified through claims of administrative rationalization (a logic of political trivialization rather than magnification, as in the case of anticorruption programs) encourages the concentration of power and resources in terms that are inscrutable to the public. Like the first scenario, this too fosters a process of political closure.

These are not the only confluences of democratic ideals and authoritarian outcomes resulting from neoliberal interventions into Customs. Providing a striking example of how neoliberal reforms allow the "shadow powers" of both the public and private realm to "remain sufficiently entrenched to guarantee continuing violence with impunity" (Gledhill 2004, 342), a similar dynamic can be found in the neoliberal push to demilitarize the state apparatus. Although Customs' oversight of persons, territory, and trade has expanded under the neoliberal mantle, as we have seen, numerous other state bodies and functions have fallen by the wayside. Motivated by the professed imperatives of democratic consolidation as much as economic efficiency, among the state sectors faced with demise are a range of paramilitary agencies and loyalists. Ever capacious, Customs accrues the agents and outlooks of these defunct regimes, ultimately rendering the exercise of force and the old lines of military cronyism ever more central to Customs mandate. While enlarging Customs' sovereign might, this shift once again comes at expense of accountability and the formulation of clear lines of authority in relation to the public, within the Customs service, and between Customs and other state agencies.

The etiology and outcome of reform in these cases and others is surely colored by Ghana's distinctive political history as the legacy of neoliberalism's political predecessors—colonial, military, socialist, or populist rule—maintain a persistent hold on the political landscape. But they cannot be wholly attributed to an inherent political pathology and labeled an "African problem." Along with the lingering import of historical determination, neoliberal interventions bring their own systemic inadequacies and structural flaws. In these examples it becomes apparent that the highly proceduralist approach to good governance, a top-down and rule-bound formulation, is vulnerable to abuse and provides little formal means for negotiation. At the same time, the strongly ideological tone of this widely applied political platform, focusing on the unquestionable moral "good" of governance, provides a ready-made cover for the pursuit of less savory agendas all the while diverting attention from public articulation of substantive collective goals. In short, with state allocation of material resources largely undermined by neoliberal economic austerity or pushed behind the scenes and onto parapolitical bodies and spaces, the good governance platform heightens the rhetoric of democratization while the real terms of participation are both reduced and obscured.

In these examples Customs restructuring can be compared with two prevailing models of late-modern governmental reform, both strongly technopolitical in orientation. On the one hand, Harvey argues that neoliberal reforms "put strong limits on democratic governance, relying instead upon undemocratic and unaccountable institutions (such as the Federal Reserve and the IMF) to make key decisions. This creates the paradox of intense state interventions and governments by elites and 'experts' in a world where the state is supposed not to be interventionist" (2005, 69). Even if some aspects of Customs work move outside the public eye, the neoliberal restructuring of Customs operations in Ghana, however, continues to rely on the very possibility of co-presence. In these situations, the ascendance of Customs' wide-ranging technocratic prowess betrays the type of bureaucratic license described by Judith Butler (2004, 61–62) in conditions of late-modern political emergency (Butler's case in point being the U.S. "War on Terror").

Less the sort of executive writ that lies above the law, as in traditional conceptions of sovereignty (Agamban 1998), this is a type of administrative sovereignty that comes from being "below the law," that is, mere "paralegal" procedure, thus allowing for unexamined and expanding power. But distinct from the scenario Butler describes, in the case of Customs reform in Ghana the subjects and agents of rule (the traveling/trading civilian and Customs official) already exist in affective relation, drawing together technocracy and intimacy in ways different from those anticipated by Butler.[8] Sketched below, this sociality impacts the political tenor of neoliberal reform and its potential to delimit or enlarge both the grip of state discipline and the popular production of alternatives.

The Social Life of Sovereignty

As the affective and moral engagements between Customs officials and their subjects makes clear, the retooling of Ghanaian sovereignty in the neoliberal context does not hinge on political and economic dynamics alone. As stated at the outset, sovereignty is always a social relation (Biersteker and Weber 1996), operating in and through social relations, sentiments, moral codes, and collective and individual bodies. The remaking of sovereignty, to extend Marcus and Fischer's classic statement (1986, 78), like other "dominant and emergent trends in global systems of political economy . . . while structured, is also inherently social . . . complexly registered in language, emotions and imagination." In Ghana, due to the pre-existing ties between Customs officials and state subjects, along with the intensity of transition, the moral and affective cast of neoliberal reform is particularly vivid. A fundamental feature of state authority overlooked by Ong (1999, 2006) in her examination of graduated sovereignty, not only are subjectivity and sociality the grounds on which sovereignty is known and expressed, they are also the place where it is made, where diverse and otherwise remote determinations come together and are integrated and orchestrated in practice. Customs officers in this regard are key interlocutors. Much more than a neutral conduit for the transmission of neoliberal imperatives, as in any act of transmission they contribute to the making of meaning at the same time they are changed by the neoliberal project.

As we have seen above, the political implications of Customs officials' moral and affective engagement with the subjects of neoliberal reform are manifold. Officers' deep knowledge and identification with the targets of reform in many ways intensify their impact, enabling officials to press new policies on the back of existing relations and interventions. This is clear, for instance, at Aflao as well as Kotoka International Airport, where Customs officers use their familiarity with the border zone's social makeup and related cultural codes and styles of comportment to intensify their discipline of mobile populations through means documentary, discursive, and embodied. By the same token, foreknowledge and identification can also temper the imposition of new governing rubrics, as evident in the type of "sympathetic corruption" practiced by officers in the Aflao Baggage Hall. Here too we see the blurring of the boundary between agents and targets of neoliberal management, with Customs officers subject to the impositions of their superiors from headquarters and private Customs proxies and thus sensitized to the plight of those they are expected to govern.

The play of empathy cuts both ways, both expanding and curbing the grip of the state. At the airport, we witness an extraordinarily strong tie between Customs officers and African travelers (specifically those caught up in transnational migration) built on a combination of highly personalized disdain and longing, with rather striking political implications. The selective application of new regulatory modes gleaned from international standards renders the transnational-migrant traveler doubly surveilled as insiders and outsiders, natives and strangers, threats and objects of desire.[9] These trends bear a connection to the dually democratic and autocratic features of the neoliberal, though not in predictable or uncomplicated ways. Blurring the boundary between sovereign and citizen, African transnationals, though disabled by the impositions they face, are not passive in the face of Customs exactions. Rather they use their experience of exclusion abroad to reinstate what they take to be the proper terms of rule at home, delimiting the terms of both citizenship and sovereign authority. Remarkably, this popularization of governance is not undermined by the fast pace of travel or the technical terms of its expression but codified and conveyed as a means of cementing connections among a highly mobile community.

The implications of the popularization of the neoliberal project of governance in moral terms and its role in policing the boundaries of the state through unscripted "para-political" channels is equally striking in case of controversies surrounding car clearance and importation.

Here we see not just the identification of the agents and subjects of rule around common cultural codes and status aspirations, but a concomitant popularization of neoliberal ideas spreading from the arcane realms of governance to the rhetoric of religion and popular culture. A testament to what Gledhill calls "the neoliberalization of everyday life" (2004, 338), this sort of ideological transposition results from Ghana's, and hence, Ghanaians', prolonged exposure to neoliberal policies and their attendant rhetoric. Underwriting the expression and achievement of popular sovereignty, such mass-mediated forms of culture have come to be used by the public to discipline the state: curbing state privilege and state claims to private persons and property. The result is a stunning example of neoliberal democratization where commodities and consumption provide the foundation of public interest and the market emerges as both a space of popular debate and a model for social order.

Sovereignty, Territoriality, and the Networked Frontier

Amidst these shifts, where does sovereignty lie? Does Customs' restructuring conform with predictions regarding the deterritorializing effects of neoliberal globalization? Does the hypermobility of commodities and capital, the uprooting of culture from localized understandings and sites of production, and the rise of supranational power blocs (Appadurai 1996a; Robinson 2004; Ruggie 1993) threaten national boundaries— since the seventeenth century the fundamental marker of modern state sovereignty? Or does Customs reform create the sort of parcellized or zonal political-economic configurations highlighted in the case of Asian economic restructuring by scholars such as Ong (2006). Might there be another mode of large-scale spatial patterning in the works brought about by neoliberal appropriation of boundary-based systems of fiscal governance in the African setting?

To begin with, the persistence and expansion of Customs operations in Ghana is compelling proof that neoliberal reforms do not bring about the diminution of the state's sovereign authority at the territorial frontier. Whether at the Aflao land border, Tema Harbor, or Kotoka International Airport, the ranks and operations of Customs are growing along with their international clout. Even Ghana's international financial institution-motivated anticorruption crusade, while exposing Customs officers to greater scrutiny, keeps Customs in the public eye, heightening rather than lessening their imprint on the border landscape, all the while sowing new forms of order and disorder. Likewise new modalities of surveillance, even if contested and imperfectly applied, thicken the regulatory modalities put into play at the boundary line.

These signs of territorial oversight nevertheless only tell a small part of the story regarding the broad range of substantive transformations occurring at Ghana's numerous border zones. Hence, in probing the territorial expression of sovereign rule in neoliberal times, the Ghanaian situation once again cannot be reduced to a singular question of state presence or absence. To fully understand the process of sovereign realignment—territorial and otherwise—we need to defer to a much wider range of indicators regarding the means and meanings as well as context and configuration of rule at the state's multiple borderlines. On the one hand, as revealed in the historical genealogy of the Aflao border examined in chapter 3, what counts as state presence varies over time and in place, whether an embodied *cordon sanitaire*, practices of verbal interrogation, ceremonial display, the assertion of force, or written records and receipts. Equally significant, as demonstrated in nearly all of the book's chapters, state power at the frontier is never fully what it appears to be (Andreas 2000). Rather, the regulatory processes visible at the border zone always operate in a networked relation with other nodes and codes of authority.[10] In classic models of the nation-state, the hierarchical control of central government anchors this configuration (Agnew 2005). Made clear in the Ghanaian case, it also may encompass the influence and imperatives of multinational corporations and multilateral institutions as well as historically precedent political and economic orders. Thus any sort of intensive investigation of border territories, this book argues, must necessarily be supplemented by an examination of how the regulatory capacities of the state in a given location are situated within and a product of a more extensive field of power.[11]

Such an approach to territorial borders, paying close attention to their position within networks of influence and control, while of general significance is especially relevant in the case of late-modern/late-capitalist state reform. An approach to the constitution of sovereign power (territorial and otherwise) through the logic of the network makes it possible to track the changing organization of state authority—the shifting loci of command and control, obligation and delegation—that mark the late-modern moment more generally. Equally important, they again bring to the fore an appreciation of the strongly infrastructural dimensions of late-modern sovereignty (Mann 1986, 2008) and thus shed light on the how the ascendance of state control through administrative realms such as Customs serves as a defining characteristic of twenty-first-century politics. While it is possible to see these developments in state's infrastructural authority as fully consistent with the existing political proclivities and organizational logics (pace Roitman 2005, 196), the Ghanaian evidence suggests a qualitative change afoot, giving rise to a new balance of power within the state apparatus. Even if some of the "ends" of the state remain the same, there are new mechanisms for the production of sovereign authority, and thus new effects, even if unacknowledged or unanticipated.

Specifically, though states such as Ghana maintain a centralized organization, they coexist and compete with other centers of power, public and private, international as well as domestic, ephemeral as much as historically embedded. These conditions, as we have seen, lead to an overall dispersal or horizontal configuration of power tempering the state's claims to absolute hierarchical control. But rather than the kind of zonal arrangement discussed by Ong (2006), producing discrete islands of regulatory authority—a situation evident in Asian industrial zones as well as African enclaves of natural resource extraction such as Angola and Sierra Leone (Reno 1998)—in this African case, the new network and the old boundary are fused. Rather than productive spaces where states renounce their ultimate authority, in the Ghanaian instance the regulation and fostering of mobility across the frontier brings profit and power to select elements and agents of the state at the same time regulatory authority is exercised by other bodies. Under such conditions, frontiers are marked by uneasy terms of cooperation among the authors and agents of the diverse regulatory regimes at play. As a result, territoriality and sovereignty are intertwined but not necessarily coterminous.

A further impetus to peering behind the attributes of state sovereignty in a given location to track the networked relations of sovereignty's production, each border I research—from the Aflao land frontier, to the Tema Harbor and Ghana's international airport—draws upon different modes of control, involving distinct forms of institutional and social participation and international connection and relying upon diverse meanings, media and affective and moral coordinates. Shattering the narrow foundations of most anthropological investigations of African borders, the diversity of governing processes in play reflect the unique functionality of each frontier, whether the priority of the movement of persons versus things or the balance of transoceanic versus transcontinental flows. Not only does this orientation undermine the conception of land frontiers as model boundaries,[12] it situates each border zone in its rightful global/transnational context without losing site of its specific, but always historically constructed, local mooring.

Even at the Aflao land frontier, on the surface the most conservative of the boundary zones I explore, global mobility reshapes autochthony, with the terms of state authority and local accommodation impacted by consumption regimes and models of governance imported from the subregion and the world over. By the same token, the operations of the most multinationalized space of border control—the Accra GSL office—is marked by local aspirations and considerations. In this regard, Sassen's (2006, 419) observations, bringing together Ruggie's (1993) notion of territorial unbundling with the possibility of what might be called territorial "recycling" appears apt. As Sassen sees it, "critical components of authority deployed in the making of the territorial state are shifting toward becoming strong capabilities for detaching that authority from its exclusive territory and onto multiple bordering systems" (2006, 419). This multiplicity of bordering processes and allied political economic fields are very much present in Ghana's frontier zones.

So constituted, the view from the Aflao land frontier provides a stark example of disconnect between the density or quantity of border controls (what we take to stand as the territorial expression of state sovereignty) and the actual coherence of the state project. At this boundary the tensions of territorial rule hinge not only on the inherent challenge of claiming control over mobile persons and things, but equally, the uneasy layering of national political logics and regulatory modes. Reflecting the unsettled legacy of political reform in Ghana, movement through the space of the Aflao frontier zone is akin to moving through the state over time. Here the specter of long gone ruling regimes is brought back to life, signaling the tenuousness of political platform of the day however assiduously pursued by the agents of Customs central command.

International financial institutions' conditional "good governance" initiatives "thicken" the expression of state power at the Aflao frontier in other ways, yet equally incite a disarticulation of authority both geographic and political. This occurs as Customs officers seek autonomy from the violent exactions of Customs administrative center and ally themselves with border-crossers and residents, and all groups—travelers, traders, and state agents combined—pursue increasingly temporary and peripatetic strategies of control. This sort of spatial dispersal finds a parallel in the farming out of Customs operations to yet another node of the Aflao border network: private multinational bodies minimally on-site at the frontier post and headquartered in Ghana's national capital, but not at Ghana Customs' head office. Ultimately boosting the range of state-based controls pursued at the frontier and national space more generally, at stake here is neither a process of recentralization nor decentralization, but a multisited verticalization of control where there are multiple centers of authority in a networked but unsettled relation.

A close reading of the shape and substance of Customs practices at Tema exposes a different combination of regulatory dispersal and intensification of territorialized authority along with the overlap of different regulatory fields. If the Aflao frontier is characterized by the persistent yet increasingly tenuous grasp of the centralized state, at Tema Harbor Customs and its proxies have a broad presence, yet are more and more remote due to the specific inspection technologies employed by Customs and its partners at the port. Grounded in a dispersed corporate network that exists well beyond Ghana, the harbor in all of its vast material concreteness is absorbed into an increasingly virtualized global network of electronic communication. The proliferation of regulatory agencies ruling over the harbor site and the goods that move through it is paralleled by dispersion of knowledge on which the regulatory bodies rely. In this setting the breadth, vastness, and generality of the x-ray imagery and electronic data exchange exist side by side but also inspire the defense of older forms of authority based on physical familiarity and co-presence. Likewise, the perfection of the GCNET electronic data interface bolsters the state's claims to territorial control and coherence at the same time it boosts Ghana's standing in an in international field of standards making. Here we find a compelling example of Sassen's contention that "state border capabilities centered on nineteenth and twentieth century geographic concepts of the border could switch into nongeographic bordering capabilities operating both transnationally and subnationally" (Sassen 2006, 417). Instead of a question of either/or, here the national and supranational exhibit a tense interdependence.

The airport too is a frontier that is endowed through diverse and dispersed means. Although it has long stood as a national icon and security zone and appears ever amenable to rebuilding and renewal as the recent redesign well attests, KIA is a space that thrives on all sorts of external accreditation. These include international financing and international aviation agreements, the work of international architects and construction firms, and international training programs for Customs personnel, along with the cosmopolitan aspirations and imaginations of Customs officers gleaned from their interactions with international travelers and transnationals. Thus it is a space both national and extranational; but unlike the harbor, it remains deeply personalized with the terms of power intensely negotiated between travelers and customs officials. The question of who commands the national and on what terms emerges as a touchstone, point of contention, and source of power for travelers and

Customs alike, and ever functional to both international regulatory agencies and multinational capital, whether invested in trade, state services, or infrastructure. Yet as a site for the joint production of sovereignty and citizenship in the midst of flows, at KIA political relations, alongside their technocratic entailments, are constructed via means deeply felt, with affect serving as a highly portable and enduring ground for the constitution of both political sociality and subjectivity in the course of movement.

Conclusion

Boldly evident in the case of Customs restructuring, Africa's leading developing states, dependent on international interventions and well versed in processes of reform, are important sites for the formulation and testing out of neoliberal governing strategies, even those that require a panoply of high-tech investments, extensive international exchange, and the broad distribution of expert knowledge. Under such conditions states such as Ghana stand as beacons of governmental innovation, generating and displaying models of rule and modalities of sovereignty to be replicated in the more- and less-developed world.

As demonstrated by the Ghanaian example, in these moves we witness the revival sectors of the state apparatus typically considered the most retrograde. Here we see a technopolitical orientation inherited from the colonial period gaining relevance anew in the face of the premium placed by neoliberal initiatives on fiscal management and multipurpose rule. Distinct from the proclaimed expansion of structures of representative rule, the result is an increasingly bureaucratic rendering of sovereignty. Shoring up the state through the cultivation of discrete territorial claims and the activation of new means of control and accreditation, under these circumstances claims to sovereignty are at once heightened and flattened as the organs of national governance find themselves situated in expanding and diversified networks of power.

In a nation-state whose fate, identity, and worldview over the past three decades have been fundamentally shaped by neoliberal interventions, shifts in the terms and modalities of Customs bureaucratic *cum* fiscal regulation do not operate at a distance from the lives and outlooks of those who in inhabit the polity. Customs officials, at once enmeshed in the details and technocratic discourses of reform and in close contact with the public—to which they themselves belong—play a central role in negotiating the forces of sovereign transformation. Far from being a static and faceless bureaucratic corps, Customs officers' implementation of changing codes of governance involves a concomitant reworking of ways of being and knowing, of self, sociality, and morality to alter the ontology of sovereign power.

The affective, intellectual, and embodied engagements on which such bureaucratic reforms depend makes the recalibration of sovereignty about much more than the redistribution of material resources and the terms of command and control. It is thoroughly bound up with the forms of life inhabited by both the agents and subjects of rule. In Ghana, then, the modes of sovereignty moored in Customs administration, though expressed through means arcane and banal: counting and classification, scanners and inspections, examinations and interrogations, x-rays, stamps, documents, exchange rates, and electronic data bases, uniforms, bribes and gunpoints, training sessions, ceremonies and visitations, are fully a "regime of living," to borrow a term from Collier and Lakoff (2005, 23). Encoding a vast genealogy of power with fiscality and bureaucracy jointly at the fore, these practices and perspectives at once invoke an earlier history of the modern state and impel an alternative future for the state system.

Notes

1. Qualifying Gledhill's sweeping claim, the study of Customs in the neoliberal context allows us to consider how and why state authority is sustained via particular arenas of rule.
2. For a discussion of the factors behind Ghana's economic downturn see Herbst (1993).
3. Following the tenets of the neoliberal creed, state assets and activities in Ghana were opened to market forces and the government ostensibly removed from the economic arena via massive programs of privatization and administrative streamlining by way of retrenchment, rationalization and outsourcing (Chalfin 1996; Harrigan and Oduro 2000). Even those areas of government geared to public provisioning— from health and education to utilities and basic infrastructure—were reformed to emulate a market model of competitive, cost-effective and profit-bearing activity, or cease operation (Crook and Ayee 2006), undermining not only the legacy of socialism (African and otherwise) but also mainstream welfarism.
4. The largest and fastest growing arena of economic activity in Ghana, from 1993 to 1998, merchandise exports and imports' share of GDP grew from 18 and 29 percent respectively to 28 and 39 percent. Speeding up this economic trajectory, between 1995 and 2005 growth of merchandise imports averaged 10 percent annually, with exports holding steady at 4 percent per annum (WTO 2008).
5. Less a confession, I share this as a warning to others who seek to tread a similar path of inquiry within organizations, state-based or otherwise, where the distribution of power and resources is highly stratified and largely unchecked.

6. Euphemistically referred to as "Item 13," Hasty (2005a) describes the ubiquity of such distributions in the work of Ghanaian journalists.

CHAPTER ONE

1. This act, involving British administrators and local chiefs, is known as the Bond of 1844 and was an effort to legally define the jurisdiction which had developed around Britain's informal protectorates (Adu Boahen 2000 [1975]: 41).
2. Ghanaian sources indicate that Customs annually collects anywhere from 40 to 70 percent of national revenue, depending on accounting. The Republic of Ghana Budget and Economic Policy Statement (2005), for instance, lists the tax share contributed by Customs at 37.7 percent for 2004 and 38.6 percent for 2003. For the period 1999–2003, World Customs Organization (2004) documents, in contrast, suggest the contribution of Customs revenue to national revenue stands at roughly 20 percent. According to Customs professionals, however, this figure is difficult to gauge depending on whether or not foreign direct assistance is included as a source of national revenue. In Ghana, Customs also collects revenue on behalf of other state organizations.
3. Similar to Ghana, in the West African subregion alone, in 2000 Customs accounted for 40 percent of government revenue in Senegal, 46 percent in Benin and 60 percent in Niger, with strikes of Customs officers in Niger threatening to bring down the whole state apparatus (Arifari 2006, 184).
4. In my effort to highlight the specific historical genealogy of Ghana's Customs Service and its close association with modern state formation, these comments are not meant to discount the role played by tariffs, tolls, and other modes of financial administration in non-Western or nonmodern polities. Cutting across a range of eras and regions, throughout history the exercise of power by officials over goods and revenue through a variety of modes of tax farming and trade control has been closely associated with the constitution of authority (Asakura and WCO 2003). This is no less true in precolonial Ghana than elsewhere in world. The Asante empire alone oversaw various forms of tribute, trade tolls, and commercial monopolies (Wilks 1961, 1989). Likewise, in northern Ghana, despite a political fabric marked by stateless societies, Hausa and Dyula long distance trade caravans were obliged to exchange wealth for protection and the right of passage (Chalfin 2004).
5. Although fiscal regimes of all kinds have been and remain important to state craft, it is worth noting the distinction between the taxation of that which is stablilized, whether consumers, fixed property or income, typically glossed as "direct taxation," and "indirect taxes" such as Customs levied on that which is mobile, whether merchants or commodities.

These are interrelated yet distinct fiscal regimes with different political entailments. This is a point addressed by Roitman (2005) in the case of northern Cameroon, where a direct tax regime was central to the colonial project.

6. Theorized along somewhat similar lines, Peter Sahlins (1989) provides a parallel example of the role of Customs collection in the definition of the French-Spanish borderlands during the eighteenth century.

7. Ardant also presents striking evidence regarding the particular importance of Customs income to federalist nations, including the German empire and the United States in the late nineteenth century (1975, 222).

8. In a passing remark, for instance, Thomas Hansen notes, "Most of the administrative functions, rules, and technologies of governance of the late colonial administration lived on in the Indian state, not least in the realm of policing, taxation, and the legal machinery" (1999, 46). This founding armature of the colonial state remains well ensconced around the world. A project beyond the scope of this work, a whole history could be written regarding the similar governmental designs of British imperial possessions in Africa, India, and the Near East along with the lingering presence of the arcane bureaucratic procedures left over from imperial past from the perspective of Customs. While this legacy may be most marked in the case of the British empire, the logics of French and Spanish imperialism likely linger in Customs as well.

9. Though they are posed as tangential to his wider argument, Anderson does makes mention of Customs in the context of Hungarian/Austrian imperialism (1991, 107) and with regard to the Spanish colonies in the Americas, which, in his view, remained competitive units due to their separate economic administration (52–53).

10. I borrow this term from Ardant (1975, 168).

11. The tremendous dependence of the state on Customs revenue is common throughout the nations of Africa, as is true in less developed countries elsewhere in the world (World Customs Organization 2003). Yet even in the United States, prior to World War I and the imposition of the income tax, Customs provided the primary share of government revenue (Andreas 2000). While U.S. Customs in 2006 collected roughly 3 percent of government revenue, Customs revenues for the European Union netted nearly 12 percent, occupying the low end of the global average of approximately 20 percent of state revenue (WCO 2006a).

12. Mann's generalized comments on infrastructural authority in Africa are instructive in regard to Ghana Customs. As Mann sees it, "Post-independence states thus inherited and perpetuated uneven infrastructural power, except that the external links became as much with the overall global economy as with the former colonial power. Internally, infrastructural power is quite developed along particular segments of the country, but it then flows out

of the country through the economic power infrastructures of multinational corporations, stopping on the way in the capital to provide a cut of the profits to the centralized political elite" (2008, 364).

13. The few exceptions to this premise are the principalities of Liechtenstein, Monaco, and San Marino, which share Customs administrations with the neighboring governments of Switzerland, France, and Italy respectively. A number of states that are not autonomous, such as Hong Kong and Macau, maintain independent Customs authorities.

14. Following the same logic, an early step of the U.S. Coalition Provisional Authority toward state-building in Iraq was the resurrection of the Customs Service (USCBP 2005).

15. Restricted neither to the African continent nor developing economies, the pressures and prerogatives of WTO membership equally apply to the economically dominant states of Asia and the North Atlantic core.

16. GATT's earliest charter included 45,000 tariff concessions, www.wto.org/thewto_e/whatis_e/tif_e/fact4_e.htm.

17. In 2007 the African continent is strongly represented in the WCO, with forty-seven members spanning three administrative regions, a fact that gives Africa exceptional clout in the organization's policy negotiations and renders African Customs authorities attractive targets for bilateral delegations, trade capacity building and aid in the pursuit of support in the WCO's highly competitive elections.

18. Such lobbying was easily observable during my visits to WCO meetings at the headquarters in Brussels.

19. With a worldwide reach, between 1982 and 2002, the World Bank carried out 117 Customs-related projects spanning Africa, Middle East, Latin America, and South Asia, as well as extensive investment in the transitioning states of Europe and Central Asia (DeWulf and Sokol 2004, 165).

20. See Putnam, Leonardi, and Nanetti 1993 for an early statement of the relationship between good governance and economic development.

21. Part of the Bush administration's self-declared "International Trade Agenda" (USAID 2001), the United States displays a wide-ranging investment in Customs-related assistance in Africa and Latin America as well as Central Asia and Eastern Europe. With the proliferation of regional free-trade agreements, USAID work on the Customs front has been expanded and further institutionalized through multiyear and multicountry initiatives such as FASTrade. Initially focused on Central Asia and Central America, they are poised to branch out and incorporate USAID missions in other regions, including Africa (USAID 2005a–c).

CHAPTER TWO

1. Seen from this point of view, the crucial and continuing role of state institutions and legal regimes in securing the conditions for capital mobility

and the cultivation of market relations via banks, dispute mechanisms, provision of information and infrastructure should not be underestimated as the Regulation School has long reminded us (Jessop 1999).

2. As Humphrey puts it: "analysis of sovereignty need not be opposed to studies of governmentality . . . both concepts are essential in explaining how political life emerges and may be constituted" (2004, 435).

3. This claim is foreshadowed by the insights of Hall (1984, 14), who states, "Administering Society is every bit as much a part of the state's powers as policing society."

4. Developing a semiotic perspective on state power rather than a governmental one, Herzfeld's (1992, 1997, 2005) work on bureaucracy provides an important step in this direction.

5. Informed by a rather different set of theoretical concerns regarding rule bound social behavior, anthropological investigation of the inner working of African bureaucracies was pursued in an earlier era by G. Britain and R. Cohen (1980).

6. A question warranting further reflection, the alternative findings and approaches of research conducted in Francophone versus Anglophone African states may well be indicative of distinct historical legacies stemming from different patterns of colonial administration as well as postcolonial political reform and international engagement.

7. In several places the Blundo and Olivier de Sardan (2006) volume tellingly considers the position of individual bureaucratic realms within the wider administrative fabric of state in order explain specific episodes of corruption and malfeasance but these observations do not form the basis of a comprehensive theorization of this sort despite the evidence they provide.

8. See Sassen (2006), for example, on modeling epochal change.

CHAPTER THREE

1. In African studies, this outlook finds expression in the wide array of scholarship on informal economies (Azarya and Chazan 1987; MacGaffey 1987) as well as a more recent set of discussions of borderlands (Flynn 1997; Nugent 1996, 2002; Roitman 2005).

2. In addition to individual state initiatives, on the continent-wide level, this is evident in the recent African Union statement "Customs Standards and Cooperation" (2005).

3. In contrast to the fragmentary basis of border control within the neoliberal state, reflecting the rise and fall of different political agendas and regulatory agencies over time, for a discussion of another sort of parcellized sovereignty under feudalism see Teschke (2003).

4. Part of a much broader cultural formation, southeastern Ghana shares a common cultural heritage with the coastal zones of southern Togo and Benin as well. The Ewe languages and traditions of the Ghana-Togo borderlands

are closely linked to Togo's Mina peoples as well as the Fon of Benin, who share origin myths with the Yoruba peoples of southwestern Nigeria.

5. It is curious that where free movement is permitted, the state is emblemized in much more dramatic ways than in zones of prohibition.

6. According to promotional material accompanying the construction and unveiling of Black Star Square, the arch was meant to signify the triumph of national determination rather than denote a gateway. Indeed, though standing in the middle of a major downtown thoroughfare in central Accra, the Square, resembling the Arc de Triomphe is perpetually blocked to traffic.

7. The morphemic glosses and the translation are as follows, courtesy of James Essegbey (personal communication, February 6, 2007): *Aflao flalala, kpoklikpo de-ve, tsi-ma-dza-ma-dza gake baba didi ame.* "Aflao (praise-name) palm-forest water-NEG-fall-NEG-fall but mud slip person."

8. The border zone in this respect holds much in common with the informal yet elaborated configured urban spaces and lifeways discussed by Simone (2004).

9. To illustrate this point Hess quotes an article from a 1963 edition of Ghana's *Evening News*: "Everywhere there are signs of construction. Everywhere the spirit of the Work and Happiness Programme has caught on. Cranes and caterpillars bull-doze their way to the glorious socialist future for Ghanaians who must appreciate the value and extent of the work the party is doing for them. IT IS WORK AND HAPPINESS FOR YOU! FORWARD TO SOCIALISM! LONG LIVE THE PARTY!" (Hess 2000, 47; caps in original).

10. The Wikipedia entry for Acheampong for instance, refers to the regimes investment in "face-lift projects in cities, and the reconstruction/upgrading of stadia to meet international standards." Across Ghana, Acheampong's reign is still remembered for the many building projects undertaken in outlying regions beyond the hub of the nation's capital, from ministries and court complexes in Cape Coast (Painstil 2009) to Cocoa Marketing Board regional headquarters in Sunyani (Tachie-Menson 2007).

11. This is a popular term referring to the low cost and typically lower class private security guards hired to guard the unfinished homes of the up-and-coming in the Accra suburbs.

12. Here a useful point of comparison is provided by J. Caplan's (2001) discussion of official naming practices in eighteenth- and nineteenth-century northern European states relying on the semiotic triad of on symbol, icon, and index, and the attendant political claims these forms of signification uphold.

13. Developed and constantly updated by the World Customs Organization, a six-digit HS notation is available for every item traded across borders and contains within it a shorthand description of product, its use and material.

14. U.S. tariffs, in comparison, average 2–3 percent.

15. The document is known as the Final Classification and Valuation Report or FCVR.

16. These drinks were often among the gifts I received from Customs officers in the course of my research.

CHAPTER FOUR

1. Sassen (2006, 235) labels these configurations "transgovernmental networks."

2. See also Jourde (2005) for an application of this analytic to the itinerary of presidential pilgrimages in Mauritania.

3. Pointing to the historical embeddedness of this trend, in a study conducted among bureaucrats in Ghana thirty years earlier, Le Vine (1975) identified a the very same tendency to refer decisions up the chain of command. Affirming the structural privilege of executive officers, Blundo and Olivier de Sardan (2006, 159) note a similar convention in effect in government institutions in Niger and Benin,

4. Not only a sign of the discretionary powers of the bureaucratic executive, this example is equally illustrative of a convention evident in other West African bureaucracies of using postings in obscure locations as a form of "banishment in atonement for transgressions, professional errors and political disgrace" (Blundo and Olivier de Sardan 2006, 90).

5. The term "Long Room" is used in Customs work worldwide. Not entirely different from the conditions in Ghana, a compelling eighteenth-century description of HM Customs Longroom at the height of Britain maritime prowess follows: "The Long Room was the most important—and the most striking—part of the Custom House. This was first introduced in Thomas Ripley's building and later recreated in the new Custom House. The Long Room contained the public offices of the Customs Service. All paperwork regarding duties payable on cargoes was taken to the customs officials there. This was a complicated business. When there were almost 2000 dutiable goods, and ships carried many different goods, calculating the necessary duties for each vessel was an immense task. After all the calculations were completed and the dues paid, the Long Room officials would issue the necessary receipts. Only then could the goods be unloaded" (Port Cities: London 2007).

6. Hearsay at the World Customs Organization revealed that within Mauritius Customs, where a similar licensing plan was operating, Customs agents were illicitly buying and selling access to authorized clearing agents' ID numbers and passwords to be used on the country's automated Customs declaration system. Getting wind of this, Mauritius Customs in turn began to check the location where the electronic entries were being submitted.

7. In an effort to preserve Ghanaian industry, controlled goods included, for example, foreign-made wax prints.

8. On several occasions during the mid-1990s the imposition of Value Added Tax by the government sparked massive protests across the country, some leading to violent encounters between the public and security forces.

9. Known by the tag "Kamina 85," this group of officers circulates a newsletter and organizes yearly gatherings much like Ghana's many "old girl" and "old boy" alumni networks.

10. Demonstrating the sustained existence of such networks, a number of well-connected officers from headquarters were dispatched to the Aflao frontier right around election time in 2000 for reasons that were never well explained.

11. While this "blurring of the lines denoting civil and military status" (Roitman 2005, 162) is treated as novel or at least episodic (viz. the parallel with the brigand-chiefs of the colonial period [181]) in the Central African case, in Ghana, as recounted in chapter 1 and above, it has long been part of Customs official mission.

12. A similar proliferation of specialized and temporary units aimed at reining in the unpredictable developments of the border zone can be found in Cameroon through such bodies as the Bataillon Rapide Intervention (Roitman 2005, 175).

13. At Aflao and other land frontiers, Customs' decision to recruit local residents to the Preventive Corps without giving them training in other aspects of Customs work provoked controversy.

14. Telling evidence of this uncertainty, when the NPP's John Kufuor assumed the office of President in January 2000, the Customs Commissioner was put on involuntary leave. Though not arrested or charged with any crime, he was ordered not to leave the country or arrive at the office. Rather he stayed at home, in limbo for several months, waiting for his status to be resolved.

15. From this vantage point the "exceptional solutions" to neoliberal expectations and interventions identified by Ong (2006) across Asia, should perhaps be considered even more exceptional—and indeed, more power-laden, given the apparent stability in their functioning and design.

CHAPTER FIVE

1. The independent government likewise hardened its monopoly of agricultural export through the enlargement of colonial-era marketing boards. This was so notwithstanding the fiercely independent reputation of Ghanaian cocoa farmers, who were both a primary source of foreign exchange and whose protests has earlier served as a major impetus to the achievement of national independence (Beckman 1976).

2. Ghanaians' longstanding involvement in transoceanic cultural exchanges

are well-evidenced in numerous accounts of the colonial era, from Parker's (2000) history of colonial Accra and Newell's account of literary culture (2002) to Cole's (2001) discussion of the Ghanaian concert-party performance genre. Likewise, philosopher and culture-theorist, K. A. Appiah (1998) recounts his own family's dual Ghana-English heritage in the late-colonial and early independence period in an essay entitled "Cosmopolitan Patriots.

3. As in other socialist states, such processes of informalization are common and in many ways necessary to both survival and system reproduction (Sampson 1987; Verdery 1991).

4. Involved in the mass production of armored vehicles for World War II, South Africa has held a longstanding place in the automotive industry, largely unique for the subcontinent (Guttman 2004). Accounting for 0.8 percent of the global auto industry, of the more than 41 million passenger vehicles produced in 2002, fewer than 250,000 came from Africa. www.autoindustry.co.uk/statistics/production/world.

5. Centered on Benin's port city of Cotonou, Beuving (2004) provides a detailed description of the social and commercial networks engaged in shipping and selling cars from Europe to West African consumers.

6. Suame Magazine (Schildkrout 1996), located in Ghana's second largest city, Kumasi, is renowned as the largest used-car repair center in the subregion and possibly the continent.

7. Commercial vehicles, used for evacuating produce and supplying stores as well as transporting labor migrants, however, were often owned by European or Levantine traders and firms (Roncoli 1994, 103).

8. This was so not just in West Africa, but across the continent. With a focus on East and Southern Africa, White (2000) explores the way the memories of colonial rule in the region were much mediated by vehicular imagery, especially the rumored mysteries of police cars, fire engines, and ambulances.

9. Beuving (2004, 512–13), tracking car importation in Benin over the course of the 1990s, finds a similar pattern of explosive growth and gradual tightening. He suggests that actual rates are likely to be higher due to the many unofficial circuits of car trade and entry in the West African subregion.

10. With presidential and parliamentary elections taking place in December of 2000 and 2004, it is possible to speculate that these surges, at least in part, reflect increases in state, political party, and patron purchase or importation of cars in relation to elections and political campaigns

11. A Bill of Lading is a standard document proving goods have been loaded on a ship and is necessary for their transport or transfer.

12. Although Customs officers are typically transferred to new posts every two years or less, officers at the Car Park usually have a much longer tenure due to the experience this sort of work requires. On my first visit to the Tema Customs lot, my guide touted the skill of his coworker in identifying aspects of vehicles misidentified in their accompanying documentation. In

Ghana, even if one has limited practice in car assembly or disassembly, talk of chasses, spare parts and the rest are common parlance among car owners and operators due to the frequency of repair and the work that goes into finding and configuring spare parts under conditions of shortage. This was a lesson I learned all too well in the course of acquiring and upkeeping a used Nissan Patrol during my fieldwork.

13. In Ghana, there are strong regional/ethnic undertones to political party membership. The NDC is often associated with the Ewe of eastern Ghana, reflecting Rawlings's familial heritage and the NPP is considered an Asanti party, representing the interests of central Ghana and the cocoa-growing forest zone.

14. As one informant famously put it, ill-gotten wealth was the only means available for his family to properly observe Ramadan (Roitman 2005, 160).

15. The church Web site explains the logo: the Benz sign depicts "1.The tower of a chapel. 2. The V sign signifying victory. 3. The leaves signifying the GARLAND speaking of a crown for a victorious person" (www.vbint.org).

16. With cars already established as a public and nationalized symbol, to enter the rhetoric of market through the sign of the vehicle is to enter an inclusive field of discussion that is very different from the ethnic and regional divisions that are typically tagged as the stuff of African political culture. Although the culture of cars is surely not equalizing (and there are clear ethnic/regional undertones in the NPP's rise to power), given its vernacular form, it is one in which access, at least on a symbolic level, is relatively open as almost all urban Ghanaians can read its nuance and glean a level of self-recognition.

CHAPTER SIX

1. Of note, the Black Star decorating Ghana's national flag is derived from the emblem of the Black Star Shipping Line founded by Marcus Garvey in 1919.

2. Ghana's Minister of Trade, in a December 5, 2000, speech commissioning the GSL Scanner in Tema, noted that the volume of maritime-cargo clearance in Ghana grew from 80,000 TEU (20-foot cargo containers) in 1991 to 250,000 TEU in 1999.

3. This expansive commercial circuitry rendering Ghana second only to South Africa in port growth in sub-Saharan Africa (United Nations Conference on Trade and Development 2007, 87).

4. The case of cheap Asian rice displacing the consumption of domestically produced grains in Ghana is a particular glaring example of this new form of import substitution.

5. As many of the same firms hold contracts for port and trade security post-9/11, this development suggests that the current maritime security agenda

(see Chalfin 2007; WCO 2006b) is less a radical departure than an expansion of regulatory rubrics earlier in place.

6. Although the employment of mercenary armies in this manner appears to be a new turn for modern nation-states, the practice has a long history. In the eighteenth century we see another variation on this theme in the process of "privateering" where states authorize the deployment of private naval vessels against foreign shipping (Thomson 1994, 9).

7. I am indebted to Neil Englehart ("Must States Be Sovereign?" unpublished paper, 2001) for a discussion of this distinction in relation to globalization.

8. The Swiss company SGS has carried out customs work in Mozambique, the Philippines, and Indonesia (*Business Asia* 1997, 12; *Economist* 1991). Likewise, the British firm Crown Agents is charged with managing the customs service of both Mozambique and Angola (Crown Agents 2003).

9. Until 1993 Pre-Shipment Inspection (PSI) in Ghana was monopolized by one company. At that time, responding to the overall climate of liberalization, PSI was opened to competition and became the purview of multiple firms, SGS and Bureau Veritas among them.

10. They include Benin, Chad, Comoros, Cote d'Ivoire, Ghana, Kenya, Niger, Nigeria, Senegal, Tanzania, Togo, Columbia, Ecuador, and Peru.

11. Both prior to and in the wake of 9/11, security initiatives employing new surveillance technologies are changing the face of international shipping. These include continuous monitoring of containers, new rules of notification and verification, and the strict enforcement of international standards (Cottrill 2002; Edmonson 2002; Young 2002).

12. After opening up the contract for Destination Inspection to competitive bidding in 1999, COTECNA was awarded the sole right to serve as an agent for the state in this regard. COTECNA's capture of the contract was explained by the company's chair to be a result of their offer to undertake inspection through a joint-shareholding arrangement taking the form of GSL. According to my contacts at GSL, the plan received the endorsement of the Minister of Trade at the time.

13. The involvement of Ga dignitaries in the commissioning needs to be recognized as meager recompense for the massive displacement of the resident Ga community when Tema harbor was built in the 1950s.

14. The establishment of the "scanner gate" as it was provisionally labeled, foreshadowed a larger project of port expansion and reorganization. Beside the GSL device—yet outside the official boundaries of the port—construction teams were breaking ground for the country's first container terminal. Financed by the Ghanaian Antrak Group and a foreign partner, SDV, to accommodate the growth of maritime commerce, both the Ghana Ports and Harbors Authority and the Customs Service considered the new terminal of critical importance to their own operations within the port, despite its private ownership and location (Chalfin 2009).

15. With the harmonized system every commodity is assigned an eight-digit code denoting type of good—such as apparel—and attendant specifications, men's apparel, socks, cotton, down to the most detailed specification.

16. This was supposed to be based on market research, but more often was a matter of decree. All wax prints coming into the country would be given a uniform and fixed value, as would all women's shoes, building materials, and so on.

17. The role of documentation—whether taking the form of passports (Torpey 2000), identity cards (Caplan 2001), censuses, maps (Appadurai 1996a), and more recently, retina scans and other sorts of body imaging (Lyon 2001)—in the expression of state power and the creation of modern political subjects is widely recognized.

18. Personal email correspondence of interviewee, April 25, 2001.

19. Personal email correspondence of interviewee, May 1, 2001.

20. A case by no means restricted to Ghana, private customs authorities are not above the law. As Arifari (2006, 202) finds in the case of Benin, Bureau Veritas employees were charged and imprisoned for regular misclassification.

21. Ong (1999), for example, discusses the way "different production sites become institutional domains that vary in their mix of legal protections, controls and disciplinary regimes" (215). Using Malaysia as her case study, she contrasts the environment of control and containment experienced by immigrant labor working in factory settings (218) with the differential positioning of laborers versus investors, with the much lighter hand of the state within Multimedia Corridors designed to attract foreign capital and foster an entrepreneurial elite involved in the development of high-tech products and services (219).

22. See Monmonier (2002) for a discussion of relationship between technology and surveillance.

23. Caplan and Torpey (2001) discuss the power as well as limits of databasing, even in its most rudimentary form.

24. www.signposts.uts.edu.au/contacts/Singapore/Government/426.html.

25. www.cia.gov/cia/publications/factbook/geos/mp.html#Econ

26. Indicative of customs role in Mauritius's larger vision of off-shoring, in 2002 the Mauritius government appointed a Canadian to head the nation's Customs Service. A former officer in the Canadian Customs Services, he is also the self-described principal of a 'fiscal and trade facilitation consulting firm." (events.wcoomd.org/bio.htm)

27. Presentation, GCNET Operations Manager, Ndaba Hotel, Sandton, South Africa. October 10, 2003.

CHAPTER SEVEN

1. Initially bankrolled by British government to the tune of 23 million pounds, KIA's renovations embody the goals of neoliberal reform so well

that in 2002, after Britain's Prime Minister, Tony Blair, used the airport on his visit to Africa, his government proclaimed KIA to be "one of the few large projects successfully concluded by HIPCs in recent years" (UK Export Credits Guarantee Department 2002). Signaling the maturation of the project's neoliberal logic, a second phase of airport enhancement was financed by loans totaling more than $40 million from the Hong Kong and Shanghai Banking Corporation (HSBC), the French bank Paribas, and Ghana's Ecobank. Construction for both phases was carried out by the giants of multinational construction and contracting—Taysec, Skanska, and Siemens Plessy.

2. With Ghana at the front of the line, airport rebuilding and aviation reform is widespread and remarkably well financed across the African continent. Indeed, high-cost airport enhancements are underway from Mali to Tanzania, South Africa to Ethiopia, to name just a few countries engaged in this process.

3. Throughout the 1980s and 1990s, a series of accords targeting African airspace was put into play, the most significant being the 1988 Yamoussoukro Declaration on a New African Air Transport Policy (Economic Commission for Africa 1999, 2, and 2001, 2; Goldstein 2001, 222). Periodically revived and revised over the years (ICAO 2002), Yamoussoukro established a new baseline for African air transport, promoting private investment, restricting national control, and establishing for its signatories a set of common rules (Economic Commission for Africa 2001, 2).

4. Further, contributing to Ghana's rising rank and recognition within the space of global aviation, in the late 1990s, KIA became "one of only 5 airports in Africa to have the FAA accreditation to fly directly to the USA" (AZ World Airports On-Line 2004; FDCH Regulatory Intelligence Database 2001; Goldstein 2001, 233).

5. On the Ghana Civil Aviation Authority, see http://www.gcaa.com.gh.

6. Fostering this sort of aesthetic internationalism, overseas firms were also the source of the airport's interior designs. A telling commentary on the proliferation of such look-alike spaces of commerce and convenience, the vendor responsible for the airport's flight-status screens, on its website (PAI Group 2003) compared its work at KIA to its other projects, providing visuals of London nightclubs and the Warner Bros megaplex cinema chain.

7. As Esi Dogbe (2003) suggests, for these reasons the airport is also very much a space of collective fantasy and frequently appears in popular Ghanaian videos.

8. That Rawlings continued to be addressed as flight lieutenant (the rank he held when he led his 1979 coup) throughout his long tenure as head of state illustrates the deep tie between the control of airspace and political might.

9. Again affirming the link between the airport and executive power, when J. A. Kufuor assumed the presidential post in 2001, he chose not to reside

in Christianbourg Castle, as had his predecessors, but to remain at his private home located in the prestigious Airport Residential Area adjacent to KIA.

10. See Andreas (2000) and Heyman (1995) for a parallel discussion of changing perceptions of border authorities under new political circumstances with regard to U.S. border agents on the U.S.-Mexican frontier.

11. Even in bilateral programs, the crafting of a global Customs agenda was evident. This outlook was part and parcel of a seminar carried out by the U.S. Customs Service and the U.S. Bureau of Alcohol, Tobacco, and Firearms in October 2000. Including Customs officers from Anglophone states across the West African subregion—Nigeria, Liberia, and Sierra Leone—the seminar took place at an exclusive Accra hotel. Signaling the expanding U.S. role as an international security hegemon even before September 11, 2001, its focus was "The New International Criminal" and "International Criminal Organizations."

12. On this point, see Coutin (2005) for a discussion of the legal fictions of citizenship at work in situations of transmigration.

13. In postcolonial locations such as Ghana, where the hand of neoliberalism and the legacies of imperial rule have long made the pace and scale of extroversion arbiters of survival, this process is well evidenced. But also in the United States, following September 11, 2001, one can see how the spaces and personages of transience are becoming increasingly central to the making of national policy and the proving of state power not just for the so-called alien but also for the citizen

14. Sharing this disapproval, the author of a popular newspaper column, "The Imported Ghanaian," in an entry entitled "Call the Fashion Police," poked fun at the flamboyant outfits worn by the Ghanaian "boggers" (i.e., burghers) when they return to Ghana (Sumprim 2000, 3).

15. These behaviors strike a provocative parallel with what Blundo and Olivier de Sardan (2006, 117) describe as the mimetic aspects of corruption, with public officials reproducing the behavior of elites. Here the homemade database, while not exactly illegal and not fully legitimate either, served as a form of political commentary.

16. As Blundo and Olivier de Sardan remind us, "Illicit practices are not associated with the ignorance of the law or regulations on the part of officials. On the contrary, such practices are facilitated by good command and knowledge of the relevant information and rules" (2006, 84).

17. Helpful to capturing the way such localized encounters reference much more abstract and geographically dispersed orders is Karin Cetina and Urs Bruegger's discussion of "global microstructures," that is, "patterns of relatedness and coordination that are global in scope but microsocial in character and that assemble and link global domains" (2002, 907).

18. This is not to say that the airport is not vulnerable to the possibility of the law's suspension, as Mateo Taussig-Rubbo's (2007) research on the juris-

dictional uncertainty and abusive practices of asylee interrogation at Los Angeles International Airport makes clear.

CONCLUSION

1. For examples from Japan, see Helleiner (1992) and Miyazaki (in press).
2. Evidence from around the world readily substantiates the breadth of these trends. Mitchell (2002, 281), addressing the case of Egypt, vividly describes what might be characterized as the hidden underbelly of the country's apparent neoliberal success, pointing to the increasing consolidation of wealth and regulatory power in a heavily subsidized state-based financial sector. Jonathan Fox (2000) despite a rather different research problem, provides evidence of similar trends in Asia and Latin America. In his examination of World Bank responsiveness to civil society environmental concerns, he notes the increasing autonomy of national financial authorities of borrowing governments in Brazil and India. Scholars working in Eastern Europe, highlighting the case of neoliberal reform in Hungary, note the "bureaucratic redesign of the Hungarian State generated 'finance driven' form of economic governance with the state bureaucracy reconfigure around the fiscal controls of the Finance Ministry (Phillips et al. 2006, 585). Babb's (2001) research on the rise of neoliberalism in Mexico provides a fascinating discussion of the concomitant rise of the economist and the economics profession accompanying the ascendance of the state's fiscal authority.
3. Taking an alternative comparative approach, Simmons and Elkins (2004) examine these dynamics through the lens of "policy diffusion."
4. Harvey's (2005) discussion of the early formulation of neoliberal reforms in Chile works from a similar crisis-based premise of innovation.
5. See Callaghy (2009) for preliminary discussion of the changing "demand side" dynamics of African development finance.
6. Working from an Egyptian case study of the critical role played by field research in NGO funding and development, Elyachar (2006) speaks to a similar interplay of academic and applied experiments in neoliberal times.
7. The authoritarian underpinnings of neoliberal reform has not gone unnoticed, as early accounts of implementation in Ghana and elsewhere point to the necessity of a strong state (Callaghy and Ravenhill 1993). Evidence from Latin America, in particular, suggests that platforms of democratic reform combined with neoliberal economics fan old authoritarian flames (Oxhorn and Ducatenzeiler 1998). Taking a different point of view here, I am suggesting that governmental directives explicitly meant to temper these tendencies revive them anew.
8. Such a merging of affective identification and fiscal proceduralism is explicitly explored in Roitman (2005) study of cross-border exchange and governance in the Chad Basin. Her largely localized account, however,

despite its international context, overlooks how these relations are structured by wider processes of governmental reform and broader conditions of political economy. This orientation runs the risk of presenting this confluence as a natural or inevitable part of Africa's politic landscape indicative of the regulatory void brought about by the breakdown of formal state apparatus. The account I present argues for very different sort of structural determination. It is corroborated by Perry's (2009) research on smuggling in the Senegal Gambia border zone, also carried out in and cognizant of the context of neoliberal reform.

9. Of note, the transnational migrants are the target of government exactions at home are also subject to the scrutiny of state authorities in their host countries abroad, where they find themselves the target of numerous exceptions and exclusions despite the neoliberal opening of the market on which their mobility is predicated (Fikes 2009).

10. Analyzing rural politics on the national level in West Africa via a center-periphery framework, Boone (2003) works from a related perspective.

11. Responding to an earlier set of studies privileging border policy over practice, such a networked perspective on African border zones is lacking in most recent research anthropological research on borders marked by a strongly localized focus (Flynn 1997; Herbst 2000; Roitman 2005), with few exceptions (pace Boone 2003; Hughes 2006).

12. Although celebrated for recognizing the position of African populations within modern nation-states and even their investment in "unnatural" political frontiers imposed by colonial regimes, this point of view harks backs to the assumptions of an older anthropology that saw African societies as not only bounded but rooted in particular locations (Gupta and Ferguson 1997).

References

Abrams, P. 1988. Notes on the difficulty of studying the state. *Journal of Historical Sociology* 1 (1): 58–89.

Abugri, G. S. 2001. One for the road: A letter to Jomo. *Daily Graphic*. May 4.

Accra Mail. 2001a. Alarm blow: Mother of all car looting capers. February 22.

———. 2001b. X-ray scanner attracts Israelis. August 27.

———. 2002. Customs arrests couriers. April 8. Retrieved from http://www.accra-mail.com.

Adam, C., and S. A. O'Connell. 1997. *Aid, taxation, and development: Analytical perspectives on aid effectiveness in Sub-Saharan Africa*. Oxford: Centre for the Study of African Economies.

Adjei-Bediako. 2000. Tony Aidoo must be ashamed. *Chronicle* (Ghana), March 5.

Adu-Boahen, A. 2000 [1975]. *Ghana: Evolution and change in the nineteenth and twentieth centuries*. Accra: Sankofa.

Agamben, G. 1998. *Homo sacer: Sovereign power and bare life*. Stanford, Calif.: Stanford University Press.

Agnew, J. 2005. Sovereignty regimes: Territoriality and state authority in contemporary world politics. *Annals of the Association of American Geographers* 95 (2): 437–61.

Akyeampong, E. 2005. Diaspora and drug trafficking in West Africa: A case study of Ghana. *African Affairs* 104 (416): 429–77.

Allman, J. 2004. Fashioning Africa: Power and the politics of dress. In *Fashioning Africa: Power and the politics of dress, African expressive cultures,* ed. Jean Allman. Bloomington: Indiana University Press.

Allotey, J. A. 2001. Opinion: Cars, cars and still cars. *The Independent* (Ghana), January 23.

Alvarez, R. R., Jr. 1995. The Mexican-U.S. border: The making of an anthropology of borderlands. *Annual Review of Anthropology* 24:447–70.

Amissah, J. 2001. I have not bought any Audi car from CEPS. *Daily Graphic* (Ghana), March 3.

Ampofo, O. 2005. Mr. President, act to control public funds. GhanaHomePage, July 15. Retrieved from http://www.ghanaweb.com/GhanaHomePage/features/artikel.php?ID=85843.

Anas, A. 2001. CEPS official reacts to *Crusading Guide* story. *The Crusading Guide* (Ghana). April 19.

Anders, G. 2002. Freedom and insecurity: Civil servants between support networks, the free market and the civil service reform. In *A democracy of chameleons: Politics and culture in the New Malawi*, ed. Harri Englund. Uppsala: Nordiska Afrikainstitutet.

Anderson, B. 1991. *Imagined communities: Reflections on the origin and spread of nationalism*. London: Verso.

Andreas, P. 2000. *Border games: Policing the US-Mexico divide*. Ithaca, N.Y.: Cornell University Press.

Anim-Asante, J. 1988. A descriptive list of the records of the Customs Department in the National Archives of Ghana, Accra. Department of Library and Archival Studies, University of Ghana, Legon.

Anyemedu, K. 1991. Export diversification under the Economic Recovery Program. In *Ghana: The political economy of recovery*, ed. D. Rothchild. Boulder, Colo.: Lynne Rienner Publishers.

Anzaldúa, G. 1987. *Borderlands: The new mestiza = La frontera*. San Francisco: Spinsters/Aunt Lute.

Appadurai, A. 1996a. *Modernity at large: Cultural dimensions of globalization*. Minneapolis: University of Minnesota Press.

———. 1996b. Sovereignty without territoriality: Notes for a postnational geography. In *The geography of identity*, ed. P. Yaeger. Ann Arbor: University of Michigan Press.

Appiah, K. A. 1998. Cosmopolitan patriots. In *Cosmopolitics: Thinking and feeling beyond the nation*, ed. P. Cheah, B. Robbins, and Social Text Collective. Minneapolis: University of Minnesota Press.

Apter, D. E. 1972. *Ghana in transition*. 2nd rev. ed. Princeton, N.J.: Princeton University Press.

Arasaratnam, S. 1998. Trade and political dominion in South India, 1750–1790. In *The East India Company: 1600–1858*, ed. P. J. N. Tuck. New York: Routledge.

Ardant, G. 1971. *Histoire de l'impot Tome 1: De l'Antiquite au XVIIe siecle*. Paris: Fayard.

———. 1972. *Histoire de l'impot Tome 2: Du XVIIIe siecle au XXe siecle*. Paris: Fayard.

———. 1975. Financial policy and the economic infrastructure of modern states and nations. In *The formation of national states in Western Europe*, ed. C. Tilly.

Studies in Political Development 8. Princeton, N.J.: Princeton University Press.

Aretxaga, B. 1995. Dirty protest: Symbolic overdetermination and gender in Northern Ireland ethnic violence. *Ethos* 23 (2):123–48.

———. 1999. A fictional reality: Paramilitary death squads in Spain. In *Death squad: The anthropology of state terror*, ed. J. Sluka. Philadelphia: University of Pennsylvania Press.

———. 2003. Maddening states. *Annual Review of Anthropology* 32:393–410.

Arhinful, D. 2002. We think of them: Money transfers from the Netherlands to Ghana. In *Merchants, missionaries, and migrants: 300 years of Dutch-Ghanaian relations*, ed. I. van Kessel. Amsterdam: KIT Publishers.

Arifari, N. B. 2006. We don't eat the papers: Corruption in transport, Customs, and the civil forces. In *Everyday corruption and the state: Citizens and public officials in Africa,* ed. G. Blundo and J-P. Olivier de Sardan. London. Zed Press.

Armah, A. 1969. *The beautyful ones are not yet born.* Oxford: Heinemann Publishers.

Armstrong, R. 1996. *Ghana's country assistance review: A study in development effectiveness.* Washington, D.C.: World Bank.

Arrighi, G. 2000. Globalization, state sovereignty and the "endless" accumulation of capital. In *The ends of globalization*, ed. D. Smith, D. Solinger, and S. Topik. London: Routledge.

Arthur, P. 2006. The state, private sector development, and Ghana's "golden age of business." *African Studies Review* 49 (1): 31–50.

Aryeetey, E., and F. Tarp. 2000. Structural adjustment and after: Which way forward? In *Economic reforms in Ghana: The miracle and the mirage*, ed. E. Aryeetey, J. Harrigan, and M. Nissanke. Oxford: James Currey.

Aryeetey, E., and J. Harrigan. 2000. Macroeconomic and sectoral developments since 1970. In *Economic reforms in Ghana: The miracle and the mirage*, ed. E. Aryeetey, J. Harrigan, and M. Nissanke. Oxford: James Currey.

Asakura, H., and World Customs Organization. 2003. *World history of the customs and tariffs.* [Brussels]: World Customs Organization.

Asante, S. K. B. 1975. The neglected aspects of the activities of the Gold Coast Aborigines Rights Protection Society. *Phylon* (1960–) 36 (1): 32–35.

Ashley, R. 1984. The problem of neorealism. *International Organization* 38: 225–86.

Augé, M. 1995. *Non-places: Introduction to an anthropology of supermodernity.* London: Verso.

Austen, R. A. 1987. *African economic history: Internal development and external dependency.* London: J. Currey.

Austin, D. 1964. *Politics in Ghana.* London. Oxford University Press.

Auto Industry. 1990. Africa report. 35 (3): 12.

———. 2006. World vehicle production since 1997 by region. Retrieved from http://www.autoindustry.co.uk/statistics/production/world.

————. 2007. World vehicle production statistics since 1997 by region. Retrieved June 5, 2007, from http://www.autoindustry.co.uk/statistics/production/world.

AZ World Airports On-Line. 2004. Kotoka International Airport (ACC/DGAA). Retrieved from http://www.azworldairports.com/airports/p1610acc.htm.

Azarya, V., and N. Chazan. 1987. Disengagement from the state in Africa: Reflections on the experience of Ghana and Guinea. *Comparative Studies in Society and History* 28 (4): 106–31.

Azhar Architecture. 2005. Kotoka Airport, Accra, Ghana. Retrieved from http://www.azhararchitecture.com/profile_experience.htm.

Babb, F. 1999. Managua is Nicaragua: The making of a neoliberal city. *City and Society* 1 (2): 27–48.

Babb, S. L. 2001. *Managing Mexico: Economists from nationalism to neoliberalism.* Princeton, N.J.: Princeton University Press.

Barthes, R. 1972. *Mythologies.* New York: Noonday Press.

BBC. 2006. The story of Africa between world wars: Air and road. BBCWorldservice .com. Retrieved from http://www.bbc.co.uk/worldservice/africa/features/storyofafrica/13chapter9.html.

Beckman, B. 1976. *Organising the farmers: Cocoa politics and national development in Ghana.* Uppsala: Scandinavian Institute of African Studies.

Berry, S. 1993. *No condition is permanent: The social dynamics of agrarian change in sub-Saharan Africa.* Madison: University of Wisconsin Press.

Beuving, J. J. 2004. Cotonou's Klondike: African traders and second-hand car markets in Benin. *Journal of Modern African Studies* 42 (4): 511–35.

Biersteker, T., and C. Weber. 1996. The social construction of state sovereignty. In *State sovereignty as social construct,* ed. T. Biersteker and C. Weber. Cambridge: Cambridge University Press.

Biney, K. 2001. Ato Dadzie must face trial. *Guide* (Ghana), January 29.

Blay-Amihere, K. 2001. Back on the block: Getting it right at Accra International Airport. *The Independent* (Ghana), March 29.

Blundo, G., and J.-P. Olivier de Sardan. 2006. *Everyday corruption and the state: Citizens and public officials in Africa.* New York: Zed Press.

Boachie, J. 2003. The liberalization experience: The case of Ghana. Paper read at Aviation in Transition: Challenges and Opportunities of Liberalization, ICAO Worldwide Air Transport Conference, March 22–23.

Bodin, J. 1992. *On sovereignty: Four chapters from six books of the Commonwealth.* Cambridge: Cambridge University Press.

Boone, C. 2003. *Political topographies of the African state.* Cambridge: Cambridge University Press.

Botwe, F. O. 2001. CEPS told to provide vehicles to DAs. *Chronicle* (Ghana), March 15.

Bourdieu, P. 1984. *Distinction: A social critique of the judgment of taste.* Cambridge: Harvard University Press.

Bowie, K. 1993. Assessing the early observers: Cloth and the fabric of society in nineteenth-century northern Thailand. *American Ethnologist* 20 (1): 138–58.

Brandon, R. 2002. *How the car changed life.* New York: Macmillan.

Britain, G., and R. Cohen. 1980. *Hierarchy and society: Anthropological perspectives on bureaucracy.* Philadelphia: Institute for the Study of Human Issues.

Broadman, H. 2007. *Africa's silk road: China and India's new economic frontier.* Washington, D.C.: World Bank.

Bruner, E. 1996. Tourism in Ghana. *American Anthropologist* 98 (2): 390–404.

Brydon, L., and K. Legge. 1996. *Adjusting society: The World Bank, the IMF, and Ghana.* Oxford: Taurus.

Business Asia. 1997. Clean up at last. 29 (17): 12.

Business Times Singapore. 2002. SNS is now CrimsonLogic. August 19.

———. 2004a. CrimsonLogic gains a foothold in Latin America. February 23.

———. 2004b. Portal lets logistics firms submit to the US. February 23.

———. 2004c. CrimsonLogic carving own niche. April 19.

Butler, J. 2004. *Precarious life: The powers of mourning and violence.* New York: Verso.

Callaghy, T. 2009. Africa and the world economy. In *Africa in world politics: Reforming political order,* 4th ed., ed. John Harbeson and Donald Rothchild. Boulder, Colo.: Westview Press.

Callaghy, T., and J. Ravenhill. 1993. *Hemmed in: Responses to Africa's economic decline.* New York: Columbia University Press.

Caplan, J. 2001. "This or that particular person": Protocols of identification on nineteenth-century Europe. In *Documenting individual identity: The development of state practices in the modern world,* ed. J. Caplan and J. Torpey. Princeton, N.J.: Princeton University Press.

Carson, E. 1972. *The ancient and rightful customs: A history of the English Customs Service.* London: Faber and Faber Ltd.

Carter, D. 1997. *States of grace: Senegalese in Italy and the new European migration.* Minneapolis: University of Minnesota Press.

Carter, G. 1958. *The commonwealth in Africa.* Toronto: Canadian Institute of International Affairs.

Center for International Development, Harvard University. 2004. Trade facilitation summary. Global Trade Negotiations. Retrieved from http://www.cid.harvard.edu/cidtrade/issues/tradefac.html.

Cetina, K., and U. Bruegger. 2002. Global microstructures: The virtual societies of financial markets. *American Journal of Sociology* 107 (4): 905–50.

Chalfin, B. 1996. Market reforms and the state: The case of *Shea* in Ghana. *Journal of Modern African Studies* 34 (3): 421–40.

———. 2001a. Border zone trade and the economic boundaries of the state in northeast Ghana. *Africa* 71 (2): 197–224.

———. 2001b. Working the border: Constructing sovereignty in the context of liberalization. *Political and Legal Anthropology Review* 24 (1): 129–48.

———. 2003. Working the border in Ghana: Technologies of sovereignty and its others. *School of Social Science Occasional Paper* 16. Princeton, N.J.: Institute for Advanced Study.

———. 2004. *Shea Butter republic: State power, global markets, and the making of an indigenous commodity.* New York: Routledge.

———. 2006. Enlarging the anthropology of the state: Global Customs regimes and the traffic in sovereignty. *Current Anthropology* 47 (2): 243–76.

———. 2007. Customs regimes and the materiality of global mobility: Governing the port of Rotterdam. *American Behavioral Scientist* 50 (12): 1610–30.

———. 2008a. Sovereigns and citizens in close encounter: Airport anthropology and Customs regimes in neoliberal Ghana. *American Ethnologist* 35 (4): 519–38.

———. 2008b. Cars, the Customs Service, and sumptuary rule in contemporary Ghana. *Comparative Studies in Society and History* 50 (2): 424–53.

———. 2009. Recasting the port of Tema: The political economy of Ghana's maritime frontier. *Politique Africaine* 114.

Channel Business. 2002. Big red sun rises in Toronto. October 9.

Chazan, N. 1983. *An anatomy of Ghanaian politics: Managing political recession, 1969–1982.* Boulder, Colo.: Westview Press.

Chronicle (Ghana). 2000. CEPS boss defies court order. November 8.

———. 2001. Tony Aidoo—rejoinder. February 14.

Cohen, L. 2005. Operability, bioavailability, and exception. In *Global assemblages,* ed. Ong and Collier.

Colatrella, S. 2001. *Workers of the world: African and Asian migrants in Italy in the 1990s.* Trenton, N.J.: Africa World Press.

Cole, C. 2001. *Ghana's concert party theater.* Bloomington: Indiana University Press.

Collier, S. 2005. Budgets and biopolitics. In *Global assemblages: Technology, politics and ethics as anthropological problems,* ed. Ong and Collier.

Collier, S. J., and A. Lakoff. 2005. On regimes of living. In *Global assemblages,* ed. Ong and Collier.

Collier, S. J., and A. Ong. 2005. Global assemblages, anthropological problems. In *Global assemblages,* ed. Ong and Collier.

Collins, J. 1994. The Ghanaian Concert Party: African popular entertainment at the crossroads. Ph.D. diss., State University of New York at Buffalo.

Colonial Secretary's Office. 1934. Letter to Gold Coast Comptroller of Customs. No. 1207/31/39. Ghana National Archives.

Comaroff, J., and J. L. Comaroff. 1993. *Modernity and its malcontents: Ritual and power in postcolonial Africa.* Chicago: University of Chicago Press.

———. 1999. Introduction. In *Civil society and the political imagination in Africa: Critical perspectives,* ed. J. L. Comaroff and J. Comaroff. Chicago: University of Chicago Press.

———. 2001. Millennial capitalism: First thoughts on a second coming. In *Millennial capitalism and the culture of neoliberalism, ed.* J. L. Comaroff and J. Comaroff. Durham, N.C.: Duke University Press.

Coomson, K. 2001. More revelations on bootlegged cars. *Chronicle* (Ghana), February 9–12.

Cooper, F. 2002. *Africa since 1940: The past of the present, new approaches to African history*. New York: Cambridge University Press.

Corrigan, P., and D. Sayer. 1985. *The great arch: English state formation as cultural revolution*. New York: Blackwell.

COTECNA. 2002a. Our services. November 6. Retrieved from http://www .cotecna.com/prod/gov_services_home.asp.

———. 2002b. Introduction. November 6. Retrieved from http://www.cotecna .com/corp/corp/_aboutUsIntro.asp.

———. 2002c. Company history. November 6. Retrieved from http://www .cotecna.com/corp/corp_about UsHistory.asp.

———. 2006. COTECNA Corporate Presentation. COTECNA Inspection.

Cottrill, K 2002. Security in the Spotlight. *Trafficworld*. July 22.

Coutin, S. 2005. Being en route. *American Anthropologist* 107 (2): 195–206.

Crawford, G. 2009. Making democracy a reality'? The politics of decentralisation and the limits to local democracy in Ghana. *Journal of Contemporary African Studies* 27 (1): 57–83.

Crook, R., and J. Ayee. 2006. Urban service partnerships. *Development Policy Review* 24 (1): 51–73.

Crown Agents. 2003. *Outlook: Newsletter of Crown Agents Procurement and Consultancy Services*. July.

Crusading Guide (Ghana). 2001. CEPS Official Lies. April 10: 1.

Customs Cooperation Council. 1955. The activities of the council and the implementation of the Brussels conventions of 15 December 1950. *Bulletin no. 1.*

Daily Graphic (Ghana). 2000a. Customs, excise and preventive service, notice to owners of seized cars. October 27.

———. 2000b. Where is car number. September 25.

———. 2001a. List of beneficiaries of vehicles. January 23.

———. 2001b. X-ray scanner detects undeclared goods. February 7.

Daily Guide (Ghana). 2001. CEPS blows whistle. February 27.

Darkwah, A. 2002. Going global: Ghanaian female transnational traders in an era of globalization. Ph.D. diss., Department of Sociology, University of Wisconsin–Madison.

Dávila, A. 2004. *Barrio dreams: Puerto Ricans, Latinos, and the neoliberal city*. Berkeley: University of California Press.

De Wulf, L., and J. B. Sokol, eds. 2004a. *Customs modernization handbook*. Trade and Development Series. Washington, D.C.: World Bank.

———. 2004b. *Customs modernization initiatives: Case studies*. Washington, D.C.: World Bank.

Dean, M. 1996. Foucault, government and the enfolding of authority. In *Foucault and political reason: Liberalism, neo-liberalism, and rationalities of government,* ed. A. Barry, T. Osborne, and N. Rose. Chicago: University of Chicago Press.

———. 1999. *Governmentality: Power and rule in modern society.* Thousand Oaks, Calif.: Sage Publications.

Deleuze, G., and F. Guattari. 1987. *A thousand plateaus: Capitalism and schizophrenia.* Minneapolis: University of Minnesota Press.

Department Export Credits Guarantee. 2002. Ghanaian airport upgrade makes successful landing. Retrieved from http://www.nds.coi.gov.uk.

Devries, J. 1976. *The economy of Europe in an age of crisis.* Cambridge: Cambridge University Press.

Dirks, N. 2007. Imperial sovereignty. In *Imperial formations,* ed. A. L. Stoler and C. McGranahan. Sante Fe, N.M.: School of American Research Press and James Curry.

Dispatch (Ghana). 2001. List of beneficiaries of vehicles, final list of beneficiaries under the transitional arrangement. January 22.

Dogbe, E. 2003. Elusive modernity: Portraits of the city in popular Ghanaian video. In *Leisure in urban Africa,* ed. P. Zeleza and C. Veney. Trenton, N.J.: Africa World Press.

Donkor, M. 2001. CEPS impounds 70 vehicles . . . for non-payment of tax. *Daily Graphic* (Ghana), September 13.

Donnan, H., and T. Wilson. 1999. *Borders: Frontiers of identity, nation and state.* Oxford: Berg.

Dordunoo, C. 2000. Fiscal trends, 1970–1995. In *Economic reforms in Ghana: The miracle and the mirage,* ed. E. Aryeetey, J. Harrigan, and M. Nissanke. Trenton, N.J.: Africa World Press.

Dunn, E. 2005. Standards and person-making in East Central Europe. In *Global assemblages,* ed. Ong and Collier.

Duodu, S. 2001. Idrissu Mahama dashed stolen expensive care. *Evening News* (Ghana), March 27.

Duodu, S., and Bouna, P. 2001. Government retrieves cars, ex-officials can't pay new prices. *Evening News* (Ghana), January 30.

Durkheim, E. 1964. *The division of labor in society.* New York: Free Press.

Dwemoh, E. R. K. 1969. *Ghana Department of Civil Aviation Ghana: What it does.* Republic of Ghana.

Earle, T. 1994. Wealth finance in the Inka empire: Evidence from the Calchaqui Valley, Argentina. *American Antiquity* 59 (3): 443–60.

Economic Commission for Africa. 1999. Decision relating to the implementation of the Yamoussoukro Declaration concerning the liberalisation of access to air transport markets in Africa. Annex 1:ECA/RCID/CM.CIVAV/99/RPT.

———. 2001. Liberalization of air transport markets access in Africa. Sub-regional meeting on the implementaion of the Yamoussoukro Decision. Bamako, Mali, March 12–14, ECA/RCID/TPTCOM/MTG/2001/2.

Economist 1991. Lost in the Forest. 320 (7722): 30.

———. 1999. The desert blooms. November 20.

Edmonds, A. 2007. The poor have the right to be beautiful: Cosmetic surgery in neoliberal Brazil. *Journal of the Royal Anthropological Institute* 13 (2): 363–81.

Edmonson, R. 2002. Cargo-reporting: as clear as haze. *Journal of Commerce.* December 2–8.

Ellis, S. and J. MacGaffey. 1996. Research on sub-Saharan Africa's unrecorded international trade: Some methodological and conceptual problems. *African Studies Review* 39 (2): 19–41.

Ellison, J. 2009. Governmentality and the family: Neoliberal choices and emergent kin relations in southern Ethiopia. *American Anthropologist* 111 (1): 81–92.

Elyachar, J. 2006. Best practices: Research, finance, and NGOs in Cairo. *American Ethnologist* 33:413–26.

Engelschalk, M., and T. Minh Le. 2004. Two decades of World Bank lending for customs reform: Trends in project design, project implementation, and lessons learned. In *Customs modernization handbook*, ed. De Wulf and Sokol.

Evening News (Ghana). 2001. CEPS explains position on confiscated vehicles. January 16.

———. 2001a. CEPS pays c/50 bn to Private Company. March 26.

———. 2001b. Review GSL agreement. March 16.

FDCH Regulatory Intelligence Database. 2001. United States committed to helping improve Africa's air safety. Agency Group 06, June 28.

Ferguson, J. 1993. De-moralizing economies: African socialism, scientific capitalism, and the moral politics of structural adjustment. In *Moralizing states and the ethnography of the present*, ed. S. F. Moore. Arlington, Va.: American Anthropological Association.

———. 1994. *The anti-politics machine: "Development," depoliticization, and bureaucratic power in Lesotho.* Minneapolis: University of Minnesota Press.

———. 1999. *Expectations of modernity: Myths and meanings of urban life on the Zambian copperbelt.* Berkeley: University of California Press.

———. 2006. *Global shadows: Africa in the neoliberal world order.* Durham, N.C.: Duke University Press.

Ferguson, J., and A. Gupta. 2002. Spatializing states: Toward an ethnography of neoliberal governmentality. *American Ethnologist* 29 (4): 981–1002.

Fikes, K. 2009. *Managing African Portugal: The citizen-migrant distinction.* Durham, N.C.: Duke University Press.

Fine, B., and K. Boateng. 2000. Labour and employment under structural adjustment. In *Economic reforms in Ghana: The miracle and the mirage*, ed. E. Aryeetey, J. Harrigan, and M. Nissanke. Oxford: James Currey.

Flynn, D. K. 1997. "We are the border": Identity, exchange, and the state along the Benin-Nigeria Border. *American Ethnologist* 24 (2): 311–30.

Foucault, M. 1979. *Discipline and punish: the birth of the prison.* New York: Vintage Books.

————. 1991. Governmentality. In *The Foucault effect: Studies in governmentality*, ed. G. Burchell, C. Gordon, and P. Miller. Chicago: University of Chicago Press.

Fox, J. 2000. The World Bank inspection panel: Lessons from the first five years. *Global Governance* 6 (3): 279–308.

Gaonkar, D. 2003. On alternative modernities. In *Alternative modernities*, ed. D. Gaonkar. Durham, N.C.: Duke University Press.

Geertz, C. 1973. *The interpretation of cultures*. New York: Basic Books.

————. 1983. Centers, kings, and charisma. In *Local knowledge: Further essays in interpretive anthropology*. New York: Basic Books.

Genoud, R. 1969. *Nationalism and economic development in Ghana*. New York: Praeger.

Geurts, K. L. 2002. *Culture and the senses: Bodily ways of knowing in an African community*. Ethnographic studies in subjectivity 3. Berkeley: University of California Press.

Ghana. 1999. *Trade and investment handbook*. Accra.

————. 2001. Trade policy reviews: First press release: Secretariat and government summaries.

Ghana, Republic of. 1999. Comprehensive development framework. Accra: Ministry of Roads and Transport.

Ghana Customs, Excise and Preventive Service (CEPS). 1993. Management Law, PNDC Law 330.

————. 1999a. CEPS image in the next millennium. *Customs Newsletter* 6, July/August.

————. 1999b. *Customs News* 2 (4). January.

————. 1999c. *Customs Newsletter* 3. January/February.

————. 1999d. Dedication to hard work the answer. *Customs Newsletter* 4. March/April.

————. 1999e. New wind blowing over CEPS. *Customs Newsletter* 5. May/June.

Ghana News Agency. 2004. CPP, NDC accuse NPP attempts to marginalize opposition. October 30.

Ghana Shippers Council. 2003. Maritime Trade Statistics, Seaborne Trade. Retrieved from http://www.ghanashipperscouncil.org/ghana_shippers_council/transport_stats/maritime_trade.asp.

Ghanaian Chronicle. 2002. Ghanaian ring busted in USA, UK. July 26.

Ghanaian Times. 2001. CEPS denies allegations of smuggling of vehicles. January 17.

————. 2001. Ghana saves c/180m thru use of x-ray scanner. February 7.

Gifford, P. 2004. *Ghana's new Christianity: Pentecostalism in a globalizing African economy*. Bloomington: Indiana University Press.

Gledhill, J. 2004. Neoliberalism. In *A companion to the anthropology of politics*, ed. D. Nugent and J. Vincent. Malden: Blackwell Publishing.

Glick Schiller, N., and G. Fouron. 1999. *Georges woke-up laughing: Long distance nationalism and the search for home*. Durham, N.C.: Duke University Press.

Gocking, R. 2005. *The history of Ghana*. The Greenwood histories of the modern nations. Westport, Conn.: Greenwood Press.

Gold Coast Comptroller of Customs. 1934. Letter to Colonial Secretary. No. 1204/31. Ghana National Archives.

Gold Coast Land Registry. 1913. Acquisition of Land. No. 560/1913. Ghana National Archives.

Gold Coast Lands Department. 1934. Letter to Comptroller of Customs. No. 3099/Lands Dept./Accra/1207/31. Ghana National Archives.

Goldstein, A. 2001. Infrastructure development and regulatory reform in sub-Saharan Africa: The case of air transport. *World Economy* 24 (2): 221–48.

Goody, E., ed. 1982. *From craft to industry: Ethnography of proto-industrial cloth production*. Cambridge: Cambridge University Press.

Gramsci, A. 1971. *Selections from the prison notebooks*. New York: International Publishers.

Green, D. 1998. Ghana: Structural adjustment and state (re)formation. In *The African state at a critical juncture: Between disintegration and reconfiguration*, ed. L. Villalón and P. A. Huxtable. Boulder, Colo.: Lynne Rienner Publishers.

Greenfield, K. R. 1918. *Sumptuary law in Nurnberg: A study in paternal government*. Baltimore: The Johns Hopkins Press.

Greenhalgh, S., and E. Winkler. 2005. *Governing China's population*. Palo Alto, Calif.: Stanford University Press.

GSL. 2000. GSL destination inspection in Ghana: The way forward. April to December.

Gualini, E. 2004. *Multi-level governance and institutional change*. Aldershot: Ashgate.

Gupta, A. 1998. *Postcolonial developments: Agriculture in the making of modern India*. Durham, N.C.: Duke University Press.

Gupta, A., and J. Ferguson. 1997. *Anthropological locations: Boundaries and grounds of a field science*. Berkeley: University of California Press.

Guttman, J. 2004. South Africa's armored cars. *World War II* 19 (7): 18–24.

Gyimah-Boadi, E. 1999. Ghana: The challenges of consolidating democracy. In *State, conflict, and democracy in Africa*, ed. R. A. Joseph. Boulder, Colo.: Lynne Rienner Publishers.

———. 2001. A peaceful turnover in Ghana. *Journal of Democracy* 12 (2): 103–18.

Hall, S. 1984. The state in question. In *The idea of the modern state*, ed. G. McLennan, D. Held, and S. Hall. Milton Keynes: Open University Press.

Hansen, K. T. 2000. *Salaula: The world of secondhand clothing and Zambia*. Chicago: University of Chicago Press.

Hansen, T. 1999. *The saffron wave: Democracy and Hindu nationalism in modern India*. Princeton, N.J.: Princeton University Press.

Hansen, T., and F. Stepputat. 2001. Introduction. In *States of imagination: Ethnographic explorations of the postcolonial state*, ed. T. Hansen and F. Stepputat. Durham, N.C.: Duke University Press.

Harper, R. 2000. The social organization of the IMF's mission work: an examination of international auditing. In *Audit cultures: anthropological studies in accountability, ethics, and the academy,* ed. M. Strathern. London: Routledge.

Harrington, J., and A. Oduro. 2000. Exchange rate policy and the balance of payment, 1972–96. In *Economic reforms in Ghana: The miracle and the mirage,* ed. by E. Aryeetey, J. Harrigan, and M. Nissanke. Oxford: James Currey.

Harvey, D. 1990. *The condition of postmodernity.* Oxford: Blackwell.

———. 2005. *A brief history of neoliberalism.* New York: Oxford University Press.

Hashmi, S. 1997. Introduction. In *State sovereignty: Change and persistence in international relations,* ed. S. Hashmi. University Park: Pennsylvania State University Press.

Hasty, J. 2003. Rites of passage, routes of redemption: Emancipation tourism and the wealth of culture. *Africa Today* 49 (3): 47–78.

———. 2005a. *The press and political culture in Ghana.* Bloomington: Indiana University Press.

———. 2005b. The pleasures of corruption: Desire and discipline in Ghanaian political culture. *Current Anthropology* 20 (2): 271–301.

Hegel, G. 1967. *Hegel's philosophy of right.* Oxford: Clarendon.

Helleiner, E. 1992. Japan and the changing global financial order. *International Journal* 47:420–44.

Herbst, J. I. 1993. *The politics of reform in Ghana, 1982–1991.* Berkeley: University of California Press.

———. 2000. *States and power in Africa: Comparative lessons in authority and control.* Princeton studies in international history and politics. Princeton, N.J.: Princeton University Press

Herskovits, M. J. 1967. *Dahomey, an ancient West African kingdom.* Evanston, Ill.: Northwestern University Press.

Herzfeld, M. 1992. *The social production of indifference: exploring the symbolic roots of Western bureaucracy.* Global issues. New York: Berg.

———. 1997. *Cultural intimacy: Social poetics in the nation-state.* New York: Routledge.

———. 2005. Political optics and the occlusion of intimate knowledge. *American Anthropologist* 107 (3): 369–76.

Hess, J. B. 2000. Imagining architecture: The structure of nationalism in Accra, Ghana. *Africa Today* 47 (2): 35–58.

Heyman, J. 1995. Putting power in the anthropology of bureaucracy: The Immigration and Naturalization Service at the Mexico–United States border. *Current Anthropology* 36 (2): 261–87.

Hirschmann, D. 2005. Changing context, credible commitment, and conflicting purposes: Incentives to pay and collect tax in Africa. Paper read at African Studies Association annual meeting, Washington, D.C.

Hobbes, T. 1968. *Leviathan.* Harmondsworth: Penguin.

Hodess, R., and Transparency International. 2004. *Global corruption report 2004: Special focus: Political corruption*. Sterling, Va.: Pluto Press/Transparency International.

Holden, L. 1998. More than a marque. The car as symbol: Aspects of culture and ideology. In *The motor car and popular culture in the 20th century*, ed. D. Thomas, L. Holden, and T. Claydon. Aldershot: Ashgate.

Hopkins, A. 1973. *An economic history of West Africa*. New York: Columbia University Press.

Hughes, D. 2006. *From enslavement to environmentalism: Politics on a southern African frontier*. Culture, place, and nature. Seattle: University of Washington Press.

Humphrey, C. 2004. Neoliberalism. In *A companion to the anthropology of politics*, ed. D. Nugent and J. Vincent. Malden, Mass.: Blackwell Publishing.

Hunt, A. 1996. *Governance of the consuming passions: A history of sumptuary law*. London: St. Martin's.

Hunter, D. 2003. A smart border for smart firms. *National Post*, April 7.

Hutchinson, C. F. 2005. *The pen-pictures of modern Africans and African celebrities: A collective biography of elite society in the Gold Coast colony*. Edited by M. Doortmont. African sources for African history. Leiden: Brill.

Iliffe, J. 1995. *Africans: The history of a continent*. Cambridge: Cambridge University Press.

The Independent (Ghana). 2001. Kenyan delegation inspects x-ray scanner. April 24.

Integrated Solutions, 1999. Customs, Excise and Preventive Service, Corporate Plan. 1999–2001. Accra.

International Civil Aviation Organization. 2002. Western and Central African Office, First meeting of Directors General of Civil Aviation. Agenda Item 4: Air Transport and Liberalization:DGCA-1-WP/14.

———. 2003. Aviation in transition: Challenges and opportunities of liberalization. Session 2: Industry challenges for the regulator. Seeking a new way. Montreal, March 22–23.

International Finance Corporation. 1997. *The private sector and development: Five case studies, Results on the ground*. Washington, D.C.: International Finance Corporation.

Intertec. 2003. Kotoka International Airport, Ghana. Reference project. Retrieved from http://www.intertec.dk.

Jackson, R. 1990. *Quasi states: Sovereignty, international relations and the third world*. Cambridge: Cambridge University Press.

Jeffries, R. 1989. Ghana: The political economy of personal rule. In *Contemporary African states*, ed. D. C. O'Brien, J. Dunn, and R. Rathbone. Cambridge: Cambridge University Press.

Jessop, B. 1999. Narrating the future of the national economy and the national state. In *State/culture: State formation after the cultural turn*, ed. G. Steinmetz. Ithaca, N.Y.: Cornell University Press.

Joseph, R. A. 1999. *State, conflict, and democracy in Africa.* Boulder, Colo.: Lynne Rienner Publishers.

Jourde, C. 2005. "The president is coming to visit!" Dramas and the hijack of democratization in the Islamic republic of Mauritania. *Comparative Politics* 37 (4): 421–40.

Kane, A. 2002. Senegal's village diaspora and the people left ahead. In *The transnational family*, ed. D. Bryceson. Oxford: Oxford University Press.

Keen, M. 2003. The future of fiscal frontiers and the modernization of customs administration. In *Changing customs: Challenges and strategies for the reform of customs administration*, ed. M. Keen and International Monetary Fund. Washington, D.C.: New York: International Monetary Fund.

Kelly, J., and M. Kaplan. 2001. Nation and decolonization: Toward a new anthropology of nationalism. *Anthropological Theory* 1 (4): 419–37.

Kelly, L. 2004. *Migration policy in the UK.* Migpol: European Migration Center.

Killick, T. 1978. *Development economics in action: A study of economic policies in Ghana.* London: Palgrave Macmillan.

Kimble, D. 1965. *A political history of Ghana: The rise of Gold Coast nationalism, 1850–1928.* Oxford: Clarendon Press.

Knipe, M. 2000. *Open skies* 2000. Retrieved from http://www.pioneer_news.com/reports/ghana/report_ghanap23.html.

Kofman, E. 1995. Citizenship for some. *Political Geography* 14 (2): 121–37.

Kondo, D. 1990. *Crafting selves: Power, gender and discourses of identity in a Japanese workplace.* Chicago: University of Chicago Press.

Kopytoff, I. 1986. The cultural biography of things: Commoditization as process. In *The social life of things*, ed. Arjun Appadurai. New York: Cambridge University Press.

———. 1987. *The African frontier: The reproduction of traditional societies.* Bloomington: Indiana University Press.

Koser, K. 2003. Introduction. In *New African diasporas*, ed. K. Koser. London: Routledge.

Krasner, S. 1999. *Sovereignty: Organized hypocrisy.* Princeton, N.J.: Princeton University Press.

Kratochwil, F. 1986. Of systems, boundaries and territoriality. *World Politics* 39 (1): 27–52.

Laderman, J. M. 2000. A cream puff in used cars? *Business Week*, May 22. Retrieved from http://www.businessweek.com/2000/00_21/b3682216.htm.

Laird, S. E. 2007. Rolling back the African state: Implications for social development in Ghana. *Social Policy and Administration* 41 (5): 465–86.

Lake, D. A. 2003. The new sovereignty in international relations. *International Studies Review* 5 (3): 303–23.

Landau, L. 2004. Immigration and the state of exception: Nativism, security, and sovereignty in refugee-affected Africa. Paper read at annual meeting of the African Studies Association, New Orleans, November 13.

Lartey, O. 2000. CEPS boss rejects 38 million duty. *The Accra Mail,* November 6.

Latour, B. 1987. *Science in action: how to follow scientists and engineers through society.* Cambridge: Harvard University Press.

Lavenir, C. B. 2000. How the motor car conquered the road. In *Cultures of control,* ed. M. R. Levin. Amsterdam: Harwood.

Le Vine, V. 1975. *Political corruption: The Ghana case.* Stanford, Calif.: Hoover Institution.

———. 2004. *Politics in Francophone Africa.* Boulder, Colo.: Lynne Rienner Publishers.

Levinson, M. 2006. *The box: How the shipping container made the world smaller and the world economy bigger.* Princeton, N.J.: Princeton University Press.

Lindberg, S. I. 2006. *Democracy and elections in Africa.* Baltimore: Johns Hopkins University Press.

Linke, U. 2006. Contact zones: Rethinking the sensual life of the state. *Anthropological Theory* 6 (2): 205–25.

Lipsky, M. 1983. *Street-level bureaucracy: Dilemmas of the individual in public services.* New York: Russell Sage Foundation.

LiPuma, E., and B. Lee. 2004. *Financial derivatives and the globalization of risk.* Durham, N.C.: Duke University Press.

Locke, J. 1960. *Two treatises of government.* Edited by P. Laslett. Cambridge: Cambridge University Press.

Lyon, D. 2001. Under my skin: From identification papers to body surveillance. In *Documenting individual identity: The development of state practices in the modern world,* ed. J. Caplan and J. Torpey. Princeton, N.J.: Princeton University Press.

———. 2003. Surveillance as social sorting. In *Surveillance as social sorting: Privacy, risk and digital discrimination,* ed. D. Lyon. London. Routledge.

Lyons, G., and M. Mastanduno. 1995. Introduction: International intervention, state sovereignty and the future of international society. In *Beyond Westphalia,* ed. G. Lyons and M. Mastanduno. Baltimore: Johns Hopkins University Press.

MacGaffey, J. 1987. *Entrepreneurs and parasites: The struggle for indigenous capitalism in Zaire.* African Studies Series 57. Cambridge: Cambridge University Press.

MacGaffey, J., and R. Bazanguissa-Ganga. 2000. *Congo-Paris: Transnational traders on the margins of the law.* London: International African Institute.

Machiavelli, N. 1950. *The prince and the discourses.* New York: Modern Library.

Maiko, D. 2004. Customs union protocol finally signed. News from Africa. Retrieved from http://www.newsfromafrica.org/newsfromafrica/articles/art_3773.html.

Malinowski, B. 1922. *Argonauts of the western Pacific: an account of native enterprise and adventure in the Archipelagoes of Melanisian New Guinea.* New York: Dutton.

Malkki, L. H. 1995. *Purity and exile: Violence, memory, and national cosmology among Hutu refugees in Tanzania.* Chicago: University of Chicago Press.

Mann, M. 1986. *The sources of social power*. New York: Cambridge University Press.

————. 2008. Infrastructural power revisited. *Studies in Comparative International Development* 43:355–65.

Manuh, T. 2000. Migrants and citizens: Economic crisis in Ghana and the search for opportunity in Toronto, Canada. Diss., Department of Anthropology, Indiana University, Bloomington.

————. ed. 2005. *At home in the world? International migration and development in contemporary Ghana and West Africa*. Ghana: Sub-Saharan Publishers.

Marcus, G. 1998. *Ethnography through thick and thin*. Princeton, N.J.: Princeton University Press.

Marcus, G., and M. Fischer. 1986. *Anthropology as cultural critique*. Chicago: University of Chicago Press.

Martin, D. 2002. *Pentecostalism: The world their parish*. Malden: Blackwell.

Martin, D. A. 2003. Immigration policy and the Homeland Security Act reorganization: Migration Policy Institute, *Insight* 1.

Maurer, W. 2001. A fish story: Rethinking globalization on Virgin Gorda, British Virgin Island. *American Ethnologist* 27 (3): 670–701.

————. 2007. What is so hard about soft law(s)? De-texturizing law's structures of feeling. Paper read at A Graduate Student–Faculty Workshop, at Department of Anthropology University of California–Irvine, May 4–5.

Mazzucato, V. 2008. The double engagement: Transnationalism and integration—Ghanaian migrants' lives between Ghana and the Netherlands. *Journal of Ethnic and Migration Studies* 34 (2): 199–216.

McLeod, M. D. 1981. *The Asante*. London: The British Museum.

Mendoza, M., P. Low, and B. Kotschwar. 1999. Trade rules in the making: An overview. In *Trade rules in the making: challenges in regional and multilaterial negotiations,* ed. M. Mendoza, P. Low, and B. Kotschwar. Harrisonburg: Brookings Institution.

Merriam, C. 1900. *History of the theory of sovereignty since Rousseau*. New York: Columbia University Press.

Meyer, B. 1998a. The power of money: Politics, occult forces, and pentecostalism in Ghana. *African Studies Review* 41 (3): 15–38.

————. 1998b. "Make a complete break with the past": Memory and postcolonial modernity in Ghanaian Pentacostalist discourse. *Journal of Religion in Africa* 28 (3): 316–49.

————. 1999. *Translating the devil: Religion and modernity among the Ewe of Ghana*. Trenton, N.J.: Africa World Press.

————. 2004a. Christianity in Africa: From African independent to Pentecostal-charismatic churches. *Annual Review of Anthropology* 33 (1): 447–74.

————. 2004b. "Praise the Lord": Popular cinema and Pentecostalite style in Ghana's new public sphere. *American Ethnologist* 31 (1): 92–110.

Migdal, J. S. 2001. *State in society: Studying how states and societies transform and constitute one another*. Cambridge studies in comparative politics. New York: Cambridge University Press.

Mintz, S. W. 1985. *Sweetness and power: The place of sugar in modern history*. New York: Penguin Books.

Mitchell, T. 1991. The limits of the state: Beyond statist approaches and their critics. *American Political Science Review* 85 (1): 77–96.

———. 2002. *Rule of experts: Egypt, techno-politics, modernity*. Berkeley: University of California Press.

Miyazaki, H. 2003. The temporalities of the market. *American Anthropologist* 105: 255–65.

———. In press. *Arbitraging Japan: The economy of hope in the Tokyo financial markets*. Berkeley: University of California Press.

Monmonier, M. 2002. *Spying with maps: surveillance technologies and the future of privacy*. Chicago: University of Chicago Press.

Nader, L. 1972. Up the anthropologist—Perspectives gained from studying up. In *Reinventing anthropology*, ed. D. Hymes. New York: Pantheon Books.

Nathan Associates. 2002. Customs-related technical assistance for trade capacity building. A resource guide. Washington, D.C.: USAID.

Navaro-Yashin, Y. 2002. *Faces of the state: Secularism and public life in Turkey*. Princeton, N.J.: Princeton University Press.

Newell, S. 2007. Pentecostal witchcraft: Neoliberal possession and demonic discourse in Ivoirian Pentecostal churches. *Journal of Religion in Africa* 37 (4): 461–90.

Newell, S. 2002. *Literary culture in colonial Ghana: How to play the game of life*. Bloomington: Indiana University Press.

Nkrumah, K. 1968. *Dark days in Ghana*. New York: International Publishers.

Nordstrom, C. 2004. *Shadows of war: violence, power, and international profiteering in the twenty-first century*. California series in public anthropology 10. Berkeley: University of California Press.

North, D. 1981. *Structure and change in economic history*. New York: Norton.

Nugent, P. 1991. Educating Rawlings: The evolution of government strategy toward smuggling. In *Ghana: The political economy of recovery*, ed. D. S. Rothchild. Boulder, Colo.: Lynne Rienner Publishers.

———. 1995. *Big men, small boys and politics in Ghana*. London: Pinter.

———. 1996. Arbitrary lines and the people's minds: a dissenting view on colonial boundaries in West Africa. In *African boundaries: Barriers, conduits and opportunities*, ed. P. Nugent and A. I. Asiwaju. London: Pinter.

———. 2001. Winners, losers, and also rans: money, moral authority, and voting patterns in the Ghana 2000 election. *African Affairs* 100: 405–28.

———. 2002. *Smugglers, secessionists, and loyal citizens on the Ghana-Toga frontier: The life of the borderlands since 1914*. Western African studies. Athens: Ohio University Press.

Nyugen, V. K. 2005. Antiretroviral globalism, biopolitics, and therapeutic citizenship. In *Global assemblages*, ed. Ong and Collier.

Okine, C. B. 2001. Minister inspects military installation. *The Daily Graphic*, February 27.

Ong, A. 1999. *Flexible citizenship: The cultural logics of transnationality*. Durham, N.C.: Duke University Press.

———. 2006. *Neoliberalism as exception: Mutations in citizenship and sovereignty*. Durham: Duke University Press.

Ong, A., and S. J. Collier, eds. 2005. *Global assemblages: Technology, politics, and ethics as anthropological problems*. Malden: Blackwell Publishing.

Orhin, I. G. 2001. Ato Dadzie admits error. *Public Agenda* (Ghana), January 23.

Owusu, M. 1994. Government and politics. In *Ghana: A country study*, ed. L. Berry. Washington, D.C.: Federal Research Division. Retrieved from http://purl.access.gpo.gov/GPO/LPS40293.

Oxhorn, P., and G. Ducatenzeiler. 1998. *What kind of democracy? What kind of market? Latin America in the age of neoliberalism*. University Park: Pennsylvania State University Press.

PAI Group. 2003. Contracts. Retrieved from http://www.paigroup.com/pai_contracts.htm.

Painstil, D. 2009. Cape Coast Ministries, court complex, low cost houses need rehabilitation. *Ghanaian Chronicle*. March 18. Retrieved from http://www.modernghana.com/news/207021/1/cape-coast-ministries-court-complex-low-cost-house.html.

Painter, J., and C. Philo. 1995. Spaces of citizenship. *Political Geography* 14 (2): 107–20.

Palan, R. 2003. *The offshore world: Sovereign markets, virtual places, and nomad millionaires*. Ithaca, N.Y.: Cornell University Press.

Panitch, L. 1996. Rethinking the role of the state. In *Globalization: Critical Reflections*, ed. J. Mittleman. Boulder, Colo.: Lynne Rienner.

Parker, J. 2000. *Making the town: Ga state and society in early colonial Accra*. Social History of Africa. Portsmouth: Heinemann.

Parry, J., and M. Bloch. 1989. Introduction: Money and the morality of exchange. In *Money and the morality of exchange*, ed. J. Parry and M. Bloch. Cambridge: Cambridge University Press.

Pedersen, P. O. 2001. The freight transport and logistical system of GhanaCDR. Working Paper 01.2, March. Copenhagen: Center for Development Research.

Pellow, D., and N. Chazan. 1986. *Ghana: Coping with uncertainty*. Boulder, Colo.: Westview.

Pels, P. 2003. Magic and modernity. In *Magic and modernity*, ed. B. Meyer and P. Pels. Stanford, Calif.: Stanford University Press.

Perkins, D., and M. Roemer. 1991. *Reforming economic systems in developing countries*. Harvard studies in international development. Cambridge: Harvard Institute for International Development.

Perry, D. 2009. Fathers, sons, and the state: Discipline and punishment in a Wolof hinterland. *Cultural Anthropology* 24 (1): 33–67.

Petryna, A. 2006. Globalizing human subjects research. In *Global Pharmaceuticals: Ethics, Markets, Practices*, ed. A. Petryna, A. Lakoff and A. Klienman. Durham, N.C.: Duke University Press.

Phillips, R., J. Henderson, L. Andor, and D. Hulme. 2005. Usurping social policy: Neoliberalism and economic governance in Hungary. *Journal of Social Policy* 35:585–607.

Philpott, D. 1995. Sovereignty: An introduction and brief history. *Journal of International Affairs* 48 (2): 353–68.

———. 2001. *Revolutions in sovereignty*. Princeton, N.J.: Princeton University Press.

———. 2003. Sovereignty. In *Stanford Encyclopedia of Philosophy*, ed. E. N. Zalta, Retrieved from http://plato.stanford.edu/entries/sovereignty.

Plange, P. K. 2001. Bad-bye Nii Okine. *Chronicle* (Ghana), January 22.

Port Cities: London. 2007. The Customs Service: The Customs in London. Retrieved from http://www.portcities.org.uk/london/server.php?show=ConNarrative.145&chapterId=2993.

Prempeh, H. 2007. Plenary speech presented at Ghana's Legacy: Fifty Years of African Independence program. Center for African Studies. University of Florida, Gainesville, March 2.

Prescott, J. R. V. 1987. *Political frontiers and boundaries*. London: Unwin Hyman.

Prince, C., and M. Keller. 1989. *The U.S. Customs Service: A bicentennial history*. Washington, D.C.: Dept. of the Treasury U.S. Customs Service.

Public Agenda (Ghana). 2001. Significant fall in car imports. March 19.

Purchasing B2B. 2003. Customs on-line. May.

Putnam, R. D., R. Leonardi, and R. Nanetti. 1993. *Making democracy work: Civic traditions in modern Italy*. Princeton, N.J.: Princeton University Press.

Rapley, J. 1996. *Understanding development: Theory and practice in the third world*. Boulder, Colo.: Lynne Rienner Publishers.

Rathbone, R. 1978. Ghana. In *West African states: Failure and promise*, ed. John Dunn. Cambridge: Cambridge University Press.

Reno, W. 1998. *Warlord politics and African states*. Boulder, Colo.: Lynne Rienner Publishers.

Riles, A. 2000. *The network inside out*. Ann Arbor: University of Michigan Press.

———. 2006. Introduction: In response. In *Documents: Artifacts of modern knowledge,* ed. A. Riles. Ann Arbor: University of Michigan Press.

Robinson, W. I. 2004. *A theory of global capitalism: Production, class, and state in a transnational world*. Themes in global social change. Baltimore: Johns Hopkins University Press.

Roitman, J. L. 2005. *Fiscal disobedience: An anthropology of economic regulation in Central Africa*. In-formation series. Princeton, N.J.: Princeton University Press.

Roncoli, M. 1994. Managing on the margins: Agricultural production and household reproduction in northeastern Ghana. Ph.D. diss., Department of Anthropology, State University of New York at Binghamton.

Rosaldo, R. 1993. *Culture and truth: The remaking of social analysis*. Boston: Beacon Press.

Rose, A. 2002. Do WTO members have more liberal trade policy? Paper read at International Business, Economic Analysis and Policy Group, at Haas School of Business at the University of California, Berkeley, November 7.

Roseberry, W. 1989. *Anthropologies and histories: Essays in culture, history, and political economy*. New Brunswick, N.J.: Rutgers University Press.

———. 1994. Hegemony and the language of contention. In *Everyday forms of state formation: Revolution and the negotiation of rule in modern Mexico*, ed. G. Joseph and D. Nugent, 355–66. Durham, N.C.: Duke University Press.

———. 2002. Understanding capitalism—Historically, structurally, spatially. In *Locating capitalism in time and space: global restructurings, politics, and identity*, ed. D. Nugent. Stanford: Stanford University Press.

Rosecrance, R. N. 1986. *The rise of the trading state: Commerce and conquest in the modern world*. New York: Basic Books.

Rosenau, J. 1995. Sovereignty in a turbulent world. In *Beyond Westphalia: State sovereignty and international intervention*, ed. G. Lyons and M. Mastanduno. Baltimore: Johns Hopkins University Press.

Rosenau, J., and E. O. Czempiel. 1992. *Governance without government: Order and change in world politics*. Cambridge studies in international relations 20. Cambridge: Cambridge University Press.

Rosenthal, J. 1998. *Possession, ecstasy, and law in Ewe voodoo*. Charlottesville: University Press of Virginia.

Rothchild, D. 1991. Ghana and structural adjustment: An overview. In *Ghana: The political economy of recovery*, ed. D. Rothchild. Boulder, Colo.: Lynne Rienner Publishers.

Rudnyckyj, D. 2009. Spiritual economies: Islam and neoliberalism in contemporary Indonesia. *Cultural Anthropology* 24 (1): 104–41.

Ruggie, J. G. 1993. Territoriality and beyond: Problematizing modernity in international relations. *International Organization* 47 (1): 139–74.

———. 2002. At home abroad, abroad at home: International liberalization and domestic stability in the new world economy. In *The globalization of liberalism*, ed. E. Hovden and E. Keene. New York: Palgrave in association with Millennium Journal of International Studies.

Sahlins, P. 1989. *Boundaries: The making of France and Spain in the Pyrenees*. Berkeley: University of California Press.

Sahn, D. 1996. Economic reform and poverty. In *Economic reform and the poor in Africa*, ed. D. Sahn. New York: Oxford University Press.

Sakyi-Addo, K. 2005. GMT impressions of Togo after the "coup." *BBC News*, February 18.

Sampson, S. 1987. The second economy of the Soviet Union and Eastern Europe. *Annals of the American Academy of Political and Social Science* 493:120–36.

Sassen, S. 1996. *Losing control? Sovereignty in an age of globalization*. New York: Columbia.

———. 1998. *Globalization and its discontents*. New York: The New Press.

———. 2000. Spatialities and temporalities of the global: Elements for a theorization. *Public Culture* 12 (1): 215–32.

———. 2001. *The global city: New York, London, Tokyo*. Princeton: Princeton University Press.

———. 2002. The repositioning of citizenship. *Berkeley Journal of Sociology* 46: 5–26.

———. 2006. *Territory, authority, rights: From medieval to global assemblages.* Princeton, N.J.: Princeton University Press.

Sawyer, S. 2004. *Crude chronicles: Indigenous politics, multinational oil, and neoliberalism in Ecuador.* American encounters/Global interactions. Durham, N.C.: Duke University Press.

Scheper-Hughes, N. 2005. The last commodity: Post-human ethics and the global traffic in "fresh" organs. In *Global assemblages,* ed. Ong and Collier, 145–68.

Schildkrout, E. 1996. Kingdom of gold. *Natural History* 105 (2): 32–47.

Schmitt, C. 1985. *Political theology: Four chapters on the concept of sovereignty.* Cambridge, Mass.: MIT.

Scott, J. 1998. *Seeing like a state.* New Haven: Yale University Press.

Sen, S. 2002. *Distant sovereignty: National imperialism and the origins of British India.* New York: Routledge.

SGS. 2003. VALUENET: Adding value to customs valuation.

Shark, D. 2001. Statement by deputy chief of the U.S. mission to the World Trade Organization. Paper read at WTO Trade Policy Review of Ghana, Geneva, February 26.

Sharma, A., and A. Gupta, 2006. "Introduction: Rethinking theories of the state in the age of globalization. In *The anthropology of the state: a reader,* ed. A. Sharma and A. Gupta. Malden: Blackwell Publishing.

Shipley, J. 2003. National audiences and consuming subjects: A political genealogy of performance in neoliberal Ghana. Ph.D. diss., Department of Anthropology, University of Chicago.

Shipton, P. 1989. *Bitter money: Cultural economy and some African means of forbidden commodities.* Washington, D.C.: American Anthropological Association.

Shore, C. 2000. *Building Europe: The cultural politics of European integration.* London: Routledge

Simmons, B. A., and Z. Elkins. 2004. The globalization of liberalization: Policy diffusion in the international political economy. *American Political Science Review* 98:171–89.

Simone, A. 2001. On the worlding of African cities. *African Studies Review* 44 (2): 15–41.

———. 2004. *For the city yet to come: Changing African life in four cities.* Durham, N.C.: Duke University Press.

Smith, D. 2001. The politics of Upper East and the 2000 Ghanauan elections. In *Deepening democracy in Ghana: Politics of the 2000 elections,* vol. 2, *Constituency studies,* ed. J. Ayee. Accra: Freedom Publications Ltd.

———. 2002a. Consolidating democracy? The structural underpinnings of Ghana's 2000 elections. *Journal of Modern African Studies* 40 (4): 1–30.

———. 2002b. Ghana's 2000 elections: Consolidating multiparty democracy. *Electoral Studies* 21 (3): 519–26.

Soifer, H. 2008. State infrastructural power: Approaches to conceptualization and measurement. *Studies in Comparative International Development* 43:231–51.

Solignac-Lecomte, H. 2002. OECD DAC workshop Ghana case study. DCD(2000)10/ANN2. May 29–30.

Spruyt, H. 1994. *The sovereign state and its competitors: An analysis of systems change.* Princeton, N.J.: Princeton University Press.

Steiner, C. B. 1985. Another image of Africa: toward an ethnohistory of European cloth marketed in West Africa, 1873–1960. *Ethnohistory* 32 (2): 91–110.

Stewart, K. 1996. *A place on the side of the road.* Princeton, N.J.: Princeton University Press.

Strange, S. 1996. *The retreat of the state: The diffusion of power in the world economy.* Cambridge: Cambridge University Press.

———. 1998. *Mad money: When markets outgrow governments.* Ann Arbor: University of Michigan Press.

Strathern, M. 2000. Introduction: New accountabilities. In *Audit cultures: anthropological studies in accountability, ethics, and the academy,* ed. M. Strathern. London: Routledge.

———. 2002. On space and depth. In *Complexities: Social studies of knowledge practices,* ed. J. Law and A. Mol. Durham, N.C.: Duke University Press.

———. 2004. *Partial connections.* Updated ed. Walnut Creek, Calif.: AltaMira Press.

Sumprim, A. K. 2000. The imported Ghanaian: Call the fashion police. *The Daily Dispatch,* October 18–24.

Swindell, K. 1995. People on the move in West Africa. In *The Cambridge survey of world migration,* ed. R. Cohen. Cambridge: Cambridge University Press.

Sylvanus, N. 2006."Chinese devils"? Perceptions of the Chinese in Lomé's Central Market. Paper read at Rethinking Africa's 'China Factor': Identifying Players, Strategies, and Practices, University of California–Los Angeles, April 27.

Tachie-Menson, R. 2007. Sunyani—A star in the dark. November 7. Ghanadot.com.

Taussig, M. 1999. *Defacement: Public secrecy and the labor of the negative.* Stanford, Calif.: Stanford University Press.

Taussig-Rubbo, M. 2007. The sovereign's gift: Reciprocity and invisibility in U.S. immigration detention camps. Ph.D. diss., Department of Anthropology, University of Chicago.

Technology Airport. 2001. Economic forecasting October. Retrieved from http://www.airport-technology.com/projects/kotoka.

Teschke, B. 2003. *The myth of 1648: Class, geopolitics, and the making of modern international relations.* New York: Verso.

Thomas, D., L. Holden, and T. Claydon. 1998. Introduction. In *The motor car and popular culture in the 20th century,* ed. D. Thomas, L. Holden, and T. Claydon. Aldershot: Ashgate.

Thomson, J. E. 1994. *Mercenaries, pirates, and sovereigns: State-building and extraterritorial violence in early modern Europe.* Princeton Studies in International History and Politics. Princeton, N.J.: Princeton University Press.

———. 1995. State sovereignty in international relations: Bridging the gap between theory and empirical research. *International Studies Quarterly* 39 (2): 213–33.

Tilly, C. 1985. War making and state making as organized crime. In *Bringing the state back in*, ed. P. B. Evans, D. Rueschemeyer, and T. Skocpol. Cambridge: Cambridge University Press.

Torpey, J. 2000. *The invention of the passport: surveillance, citizenship, and the state.* Cambridge Studies in Law and Society. Cambridge: Cambridge University Press.

Torpey, J., and J. Caplan. 2001. Introduction. In *Documenting individual identity: The development of state practices in the modern world*, ed. J. Torpey and J. Caplan. Princeton, N.J.: Princeton University Press.

Toye, J., and M. Moore 1998. Taxation, corruption and reform. In *Corruption and development*, ed. M. Robinson. London: Frank Cass.

Trouillot, M.-R. 2001. The anthropology of the state in the age of globalization. *Current Anthropology* 42 (1): 125–38.

Tsing, A. L. 2005. *Friction: An ethnography of global connection*. Princeton, N.J.: Princeton University Press.

Underhill, G. 2000. Global money and the decline of state power. In *Strange power: Shaping the parameters of international relations and international political economy*, ed. T. Lawton, J. Rosenau, and A. Verdun. Aldershot: Ashgate.

U.K. Export Credits Guarantee Department. 2002. Ghanaian airport upgrade makes successful landing. Ref no: 23/02. September 23. Retrieved from http://nds.coi.gov.uk/Content/Detail.asp?ReleaseID=43114&NewsAreaID=2, accessed February 9, 2004.

United Nations Conference on Trade and Development (UNCTAD). 2002. Trade facilitation—Ghana. Retrieved from http://r0.unctad.org/ttl/ppt-2002-11-25/ghana/ghana-present.htm.

———. 2007. *Review of maritime transport. Report by the UNCTAD secretariat*. New York: United Nations.

UN Office for the Coordination of Humanitarian Affairs. 2000. US, Ghana reach agreement on open skies. Relief web. IRIN update 679. Retrieved from http://www.reliefweb/int/w/rwb/nsf/0.

USAID. 2001. *International trade agenda*. Washington, D.C.: USAID.

———. 2005a. *Customs modernization handbook: Establishing and implementing a customs integrity program*. September.

———. 2005b. *Customs reform and trade facilitation: An entrée to the global marketplace*. Washington, D.C., February.

———. 2005c. Facilitating streamlined trade project. Booz, Allen and Hamilton. Retrieved from http://www.tcb-fastrade.com.

U.S. Customs and Border Protection (USCBP). 2005. U.S. Customs and Border Protection Team Helps Secure Iraq's Borders. Feb. 1. Retrieved from http://www.cbp.gov/xp/cgov/newsroom/news_releases/archives/2005_press_releases/022005/02012005_4.xm.

———. 2003. Container security initiative, strategic plan 2006–2011. Retrieved from http://www.cbp.gov/linkhandler/cgov/trade/cargo_security/csi/csi_strategic_plan.ctt/csi_strategic_plan.pdf.

van der Haak, B. 2003. *Lagos/Koolhaas*. Brooklyn, N.Y.: First Run Film.

Van Dijk, R. 2003. Religion, reciprocity and restructuring family responsibility in the Ghanaian Pentecostal diaspora. In *The transnational family*, ed. D. Bryceson. Oxford: Oxford University Press.

Verdery, K. 1991. Theorising socialism: A prologue to the "transition." *American Ethnologist* 18 (3): 419–39.

Victory Bible Church International. 2006. Our logo. Retrieved January 27, 2006, from http://www.vbint.org.

Walker, J. 2003. Sanctioning politics and the politics of sanctions: The EU, France and development aid in Togo. Paper delivered at London School of Economics, January 22.

Walle, N. V. de. 1999. Globalization and African democracy. In *State, conflict, and democracy in Africa*, ed. R. A. Joseph. Boulder, Colo.: Lynne Rienner Publishers.

Walsh, J. T. 2006. New customs. *Finance and Development* 43 (1). Retrieved from http://www.imf.org/external/pubs/ft/fandd/2006/03/walsh.htm.

Weber, C. 1995. *Simulating sovereignty: Intervention, the state and symbolic exchange*. Cambridge: Cambridge University Press.

Weber, M. 1968. *Economy and society: An outline of interpretive sociology*. New York: Bedminster Press.

Weiner, A., and J. Schneider, eds. 1989. *Cloth and human experience*. Smithsonian Series in Ethnographic Inquiry. Washington, D.C.: Smithsonian Institution Press.

West, H., and T. Sanders. 2003. Power revealed and concealed in the new world order. In *Transparency and conspiracy: Ethnographies of suspicion in the new world order*, ed. H. West and T. Sanders. Durham, N.C.: Duke University Press.

West Region News. 2003. Ghanaian Ministry reviews gateway project. December 21. Retrieved from http://www.africast.com/article.pho?newsID=623&str Region=West.

White, L. 2000. *Speaking with vampires: Rumor and history in colonial Africa*. Berkeley: University of California Press.

Whitfield, L. 2005. Trustees of development from conditionality to governance: Poverty reduction strategy papers in Ghana. *Journal of Modern African Studies* 43 (4): 641–64.

Wilks, I. 1961. *The northern factor in Ashanti history*. Legon: Institute of African Studies, University of Ghana.

———. 1967. Asanti government. In *West African kingdoms in the nineteenth century*, ed. D. Forde and P. Karberry. London: Oxford University Press, International African Institute.

———. 1989. *Asante in the nineteenth century: The structure and evolution of a political order*. African Studies Series 13. Cambridge: Cambridge University Press.

———. 1993. *Forests of gold*. Athens: Ohio University Press.

Williamson, J. 1993. Development and the "Washington Consensus." *World Development* 21:1239–1336.

Wilson, C. D. 1941. Report on patrols, smuggling and seizures for the month of August, 1941, Southern Section, Eastern Frontier Preventive Service. C. Duncan Wilson, Collector in Charge. Accra: Ghana National Archives.

World Bank. 1984. *Ghana: Policies and programs for adjustment*. Washington, D.C.: World Bank.

———. 1989. *Sub-Saharan Africa: From crisis to sustainable growth*. Washington, D.C.: World Bank.

———. 1992. *Governance and development*. Washington, D.C.: World Bank.

———. 1994a. *Adjustment in Africa: Lessons from case studies*. Washington, D.C.: World Bank.

———. 1994b. *Governance: The World Bank experience*. Washington, D.C.: World Bank.

———. 1995. Findings Africa region, no. 52, Nov. 1995. Retrieved from http://www.worldbank.org/afr/findings/english/find52.htm.

———. 1998. World Bank group and Singapore Trade and Development Board sign cooperation agreement. *News Release* No. 98/1649, February 26.

———. 2003. *Toward country-led development: Findings from six country case studies*. Washington, D.C.: World Bank.

World Customs Organization (WCO). 2002a. *The institution of customs*. Brussels.

———. 2002b. WCO General Secretariat document SG0144E2, October 6. Brussels: World Customs Organization.

———. 2005a Draft report to the Customs Cooperation Council on the 24th session of the Enforcement Committee: World Customs Organization.

———. 2005b. Final report of the 10th World Customs Organisation (WCO) Regional Conference of the Directors-General of Customs for West and Central Africa held in Accra, Ghana, from 23rd to 25th March.

———. 2006a. Annual survey to determine the percentage of national revenue represented by Customs duties. Brussels.

———. 2006b. Conventions sponsored or administered by the Customs Co-Operation Council—Synopsis of position as of 1 July 2006, SG0158E1b. Brussels: World Customs Organization.

World Trade Organization. 1994. Understanding on the Interpretation of Article XXIV of the General Agreement on Tariffs and Trade 1994. Retrieved from http://www.wto.org/english/docs_e/legal_e/10-24_e.htm.

———. 2000. Heads of international agencies agree to new approach on trade-related technical assistance for LDCs. *WTO Focus Newsletter* 47.

———. 2001. Statement by the Honourable Kofi Konadu Apraku, MP, Minister of Trade and Industry. Paper read at World Trade Organization Ministerial Conference, Doha, Ghana, November 11.

———. 2002. Technical assistance—Trade facilitation, communication from Japan (02-5201). September 30.

———. 2003a VAL: Method 1—Transaction Value. Electronic document, Retrieved from http://www.wto.org/wto/english/thewto_e/whatis_e/eol/e/wto03/wto3-38.htm, accessed January 25, 2003.

———. 2003b Agreement on Customs Valuation. Electronic document, Retrieved from http://www.wto.org/english/thewto_e/whatis_e/eol/e/wto03/wto3_64.htm. accessed September 5, 2003.

———. 2007. Ghana. April. Retrieved from http://stat.wto.org/CountryProfiles/GH_e.htm.

———. 2008. Trade Policy Review, Ghana. WT/TPR/S/194/Rev.1.

———. N.d. *Understanding the WTO: The GATT years from Havana to Marrakesh.* Retrieved September 25, 2009, from http://www.wto.org/english/thewto_e/whatis_e/tif_e/fact4_e.htm.

Yeboah, A. A. 2001. NDC man quizzed over cars. *Ghana Times,* February 5.

Yeboah, I. 2003. Demographic and housing aspects of structural adjustment and emerging urban form in Accra, Ghana. *Africa Today* 50 (1): 107–19.

Yeboah, K. O. 2001. Facts Behind Gateway Services Operations. *The Free Press* (Ghana), April 11.

Younger, S. 1996. Estimating tax incidence in Ghana. In *Economic reform and the poor in Africa*, ed. D. Sahn. New York: Oxford University Press.

Zaun, T., and J. Singer. 2004. How Japan's second-hand cars make it to the third world. *Wall Street Journal–Eastern Edition,* 243 (5).

Index

Abrams, Philip, 45, 194
Accra, 7, 59, 62, 76, 111
Accra Mail, allegation of Customs
    role in misallocation of
    vehicles, *150*
Acheampong, I. K., 22, 76, 116,
    152, 197, 250n10
Achimota Secondary School, 94
actuarialism, 189
Adjei-Bediako, 156
administrative sovereignty, 126, 235
Aflao "borderlanders": backbone of
    Customs officers' survival, 67–
    68; capitalizing on border, 64–
    65; entrenchment of Customs
    in lives of, 57
Aflao Border Post: clandestine trans-
    port, 66–67; colonial legacy, 87;
    contribution of residents to
    maintenance of territorial
    limits, 57; extensive cross-
    border traffic, 60; Ghana-Togo
    border, *63*; organizing feature of
    sociocultural and economic life,
    64, 65; service economy, 65–66;
    state agency presence, 62; state
    building on, 69–71; and struggle
    for border, 56
Aflao Collection, 11–12, 57;
    administrative self-help plan,
    102; aura of intimidation,
    82; busiest border crossing in
    West Africa, 59; commodity
    codes, 78; corporate-to-
    corporate transactions, 77;

"distributed sovereignty,"
    129; documentary authority,
    78–81; and ebb and flow of
    frontier, 59–68; exercise of state
    power through inspections and
    emblematization, 61–62, 86;
    fee-based inspection companies,
    114; integration into local land-
    scape, 63, 85; Landing Account,
    78, 79–*80*, 86, 106, 111; legacies
    of Ghanaian state history, 85–
    86; management of mobility, 69;
    most visible presence at Aflao
    border, 62; nation-based docu-
    mentary distinctions, 83; over-
    sight of motor vehicles, 74–75;
    Preventive Unit, 63, 64, 76, 86,
    116–25; receipt, 81; reflection
    of governmental instability, 68;
    sketch map of, *70*; substations
    and regional trade routes, *57*,
    62; tariffs, 78–79; and territorial
    sovereignty, 68–85; and tradi-
    tion of *laissez-passage*, 69; values
    calculation, 79, 86; visual and
    physical surveillance, 84
Aflao Collection, Baggage Hall offi-
    cers: ceding of power to border
    residents, 110–11, 115, 127, 236;
    custom assistants, *112*; extralegal
    gratuities for services, 111; goro
    boys, 112–13; as last bastions of
    authority, 108–14; sociology and
    division of labor among, 111–13,
    115